The Parish Behind God's Back

The Parish Behind God's Back

The Changing Culture of Rural Barbados

George Gmelch
Sharon Bohn Gmelch

Union College

WAVELAND
PRESS, INC.
Long Grove, Illinois

For information about this book, contact:
Waveland Press, Inc.
4180 IL Route 83, Suite 101
Long Grove, IL 60047-9580
(847) 634-0081
info@waveland.com
www.waveland.com

Contents

Acknowledgments

During the six years this book was intermittently in progress, many people helped out. We wish to thank our academic colleagues, Barbadian friends, and former students who offered ideas, read drafts of chapters, or provided critiques of the entire manuscript in one of its several forms: Jeff Broomes, Tracy Bush, Loran Cutsinger, Peter DiCerbo, Margaret Deutsch, Jerome Handler, Victor Johnson, Marcus O'Neale, Betsy Phelps, Barbara Scantlebury, Jeanette Springer, Karl Watson, Janice Whittle, and three anonymous reviewers. Susan Whitlock, our editor, gave us direction at an early stage and encouraged us toward final revision.

We are also grateful to Stephen Hackenberger, Colin Hudson, Wayne Hunte, and Robert Speed for teaching us about the history and environment of Barbados. Librarians Bruce Connolly and Dave Gerhan, at Union College, and Michael Gill and Alan Moss, at the University of the West Indies, Cave Hill, graciously assisted us over the years in various ways. Many thanks are due to Mary McKay, Janet McQuade, Megan Donovan, and Kerry Cassidy for their help in preparing the manuscript.

Much appreciation is owed the students we have taken to Barbados since 1983 on eight anthropology field programs supported by Union College. Their insights, experiences, and attempts to make sense of a new culture greatly contributed to our knowledge of the island. Our search for an up-to-date ethnography of an eastern Caribbean culture for the students' reading list first prompted us to think about writing this book. While the students are too numerous to mention individually, we wish to thank Johanna Campbell, Amy Dillenback, Siri Doble, Sara Finnerty, Dan Gilbert, Betsy Phelps, Annika Michaels, and J. J. Weiner for permission to quote from their field notes. Our son, Morgan, has added enormously to the pleasure of each of our field trips; he first went to Barbados when he was four months old. He is now fourteen and is as familiar with the backroads of St. Lucy as those of his hometown in upstate New York.

Our greatest debt is to the people of St. Lucy, especially the residents of Josey Hill, for their gracious acceptance of our presence there. Our neighbors Rudolph and Shirley Hollingsworth have made our time in Josey Hill especially pleasant; we thank them for their friendship, kindness, and help. We also want to thank all the families who have hosted our students over the years. Many of those in St. Lucy have become our friends and teachers as well: Siebert and Aileen Allman, Daphne Armstrong, Judy and Rosevelt Griffith, Valenza Griffith, Marcus and Janet Hinds, Uzil Holder, Gail and Victor Johnson, Marcus and Velma O'Neale, and Arlette Went. Without them this research would not have been nearly as pleasurable. This book is dedicated to them.

We use pseudonyms for most of the names of villagers who are quoted in the text. We have done this to protect their privacy and because the line between conversation and interview, between friend and "informant," was sometimes blurred. We realize that some people would have preferred to see their real names used, and we apologize to those who may be disappointed. The names we have substituted are common in Barbados. All place names and other personal names in the text—including the individuals profiled in chapter 5—are real.

Introduction

In the eastern Caribbean the expression "behind God's back" refers to a place that is remote or faraway. In Barbados the saying is used when speaking of the parishes or districts that are furthest from the capital city of Bridgetown. Although the rural parishes of St. Andrew and St. Philip are sometimes described as "behind God's back," the expression is most frequently applied to St. Lucy, the most distant and rural parish. St. Lucy has a population of about ten thousand people, spread over thirty villages. Nearly all of its residents are of African descent. Most people live close to the land, deriving some of their subsistence from gardening and livestock raising, while being tied to the wider economy through wage labor and salaried jobs and to the rest of the world through telecommunications, tourism, and travel.

Although this book focuses on life in one rural parish, what we find there holds true in large measure throughout the island. There is a certain uniformity to village life in Barbados. This contrasts with many other Caribbean islands, particularly mountainous ones, in which differences between highland and lowland environments and less developed transportation links have produced greater variation. Even the contrast between rural and urban areas is less pronounced in Barbados than elsewhere in the region. Its small size, gentle geography, and extensive network of roads allow people to travel easily between country and town, village and city, producing a homogeneity in culture, although a few regionalisms in custom remain.

In describing life in rural Barbados, we are mindful of influences emanating beyond its shores. An important aim of this book is to reveal how connected Barbados and its people, even those in its most remote parish, are to the outside world. Barbadians may live in a distant corner of the Caribbean, but they are by no means isolated. One of the first things any visitor notices are youths wearing baseball caps and T-shirts sporting the names and logos of North American athletic teams: the Chicago Bulls and Oakland Raiders. Switching on the television, one is more likely to find an American sitcom or soap opera than a Caribbean program. In conversation with local people it soon becomes apparent that nearly every family has a relative living overseas and that many people have themselves traveled to New York, Toronto, London, and beyond. Barbadians understand the extent to which their lives are influenced by the metropolitan countries of Europe and North America. They know only too well, for example, that the health of the U.S. and British economies directly affects the number of tourists who arrive on the island and the amount of money they spend. In the pages that follow we devote considerable time to discussing the impact of tourism and other global influences on the island. While the primary aim of this book is to provide a contemporary ethnographic portrait of rural Barbados today and its connections to the outside world, we also try to provide enough historical context to show how present-day patterns of village life came about. To understand any Afro-Caribbean society it is essential to know something of the historical processes through which a once enslaved people of African descent established their own communities and culture within the constraints imposed by a European colonial power.

The bulk of the data for this book was collected between 1990 and 1996 during four field trips, each lasting three months. On each occasion we lived in the St. Lucy village of Josey Hill. A good deal of our understanding of Barbadian society, however, dates back to the 1980s. In 1983 we brought our first group of American undergraduates to Barbados for an eleven-week field training program in cultural anthropology. We have returned seven times since then with small groups of students, bringing a total of sixty-eight students. Our students have contributed to this book in several important ways. They have lived individually in fifteen different villages in the northern half of the island, about half of them communities in St. Lucy. In the villages they have carried out full-time field research, which we have supervised. Our visits to the village and home of each student have contributed much to our knowledge of rural Barbados and led to a network of friendships that extends across St. Lucy and into the neighboring parishes of St. Andrew and St. Peter. Much of our understanding of Barbadian culture has come from witnessing and assisting our students in their struggles to adjust to and make sense of village life. The innocent mistakes they make often bring community norms into sharp focus.

Through their friendships with Barbadians of their own age they also have given us insight into the problems, attitudes, and values of young Barbadians. It is partly because so much of our knowledge about rural Barbadian life has come from people and experiences across the entire parish that we have made the parish of St. Lucy, rather than the single village we lived in, the setting for this book.

Our fieldwork has extended beyond the parish as well. When investigating macro-level issues such as the impact of tourism, we routinely have turned to experts and individuals directly involved, ranging from academics at the University of the West Indies, government officials, and journalists in Bridgetown to hoteliers, hotel employees, and foreign tourists along the tourist belt. While most of the village-level field data has come from daily observations and informal conversations with neighbors and other residents, when working outside the parish we have more often relied on formal, tape-recorded interviews.

This book was written with students in mind. In deciding, for example, how to organize it and what level of detail to aim for, we thought of the students we have taught over the past twenty years. In an appendix we discuss the impact that living in Barbadian villages has had on undergraduates in our anthropology program. While Caribbean villagers are not "exotic" tribal peoples like the Yanamamo, Pygmies, or !Kung, the staple of introductory anthropology courses, their cultures are equally interesting and instructive. Barbados has been involved in the most significant trends that have shaped the modern world: the disappearance of an indigenous Amerindian population; colonization by a European power; the rise of European commercialism based on sugar production; the African diaspora; a complex pattern of out-migration; and incorporation into the global community through tourism, travel, and television. Barbados, like the Caribbean generally, exhibits cultural and historical characteristics that clearly promote anthropological understanding of a broad range of issues.

The book begins with an introduction to the island and parish, followed by history and a macro-level description of Barbados' economy, before turning to the local scene—patterns of work, gender relations and lifecycle, community, and religion. Toward the end the perspective widens again to look at the global forces that influence, shape, and impinge upon the lives of villagers today. Specifically, chapter 1 introduces Barbados and the parish of St. Lucy. Chapter 2 gives a historical overview of the English colonization of the island and its transformation into an agro-industrial plantation society based on slavery. Chapter 3 examines Barbados' economy, particularly the changes that have taken place with the decline of sugar and rise of tourism. Chapter 4 profiles six village households both as a way of exploring how local people make a living and contextualizing the later ethnographic data by getting to know a few individuals. Chapter 5 discusses the life cycle and gender relations. Chapter 6 looks at community and how it has been transformed in recent decades by modernization and new technology. The next chapter deals with religion, a major institution in rural Barbadian life. Chapter 8 examines how outside influences introduced through the electronic media, travel, tourism, and emigration effect village and all Barbadian life. In "Final Thoughts," we continue this discussion of Barbados' global connections, examining the country's growing regional ties and pervasive North American cultural penetration.

Chapter 1

Island and Parish

Barbados is the most easterly of the Caribbean islands. It lies outside the great arc of volcanic islands that sweeps a thousand miles from the Virgin Islands in the north to Trinidad and Tobago in the south. Unlike its volcanic neighbors, which are steep and mountainous, Barbados has a gentle terrain that is favorable to agriculture. Its tractable and fertile landscape allowed early English settlers and the slaves they later imported to quickly bring most of the island under cultivation.

Barbados is the only Caribbean nation to have had a single colonial master. The appellation "Little England," which has become a hackneyed phrase of the tourist trade, has some legitimacy. It was coined in part from comparisons between the landscapes of the two countries, which are both green and rolling and everywhere show the hand of humans. Today Barbados is better known to North Americans and Europeans for its white sand beaches and sunny, tropical climate, which have made it a popular tourist destination. The temperature varies little throughout the year, from an average of 77°F in January to 81°F in August and September. The proximity of all parts of the island to the sea ensures comfortable year-round breezes. This, combined with the purity of the groundwater and the absence of pestilence, led one nineteenth-century English traveler to rate Barbados the healthiest place in the British Empire, which then included half the nations on earth.[1]

Over 260,000 people live on the island, which measures just 21 by 14 miles, making Barbados one of the most densely populated countries in the world. The population is spread unevenly, however. Most Bajans (the colloquial term Barbadians use for themselves) live in the capital city of Bridgetown and its suburbs, while most of the rural parishes are thinly settled.[2] Nearly three-quarters of all Barbadians are descendants of the Africans who were transported to the island to work as slaves; about 20 percent are of mixed African and European

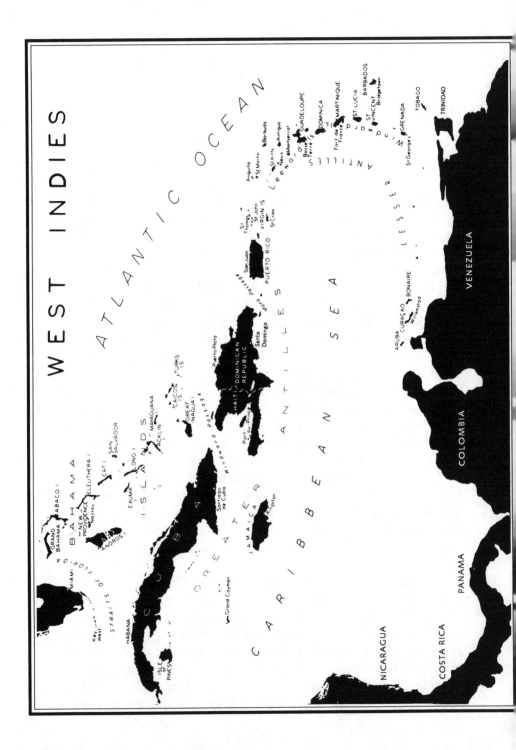

heritage; the remainder are whites—the descendants of English colonists and their indentured servants, and recent expatriates from Britain and North America. There are also small numbers of immigrants from South Asia and the Middle East. Like most small developing countries, Barbados has one principal city, Bridgetown, which overwhelms the island's other "urban" places in size and importance. Stretching outward from Bridgetown along the west and south coasts are strips of hotels and restaurants catering to tourists—a mainstay of Barbados' modern economy. Beyond the city and hotel belt the rest of the island is fairly rural. The settlement pattern consists predominantly of small villages separated by fields of sugarcane, occasionally broken by deep, tree-filled gullies.

The Parish

One of the two main ways to reach the parish of St. Lucy from Bridgetown is to drive north along Highway 1, a two-lane road with no verge or dividing line, which hugs the coast. The road cuts through a corridor of hotels and luxury homes built along the turquoise waters of the Caribbean Sea. The hotels are not the high-rises seen in San Juan or Daytona Beach; many are low, sometimes single-story resorts and cottages, with lush grounds planted in flowering trees and shrubs, their names evoking the images the Barbados Tourist Board likes to project—Golden Palm, Coral Reef Club, Sandy Lane, Coconut Creek, Paradise Beach, Glitter Bay.

Just beyond Speightstown, a small provincial town 10 miles north of the capital, the scene changes. The bustle of west coast tourist development gives way to fields of sugarcane, which before harvest form tall corridors of bamboo-like stalks and grass-like blades rippling in the wind 10 feet above the road. Here everyone is Barbadian. Most of the people waiting for buses or walking home from work and school are well dressed, but some wear the soiled clothes of road and field workers. Here and there groups of young men "lime" (hang out) on the roadside, while older men sit under the shade of a tree or in front of a rum shop, slamming dominoes down on boards resting on the top of oil drums. Turning inland, the road gradually climbs several hundred feet over uplifted coral reefs. Beneath Barbados the edges of two continental plates collide, one plunging beneath the other, the top plate, like the blade of a giant bulldozer, scraping off a mountain of oceanic

The parishes of Barbados.

sediment from the plate diving below. This sediment is the underlying land form on which the coral cap of Barbados rests. In places the road cuts deep, revealing the steep white walls of ancient reefs.

Passing through the village of Mile and a Quarter—so named because it is exactly that distance from Speightstown—a sign propped against the wall of a small grocery store warns customers and passers-by that no "indecent language" is allowed. Then the road swings north again toward the parish of St. Lucy. Substantial "wall houses" made of concrete blocks become fewer in number, and simple "chattel houses" made of wood, some still perched on crude foundations of uncemented coral stones, become more common. Soon one reaches St. Lucy's imposing parish church, originally built in the 1620s. From there the road divides, heading further north across the flat coastal plain and east to the top of yet another terrace.

St. Lucy encompasses an area of 13.6 square miles (8 percent of the island) and caps the entire northern tip of Barbados. Shortly after the British established their colony, planters divided the island into parishes, ecclesiastical and administrative units, with boundaries running from one plantation on the Caribbean coast to another on the Atlantic. St. Lucy was one of the original six parishes to be laid out. As the population grew and new churches were built, five additional parishes were soon carved out of the originals. Ten were named after saints of the Christian calendar, with St. Lucy the only female.[3]

The creation of parishes reflected both the importance of the Church of England to early settlers and their familiarity with this form of local government.[4] Parishes were important political units. Originally, each parish formed a parliamentary constituency, with parish vestries levying taxes and administering the roads, water supply, poor relief, and local education. When a British commission visited Barbados in 1939 to investigate social conditions in the English Caribbean following a series of riots on several islands, it noted "the extraordinary degree" to which the functions of government were decentralized and distributed among Barbados' parishes.

Your Majesty's Government may exercise the minimum control over the activities of the Barbados Legislature: the Barbados Government exercises hardly more over the parochial authorities in vitally important areas of education, public works and public health. . . . There is, however, a point beyond which flexibility and local participation in public work degenerate into chaotic discrepancies and lack of co-ordination, and that point seems to us to have been passed in Barbados.[5]

But it was not until twenty years later that local government was reorganized and parish councils were dissolved.[6] The parish, even now, remains the source of most Barbadians' geographical identity.[7] When asked where they come from, Bajans usually give the name of their parish—St. Andrew, St. Philip, St. Peter—rather than their district or village. Automobile license plates (rural Bajans know the number plates of most cars in their area) are also identified by parish. All cars registered in St. Lucy, for example, begin with the letter *L*, those from St. George begin with *G*, and so on. So, wherever one drives on the island, one's parish residence is displayed to others.[8]

To Bajans from the more urbanized, southern half of the island, St. Lucy is "country," and the people who live there are "country bucks." Even though the parish is less than 20 miles from the southern end of the island, it is perceived to be faraway—"the parish behind God's back." We have met Bajans who have never been to St. Lucy. Some primary school children in other parts of the island mistakenly refer to it as "St. Lucia," the name of a neighboring island. Before radio and television, townspeople claimed that news was a day old by the time it reached St. Lucy. During a cold spell in January 1996, when the nighttime temperatures fell into the low sixties, people in the southern parishes joked that folks in St. Lucy, being so far north, must be suffering from frostbite. Historically, the relative isolation of rural parishes resulted in different speech patterns; St. Lucy was said to have the most distinctive accent. In recent times, however, radio, television, and the ease of movement, and therefore contact with other Bajans, have erased most speech differences.

In a study of how Barbadians perceive different parts of the island, geographer Robert Potter found that most people dislike the north, viewing it as backward. St. Lucyians would not agree. The words they commonly use to describe their parish are *safe, kind, friendly, sharing,* and *quiet*. It is a place where neighbors still keep an eye on your house when you are away, where cows staked out at night to graze are safe from thieves, and where people still share their surplus food with one another. A neighbor of ours who spent half his life in Bridgetown put it this way: "In St. Lucy you don't find the competitive struggle that goes on in town. Here people are relaxed, and life is slow. You're surrounded by relations, and you have lots of people pulling for you." Nearly 85 percent of parish residents were born in St. Lucy, the highest of all parishes.

Foreigners who come to St. Lucy are struck by its scenery. Some guidebooks claim it's the best in Barbados.[9] The terrain is divided between a flat coastal plane and a terraced, hilly interior. Ocean swells pushed by relentless trade winds pound the 60- to 70-foot-high cliffs that are pocked with small caverns and fissures that form blow holes; when the waves surge in, great jets of spray shoot upward. Because spindrift is blown inland, the land nearest the cliffs is saturated with salt, and little vegetation grows there, giving the northeastern fringe of the parish a barren, lunar look. Further inland, as the salt lessens and the soil thickens, palm, coconut, casuarina, and mahogany trees, and clumps of sea grape green the countryside. Because Barbados was never physically connected to any other landmass—unlike Trinidad, which was once joined to the South American mainland—all of the plants on the island today, and nearly all of those that existed when Europeans arrived, reached the island as seeds carried by ocean currents or in the stomachs of migrating birds.[10] St. Lucy's rolling terrain is broken by steep gullies and ravines.[11] In the last thirty years, as villagers have stopped cooking with wood, the gullies have been reverting to bush and forest. Many contain native plants, which some people still use to make "bush teas" or medicines. The reforested gullies also provide a rich habitat for vervet monkeys, which originally arrived on the island aboard slave ships.[12] Seeing monkeys always brightened our day, but they are the bane of villagers, who grow fruit and vegetables on which the monkeys feed. Apart from the gullies most of the parish's land is planted in sugarcane. Because rainfall is lower and the soil is thinner than elsewhere on the island, St. Lucy historically was not a major stronghold of the plantocracy. Plantations in the parish tended to be smaller than the 200- to 300-acre estates that were the norm elsewhere on the island.[13]

While most of St. Lucy is agricultural, there are a few industries: the Arawak Cement Plant, the Mt. Gay rum distillery, the Superchick chicken processing plant, and the Japanese-owned Walcoal garment factory. The cement plant was built as a joint venture between Barbados and Trinidad. Its buildings loom above the cliffs on the northwest coast and are a feature that fishers and drug runners now use to get their bearings at sea.[14] There are no hotels or tourist accommodations in St. Lucy.

The residents of St. Lucy, like most Bajans, are of African descent. After emancipation, in 1838, newly freed slaves could settle anywhere. In reality, however, there was no place to go, since virtually all the island's arable land was owned by existing plantations, jobs in town were scarce, and few people had the means to emigrate. Most people ended up working for their former employers and living in settlements known as "tenantries," usually located within a kilometer of the plantation great house. They were given a house plot and a small wage in exchange for their labor.[15] In 1990 nearly 99 percent of St. Lucy's residents were classified by the government's census as "black" or "mixed." Only 42 whites, 7 East Indians, and a single Chinese person, out of a total population of 9,277, were living in the parish.[16] The anthropology students we have placed with families are sometimes the first whites to have lived in the community in living memory. And during their first few weeks they are very aware of being white.[17] They are inevitably the objects of curiosity; until they become known by name, villagers readily refer to them as "white girl" or "white boy."

From the earliest days of the colony until the mid-nineteenth century, however, a sizable white population lived in the parish. The owners and overseers of the thirty-two plantations within St. Lucy were white, as were the descendants of poor white indentured servants.[18] In the early 1700s there were over twelve hundred whites in a population of approximately four thousand.[19] Most had come to Barbados in the seventeenth century from Ireland, England, and Scotland, having been given passage to Barbados in exchange for labor. They signed contracts that tied them to a single employer for up to ten years.[20] After fulfilling their contracts, they were given a small parcel of land or money enough to buy it. Some place names in St. Lucy, such as Glendalough Street near Josey Hill, named for Glendalough, Ireland, still reflect this past.[21]

The Village

St. Lucy's villages are generally quiet places. The day begins shrilly, however, with a rooster's crow, followed by a chorus of hungry cows and sheep. Soon human voices are added to the mix as windows are opened and radios and stereos are turned on, spilling the morning obituaries, gospel music, golden oldies, and dub into the streets. Although some people have been up since 4:30 A.M., the village comes alive at about 6:00, with little seasonal variation. (Barbados lies so near the equator—13°5' north latitude—that the sun rises and sets at about the same time throughout the year.)

During the cool hours of early morning the villages are filled with activity. Passing by friends' homes, neighbors shout out greetings and check on the elderly: "Trotman! You there?"; "Mrs. O'Neale! How you spend the night?" Others greet one another in the street with "Mornin'," receiving an "Ah'right, okay" in return. Men and women are outside watering or weeding their gardens before the day heats up. Others fork the land in preparation for planting, creating high furrows or, in some cases, old-style "cane holes," which create a waffle pattern in the rich, black soil. In a distant field early risers can be seen on the horizon dragging crocus bags along, picking cotton with the weight of the dew still on. Along the roadside older women pull pigeon peas from chest-high bushes, and men lead their cows or sheep to be staked out "on the ground." Others make their way to the news seller's house to buy the *Nation* or *Advocate* before retiring to their "galleries" (porches) to read. Meanwhile, boys feed and briefly exercise their families' dogs, while the women of the house cook breakfast and iron uniforms for school.

Before long children burst from doorways and make their way to the bus stop, where they stand color coded by school—blue uniforms for St. Lucy Secondary School, peach for St. James Secondary, and here and there a distinguished Harrison College white and gray. The luckier ones catch lifts in a neighbor's or family member's car. Most of the adults with jobs outside the village also gather at the bus stop; the minority who own cars drive to work. Women who stay at home soon disappear indoors to tidy up, wash the family's "wares," and prepare the day's meal, while the remaining men gravitate toward the rum shop or the shade. During the day the main sounds are the deep-throated bleats of black-bellied sheep, punctuated by the honk of a bread man's truck, the buzz of the postman's motorbike, and the distant grind of a government bus. And so the day goes, until the second flurry of activity occurs in late afternoon with the return from work and school.

There are approximately thirty villages in the parish, roughly the number of original plantations.[22] Most villages were previously tenan-

A neighborhood in the village of Josey Hill. (Photo by George Gmelch.)

tries—that is, collections of houses built on marginal plantation land. Along St. Lucy's west coast, villages such as Half Moon Fort and Fustic, which developed as fishing and boat building communities, are oriented to the sea. Many of the island's fishing boats are hand-built on the beaches just south of Half Moon Fort. The day's catches of flying fish, kingfish, and dolphin are landed on the beaches and sold from makeshift tables and carts on the roadside. All of St. Lucy's other villages are surrounded by fields and oriented to agriculture. In most areas sugarcane dominates the landscape, with fields lining both sides of the circuitous roads. The land takes on a different character in February-March, however, once the cane is harvested. Its contours and shapes, previously hidden behind walls of cane, become visible. For the first time since the previous harvest oncoming motorists and buses can be seen at a distance rather than looming up suddenly around corners. The color of the land also changes from lush green to yellow and brown as the fields are covered with dried-out cane leaves, called "trash."

Many villages still bear the names of the plantations from which they sprang. Most plantations in turn were named for their owners; hence, British surnames such as Allman, Babb, Durhams, Greenidge, Maycocks, and Trents dot the parish. The names of other villages reveal something about their location or history. The village of Graveyard—recently renamed Cave Hill—for example, was a burial ground of many victims of the devastating cholera epidemic of 1854. Other village names, such as Seaview, Round the Rock, Mount View, Rockfield, and Church Hill, reflect location and landscape.

The settlement pattern of Barbadian villages is an untidy affair. Some houses line the roadside; others are scattered beyond the road and reached by foot path or dirt track. Rarely does a Barbadian village have an immediately recognizable center. When we first arrived we sometimes had difficulty identifying villages, since our conception of what a village looked like had been forged in Mexico and Ireland, where we had done our first fieldwork. Villages in the Mexican highlands, for example, are laid out in a grid, with a central plaza built around a large Catholic church.[23] Nothing like this exists in Barbados, where the settlement pattern has been shaped by the piecemeal sale of plantation land over the years and by the division of private land into new house spots for sons and daughters. Although Barbadian villages lack distinct centers, like the Mexican plaza, there are places where people gather and socialize—rum shops, churches, bus stops, corners, shade trees, and at night under streetlights.

Homes

One notable feature of village housing is its wide variation. Sizes range from tiny two-room "wood" houses to large, masonry "wall" houses. What is unusual from an American perspective is seeing the large and small, rich and poor, sitting side by side. In North American communities, especially in suburbs, homes in a given neighborhood are generally of the same size and price range—a pattern that reflects a segregation of population by class and income. Coming from this background, it is easy for visitors to assume that the owners of the largest wall houses must be wealthy. This is seldom the case, as many of the owners are return migrants who scrimped and saved for years.

At the other end of the housing continuum are small, wood "chattel" houses (the word *chattel* refers to movable property), with gabled roofs and a symmetrical plan featuring a central door flanked by a window on either side. They developed in response to the insecurity of the newly freed slaves who became tenants on their former plantations. Without land or financial means they built simple houses that were inexpensive, easy to construct, and capable of being disassembled and transported should their owners be evicted or able to find a better situation on another estate.[24]

The distinction between "wood" and "wall" housing has become an important social marker. "Barbadian society," notes historian Trevor Marshall, "divides itself into those that live in board and those who live in wall houses." Because of their greater cost and size and their permanence, wall houses have higher status. A wall house states for its owner, "I not only own this house, but I own the land on which it sits." We have met people in different parts of the parish who proudly recall their parents and even grandparents having, often with money earned by working on the Panama Canal or in England, built the first wall house in their village. The largest houses in St. Lucy usually have been built by return migrants or by families with substantial remittances from children working overseas. The three-bedroom wall house of one of our neighbors, Marcus Thornhill, is an example. As a young man, Marcus made six trips to the United States as a migrant farmworker, picking apples in New York's Hudson Valley and beans in

Chattel house being surrounded by a new wall house. (Photo by George Gmelch.)

Connecticut. Living frugally, he saved two out of every three dollars he earned, which, with an additional loan from a relative, he invested in a taxi cab on his return to Barbados. For the past twenty years he has been driving a taxi six days a week and is often away twelve hours a day. He also raises a few sheep, which he stakes out to graze at dawn before leaving for work. Nearly all of his savings were put into the construction of his house, which he built during vacations and on Sundays, with the help of relatives.

Despite differences in size and material, parish homes share certain features. The rigid separation between the outside and inside, characteristic of housing in northern countries, is noticeably absent. Village houses are more open to the air and elements, particularly so in chattel houses, in which the thickness of a single one-inch plank is all that separates its occupants from the outside. Here one can feel strong winds buffet the house and hear rain beat against the roof. The sounds of tree frogs, crickets, bleating sheep, and the indescribable squeal of pigs waiting to be fed easily penetrate the walls. "Jalousies," resembling shutters, allow the wind to pass through. More modern homes have louvered windows. Whatever the kind, windows are usually open during the day, allowing the breeze, but also insects and other creatures, inside. One village house we rented had four resident green lizards that we came to know well; each morning we would awake to find some portion of the group staring down at us from the wall above, heads cocked to the side watching our every move. The lizards are welcome for the insects they eat; mice and centipedes are not. Not only are the outside elements allowed indoors, but much of Barbadian living takes place outdoors. Many activities that in North America would be performed inside, such as washing and drying clothes, getting a haircut, feeding pets, and preparing food, are done in the yard in many village homes.

Some features found in traditional village chattel homes, such as gables, "hoods" or "helmets" (awnings) over the windows to shield the sun, and Victorian decorations along the eaves were once common in the estate houses of the plantocracy. As historians Henry Fraser and Ronnie Hughes note, "the small Barbadian home employed the same architectural language as that of the merchant planter."[25] Barbadian carpenters imitated the design elements that they observed in plantation homes on a smaller scale in their own village or tenantry homes. In general, however, village homes are built simply and economically.

The dimensions of board houses, for example, correspond exactly to the lengths of the lumber used.[26] Old roofing material is reused to build fences, surplus cement blocks are used in landscaping and raised garden beds, and so on. There is little building waste to be hauled away to landfills.

The interior space of many village homes, especially chattel houses, is quite small. Many bedrooms have little space to maneuver past the beds; it is nearly always a squeeze to get past the dining room table when people are seated, and bathrooms tend to be purely functional. The small interior space reflects both limited finances and the fact that the outdoors can be used for many activities.

Many village homes tend to be noisy. Walls are thin; many are partitions that do not extend to the ceiling. Frequently, curtains rather than doors separate rooms, and consequently the sounds of television, radio, stereo, and conversation spread throughout the house.

Barbadians describe themselves as house proud, and village home owners are no exception; most homes are painted annually, often at Christmas, with their "galleries" and windows trimmed in a contrasting color. Flowering shrubs and ornamental plants such as poinsettia, bougainvillea, and hibiscus border the front yard. Most people sweep their floors frequently, and villagers typically do not wear shoes indoors.[27] Walls are typically decorated with calendars, family photographs, and plaques with religious sayings such as "God is my co-pilot." The homes of older Barbadians often have photographs of the British royal family. Souvenirs and other memorabilia reveal the places families have visited or countries where sons and daughters now live—a statue of Big Ben or the Empire State Building, an ashtray from Blackpool, a pennant from Niagara Falls.

Land

About 90 percent of St. Lucy's residents own the land on which they live. Those who do not generally rent from other people in the community.[28] Land ownership is highly valued. Historically, the desire to own land and a house has been the prime reason people left the island to work overseas. Throughout the Caribbean, as many social scientists have observed, the ownership of land is the most tangible expression of freedom. When villagers are asked about the importance of land, they often describe it in terms of security: "If you own land, you always have somewhere to live"; "As long as you have land, you will always be able to feed yourself"; "Land is better than putting money in the bank."

The importance of land, however, seldom translates into a desire to keep other people off one's land, as is often the case in North America. Most private land is open, and people are free to cross it. Footpaths, worn down to the bare earth or rock, are evident in most fields and are used frequently as shortcuts. Fences, apart from backyard palings, are uncommon, and property boundaries are often difficult to make out. A hedge row of *khus khus* grass may be planted along the border, but more often boundaries are marked only with a small iron stake driven into the ground and, formerly, by red painted rocks placed at each corner. Owners who are living abroad or who, for some reason, are not using their land often give permission to others to graze sheep and cows there, which also helps keep the land fertile.[29] On a piece of flat land below Josey Hill there is a large pasture. Its owner fell ill and died some years ago. When his heirs did not make use of the land, boys in the area began playing soccer and cricket there, and some families began grazing their sheep there as well. The owners have no objection as long as no one builds a permanent structure, which might make it difficult for them to reclaim the land.

Chapter 2

Colonialism, Sugar, and Slavery

Before proceeding to the ethnographic descriptions of St. Lucy, it is important to provide some historical context. This chapter begins with a few words about the Amerindians who lived on Barbados for two thousand years prior to its "discovery" and settlement by the British; it then turns to the colonization of the island and the social conditions of slavery, an institution that has left a deep imprint on many aspects of Barbadian culture.[1] The aim here is to introduce the basic patterns of Barbadian slavery and colonial life. In trying to span two centuries of history in a few dozen pages, we inevitably oversimplify patterns of considerable complexity and gloss over some variations in slavery that occurred over time. Caribbean slavery is a rich and complex area of scholarship, often with varied interpretations by historians, political economists, and other social scientists; we therefore urge readers who desire more than a brief overview to consult the primary scholarship, notably the writings of Hilary Beckles (1990), Jerome Handler (1974), and Handler and Frederick Lange (1978), for Barbados; and B. W. Higman (1984), Franklin Knight (1990), and John Thornton (1992), for the Caribbean generally, to name just a few.

European Contact and Amerindians

The first Europeans to visit Barbados early in the sixteenth century were the Spanish, who noted little about the native population other than the presence of many settlements.[2] When English mariners arrived a century later, in 1625, followed by a settlement party in 1627, there were some material remains suggesting recent habitation but no people. The question of what happened to the Amerindians continues to perplex archaeologists. "Our best guess," according to archaeologist

Detail of St. Lucy from the oldest surviving map of Barbados (ca. 1640). The names designate plantations. (From Richard Ligon, *A True and Exact History of the Island of Barbadoes* [1657]).

Stephen Hackenberger, "is that they were either decimated by disease or were removed by slave raiders, or a combination of the two." It is well-known that, elsewhere in the Caribbean and Central America, Amerindians died rapidly of European diseases such as the flu and measles, for which they had no immunity.

Although there were no Amerindians on Barbados when English settlers arrived in 1627, during the first decade of the colony small numbers were brought to Barbados from South America.[3] And, although there were never more than a few hundred Amerindians on the island during the seventeenth century, they left an imprint. Anthropologist Jerome Handler suggests that both Europeans and Africans learned fishing and intertidal gathering techniques from them, including using poisons to fish and harvesting sea turtles by turning over the females as they came ashore to lay eggs.[4] It is also likely that hammocks, used widely by the English from the earliest days of the colony and later by African slaves, were acquired from Amerindians. Writing around 1650, Richard Ligon notes that by tarring "the strings of our hammocks . . . we avoid [ants] better than in beds."[5] (Early Barbadians also warded off ants and biting insects by lighting small fires under their hammocks.) But the greatest contribution of Amerindians to the development of Barbados was probably the domestication of plants, notably potatoes, tobacco, maize, cassava, pineapple, and cotton. Cotton and tobacco were to become the colony's first major cash crops, until they were supplanted by sugarcane. Whatever borrowing of ideas occurred between Amerindians and the colonists, it did not last for many years, as Indians once again disappeared from the island.

Africans played only a minor role in the economy during the first few decades of the colony. The early settlers relied mostly upon indentured servants from England, Scotland, and Ireland, not on African slaves, to work their small tracts of land. Most were men and women with poor prospects in their native lands who had signed labor contracts of two to ten years in exchange for a parcel of land or a start-up sum at the end of their term. Some had been kidnapped and forced into servitude. The harsh living conditions of indentured servitude probably differed little from the slavery that followed.[6]

The English economic objective in Barbados was to produce an export crop. The colonists first tried tobacco, after high prices on the London market incited "tobacco fever" in the Caribbean.[7] For a short time it dominated the island's economy so much that Barbados was once described as "wholly built on smoke."[8] But tobacco proved a precarious choice. Barbadian tobacco was of poor quality, described by one European observer as "the worst that grows in the world."[9] Once the London market became oversupplied with high-quality tobacco from the American colony of Virginia, Barbadian tobacco could not compete. By the 1630s the colonists had begun cultivating cotton, which was also in great demand in England. A visitor in 1632 noted that "the trade in cotton fills them all with hope."[10] But, as English planters on other islands soon did the same, the London market became glutted, causing prices to plummet. Barbadian planters then looked to indigo, a plant from which a rich blue textile dye is extracted. Like tobacco, indigo was grown on small holdings, which one person could manage using the labor of only one or two indentured servants. Before long, however, oversupply again led to declining profits and the search for yet another export crop.

The Sugar Revolution

In the early 1640s Barbadian planters turned to sugarcane, a decision that revolutionized the economy. Within a few decades the West Indies became known as "the sugar islands." Some sugarcane had been previously grown for cattle feed and fuel. But it was the Dutch, many of them Sephardic Jews, who had grown sugarcane on a large scale in Brazil and who had developed the technology for manufacturing sugar, who helped Barbados' colonists with capital, technology, and markets to get sugar production off the ground.[11] Dutch merchants were then the leading traders in the Caribbean, and the Dutch West Indies Company was the major purveyor of slaves.

Sugar was almost an instant success. As early as 1645, Barbados' planters believed that they had found, at last, a truly profitable staple and one that wasn't hostage to short-term price fluctuations. Sugar had several advantages. With the colonization of India and the Far East coffee and tea had become popular drinks in Europe, and sugar was in demand as a sweetener. Sugar cultivation did not require great skill, nor did the crop deplete the soil as tobacco and cotton did. The gentle topography of Barbados, in contrast to the mountainous terrain of neighboring volcanic islands, was also ideal for its large-scale cultivation and for transporting the crop and its products to port for shipment to Europe. One observer, writing in 1645, noted: "If you go to Barbados, you shall see a flourishing island, fully recovered from the crisis in tobacco and cotton production."[12]

Sugar did more than make many colonists prosperous; it radically transformed the landscape, the size of landholdings, the class structure, and the demographics of the island. As Ralph Davis noted of the new Caribbean "sugar colonies" generally, "Sugar production . . . showed a tendency to engulf whole islands in single crop cultivation and it created its own form of society."[13] Sugar could only be grown economically on large estates; hence, wealthier planters bought out the smallholders; the number of smallholdings declined from a high of 11,200 in the mid-1640s to 2,639 by 1679.[14] Many of the peasant proprietors who were bought out left the country, moving to the British colony in North America and settling in the Carolinas.

Some sugar estates were formed, however, by the opposite process. Very large holdings were broken up into more manageable, but still large, parcels of 300 to 500 acres. Sugar was so profitable that most of Barbados' arable land was put into cultivation, a combination of sugarcane and food crops. Within a few decades after the introduction of sugar, Barbados had lost most of its original forest; by some accounts Turners Hall Wood in the hilly center of the island was the only sizeable (40 acres) remaining patch.

Sugar cultivation and the manufacture of rum and molasses required an enormous amount of unskilled manual labor. The work was seasonal, with a large pool of workers needed during "crop time" to cut, transport, and quickly process the cane but few laborers needed during the off-season. Since there were not enough white indentured workers in the West Indies to meet the labor demand, planters began buying slaves, who, because they did not receive a wage, could be supported more cheaply during the off-season.

Early writings on slavery in the West Indies focused on the superior ability of Africans compared to European whites to work efficiently in the tropics.[15] "The planters discovered that the labor of Negro slaves, accustomed as they were to intense heat . . . was more efficient . . . consequently the British labourer . . . gave place to the Negro," wrote Vincent Harlow in his 1926 History of Barbados.[16] More recent scholarship, however, has shown that white indentured servants had performed reasonably well and that the planters were satisfied with their work. Rather, they turned to African slaves around the mid-1600s because the growing efficiency of the slave trade had made them a profitable economic alternative to indentured labor. Planters could buy the lifetime services of an African for a little more than they paid for a seven-year contract for a European. Furthermore, the length of service required of indentured laborers was steadily being reduced, and their interest in coming to Barbados was waning, since little land was available for purchase after their period of servitude was over.[17]

Despite high mortality rates, Barbados' slave population grew dramatically, from about six thousand in the mid-1640s to about fifty thousand by the end of the century.[18] Meanwhile, more than thirty thousand whites left the island. At the beginning of the sugar revolution Europeans outnumbered Africans by as much as five to one. Four decades later blacks outnumbered whites by three to one. Barbados changed from being over 90 percent free and white before the sugar revolution to being over 70 percent slave and black within a century.[19]

The spread of sugar estates to all corners of the island transformed Barbados into a classic monocrop colonial plantation society, with thousands of enslaved Africans producing sugar, molasses, and rum for the markets of Great Britain and North America. So successful was sugar that the value of the island's exports to England exceeded that of any other West Indian island. "Little Barbados," with its 166 square miles, writes Eric Williams in *Capitalism and Slavery*, "was worth more to British capitalism than New England, New York and Pennsylvania combined." How Barbados and the other New World colonies were viewed by their European masters can be seen in John Stuart Mill's observation that "our West Indian colonies cannot be regarded as countries with a productive capital of their own, rather they are the place where England finds it convenient to carry on the production of sugar, coffee and a few other tropical commodities."[20] In short, the colonies were looked upon as outlying agricultural or manufacturing estates belonging to a larger community.

With power rooted in its ownership of the island's sugar estates and in its control over commerce, Barbados' planter class, or plantocracy, put its stamp upon Barbadian society. This may have been more the case for Barbados than on other sugar islands due a greater proportion of planters residing on the island. Elsewhere it was typical for landowners to set up their estates so that they could be run by others—namely, a resident manager, bookkeeper, and "attorney." Their income allowed them to live a comfortable life in England and to enjoy a higher social standing than they could in the islands. In Barbados such owners were in the minority, and most acted as resident managers.

Barbadian planters, notes historian Hilary Beckles, "were proud of their English ancestry and held firmly to what they understood to be English values . . . they dressed in the finest of English clothes which were wholly unsuited to the tropics." But, isolated and conservative in their ways, with each generation becoming more acculturated to the creolized ways of the colony, they grew increasingly out of touch with fashion and custom in England. Yet they looked forward to their visits to England, where they were often received as "distant cousins who had been amputated from the trunk of civilization."[21] They had developed a distinct dialect of English in the Caribbean, and in England they were talked about as having been "Africanised." In Barbados, of course, political power was concentrated in their hands, and their belief in white racial superiority and God-given supremacy guided most of their actions toward their African laborers. They had become "colonists," with a status accorded to them in Barbados that they could not have in the "mother country."

The Slave Trade

An estimated 352,884 African slaves were shipped to Barbados between 1651 and 1807, the last year of the British slave trade.[22] They came primarily from present-day Ghana, Togo, Dahomey, western Nigeria, and neighboring territories in West Africa. The better-known ethnic groups from which they came include the Ashanti, Edo, Ibo, and Yoruba. It is nearly impossible, however, to determine the precise origins and the proportions of slaves that came from each ethnic group. The slave traders recorded only the numbers of slaves shipped from each port, not the locations where they were captured. And there are few oral traditions that might offer clues to the slaves' origins.

In the early years of the slave trade some Europeans formed raiding parties to capture Africans, sometimes luring them onto ships and then sailing off. In later years the Europeans relied upon Africans, who had practiced slavery before the arrival of white traders, to provide captives.[23] The raiders were paid for their services with European "trade goods": brightly colored woolen and cotton cloth, firearms, tools, pots and pans, and trinkets. Firsthand accounts of ship captains give testimony to the extraordinary efforts of Africans to resist capture and enslavement. In the words of Thomas Philip, the captain of the slave ship *Hannibal,* collecting a "cargo" destined for Barbados:

> The Negroes are so wilful and loth to leave their own country, that they have often leap'd out of the canoes, boats and ships, into the sea, and kept under water till they were drowned to avoid being taken up and saved by our boats, which pursued them. They have a more dreadful apprehension of Barbados than we can have of hell . . . we have likewise seen divers [diverse] of them eaten by sharks, of which a prodigious number kept about the ship in this place. . . . We had about twelve Negroes did wilfully drown themselves, and others starved themselves to death: for 'tis belief that when they die they return home to their own country and friends again.[24]

The ships sometimes spent several months on the coast collecting a full cargo of slaves before setting sail across the Atlantic. While trade goods were being off-loaded, the ships' carpenters constructed extra decks where the slaves were to travel, "lying prone all night and most of the day, for there was no room to stand upright."[25] During the first century of the slave trade conditions were particularly horrible. Chained below deck, the captives had little space and no choice but to foul his or her own place; by the time they arrived in Barbados many people were covered in sores from lying in this filth. Once a day they were brought on deck and exercised, a practice that usually involved only allowing them to jump up and down to restore circulation. In the latter half of the eighteenth century conditions improved somewhat as traders began to understand the value of scrubbing and disinfecting the decks to reduce disease and mortality and thus protect their profits.

To prevent mutiny, security on the ships was so tight that one scholar describes them as "floating prisons."[26] To discourage resistance, noted one captain in a 1694 report, it was common during the passage to "cut off the legs and arms of the most wilful to terrify the rest."[27] One analysis of insurrections aboard English slave ships in the eighteenth century found that an average of two mutinies or revolts occurred at sea each year. One of the better-known revolts took place aboard the *Thomas* in 1797. Within a few days of reaching Barbados, several of the female captives who were on deck for exercise noticed that the musket chest was unlocked. They managed to conceal some guns and to overpower the crew, bringing the ship under African control, but, since they were unable to navigate back to Africa, they drifted aimlessly for forty-two days before being spotted, attacked, and defeated by a British warship. Its commanding officer then sold them into slavery.

The African death rate during the long voyage—the "Middle Passage"—to the Caribbean varied. On the thirty-five ships surveyed by historian David Galenson mortality ranged from 1.5 percent to a high of 26 percent on one ship destined for Barbados.[28] The mean proportion of slaves who died in transit for all thirty-five ships was 12 percent.

Upon arrival in Barbados Africans were sold directly from the ship. Olaudah Equiano, who at the age of ten was captured by slave raiders near his village on the Niger River, describes his arrival in Barbados:

At last we came in sight of the island of Barbados, at which the whites on board gave a great shout and made many signs of joy to us. We did not know what to think of this . . . many merchants and planters now came on board, though it was in the evening. They put us in separate parcels and examined us attentively. They also made us jump, and pointed to the land signifying we were to go there. We thought by this we should be eaten by these ugly men, as they appeared to us; and when soon after we were all put down under the deck again, there was much dread and trembling among us, and nothing but bitter cries to be heard all the night from these apprehensions. . . . They told us we were not to be eaten but to work, and were soon to go on land where we should see many of our country people . . . and sure enough soon after we were landed there came to us Africans of all languages. We were conducted immediately to the merchant's yard, where we were all pent up together like so many sheep in a fold without regard to sex or age. As every object was new to me everything I saw filled me with surprise. What struck me first was that the houses were built with storeys, and in every other respect different from those in Africa: but I was still more astonished on seeing people on horseback.[29]

In a subsequent passage Equiano describes the sale of his shipmates to a local planter and his astonishment at the callousness of his buyers, who "without scruple" separated husbands from wives and parents from children, "most of them never to see each other again." Richard Ligon, who lived in Barbados in the late 1640s before returning to England, described Africans being sold in his *A True and Exact History of the Island of Barbados:*

> the planters buy them out of the ship, where they find them stark naked, and therefore cannot deceive in any outward infirmity. They choose them as they do horses in a market: the strongest, most youthful and most beautiful yield the greatest price. Thirty pounds sterling is a price for the best man Negro, and twenty five, twenty six, or twenty seven pounds for a woman; the children are at easier rates.[30]

Contemporary accounts suggest that slave owners in the eighteenth century expected up to one-third of their new recruits to die within their first three years in Barbados. Since the mortality rate in these early years was so high, plantation owners relied upon a steady supply of new captives. By 1780, however, as mortality declined with improved living conditions, Barbados' planters were able to eliminate their dependence on the slave trade. Enough children were being born to slave mothers and surviving to meet plantations labor demands.[31]

The Sugar Plantation

Barbados' sugar estates were agro-industrial enterprises that both grew a crop and then processed it into marketable products: sugar, molasses, and rum. Plantations were fairly self-sufficient. They grew most of their own food, had enough artisans to produce and maintain their agricultural and manufacturing technology, and were able to transport products to port.[32]

On a typical plantation the planter and his family lived in the "great house," or "mansion house." Nearby were the quarters of the overseer and bookkeeper. Grouped around the central "plantation yard" (also called the "mill yard" or, simply, the "yard") were the sugar mill boiling house, storerooms, workshops, and often stables, cattle pens, and other small buildings serving a variety of needs. Near the plantation yard was housing for the slaves—the so-called Negro yard.

Nearby was a pond that served as a water supply for both slaves and livestock.[33] But the most visible feature of the plantation until this century was the windmill, the source of energy, which turned massive rollers that crushed the cane squeezing the juice out. The juice then passed through several "coppers"—huge cauldrons—all the while being stirred by the slaves, until it was reduced to a thick brown mass of sugar crystals and molasses.

During the eighteenth and early nineteenth century, before emancipation, most medium to large Barbadian plantations (i.e., 60 to 300 acres) had between one hundred and two hundred slaves, with women outnumbering men. About 75 percent of the slaves worked in the fields. "Field slaves"—the backbone of the plantation and of the economy—were divided into three gangs. The first, or "great gang," composed of the most able-bodied men and women, performed the hardest physical labor. During "crop time," the five-month harvest season, they cut the cane and transported it to the mills for processing. In the off-season they tilled the fields, dug cane holes for a new crop, planted cane and food crops, and collected animal dung and carried it to the fields for fertilizer. The second gang, composed mostly of adolescents, performed lighter tasks such as weeding the fields and planting corn and other food crops. The third gang, often known as "grass gatherers" or the "meat pickers gang" (*meat* meaning "fodder"), was composed of children. They did the lightest tasks, such as collecting grass and fodder for livestock and tending the sheep, goats, and fowl.

During the harvest season most field slaves worked six days a week, from six in the morning until six at night, with two breaks during the day, when a meal usually consisting of yams or potatoes, corn, salt fish, and a pint of molasses and water was served. It is important to remember that, while there was a general understanding of how plantations should be run, each owner or planter had his own way of doing things, and, consequently, there were differences in what planters expected of their slaves and in how they treated them. Older women, whose age or infirmities had led to their retirement from the gangs, were assigned to do domestic chores for other slaves. They tended infants for mothers who were in the fields, cooked meals for the small children, and served as "sick nurses" in the plantation's infirmary.

Slaves feeding the fires with bagasse in the plantation boiler room. (Courtesy of the Barbados Museum and Historical Society.)

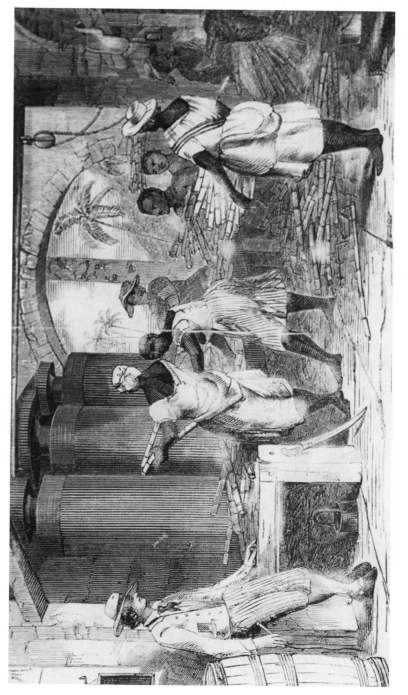

Under the watchful eye of the overseer men bring in cut canes, which the women feed into vertical rollers to be crushed. (Courtesy of the Barbados Museum and Historical Society.)

Barbados. Sugar Works. (Old Process).

No. 12. W. G. Cooper, Copyright.

B.-Series of 24.

An old postcard shows plantation workers and a windmill during crop-time in the early twentieth century. (Photo by W. G. Cooper, courtesy of Mary Kerr.)

Not all slaves worked in the fields. There were also two other categories of slaves—skilled artisans and domestics. They enjoyed more ample food rations, some privileges, and generally better treatment. Skilled artisans—blacksmiths, carpenters, coopers, and masons—performed highly valued jobs in the sugar manufacturing process. Domestic slaves such as butlers, doormen, cooks, maids, washers, nurses, carriage postilions, and attendants ran every aspect of a large household.

William Dickson described the distinctions or ranks among the slaves on Barbadian plantations as he observed them in the 1770s: "Although slavery, properly speaking, admit[s] of no distinction of rank, yet some slaves live and are treated so differently from others, that a superficial observer would take it for granted they belong to classes of men who hold distinct ranks in society." He went on to say that some skilled workers and domestics lived in such comparative ease and plenty that they do not "feel any of the hardships of slavery." On the other hand, he notes:

> The great body of slaves . . . are generally treated more like beasts of burden than like human creatures; since they cultivate the land with no assistance from cattle and suffer every hardship which can be supposed to attend oppressive toil, coarse and scanty fare, bad lodging, want of covering in the wet season, and a degree of severity which frequently borders on, and too often amounts to, inhumanity.[34]

The inequalities were such that for a domestic slave to be sent from the great house to work in the fields was not only a demotion but also a severe form of punishment. Dickson stressed that for anyone to understand the condition of slaves "it is absolutely necessary to attend to the distinctions."[35]

Like planters elsewhere, Barbadian estate owners preferred slaves born in Barbados to new imports from Africa. Those born into slavery, partially because they had known no other life, were regarded as more tractable and useful. New captives from Africa, in contrast, many having been wrenched away from family, kin, and community, knew well what freedoms they had lost and had to be "seasoned" into slavery, a process that involved, in Dickson's words, "getting over the heart breaking transition to a state so new and distressing to them as West

Indian slavery."[36] Africans were more likely to rebel and run away, and their mortality rate was higher than locally born slaves. The preference for Barbadian-born slaves was reflected in market prices; an island-born slave, male or female, was valued up to twice that of an imported slave.[37] By the late 1700s the vast majority of slaves were Barbadian born.[38]

Barbadian plantations maintained a more even ratio of men to women than was true on other Caribbean plantations.[39] Many planters made a deliberate choice to maintain an even sex ratio, perhaps realizing that not only were women productive fieldworkers but also that having an ample supply of women could mean less competition among the men, less tension, greater social stability, and more offspring.[40] In the words of Richard Ligon, who briefly managed a plantation: "We buy them so as the sexes be equal: for, if they have more men than women, the men who are unmarried will come to their master and complain, that they cannot live without wives. And he tells them that the next ship that comes, he will buy them wives, which satisfies them for the present."[41]

In the African societies from which the slaves came, polygyny—in which men may have more than one wife—was often the ideal, although it was usually achieved only by older and more influential men. On Caribbean plantations slaves maintained their preference for polygynous unions. Men and women, notes Beckles, "had no reason to believe this norm should not continue," and, consequently, men kept one "wife" on their plantation and sought others on other plantations.[42] The planters apparently had little reason to object to the practice. It is evident from the advertisements they placed in newspapers when they sought assistance locating a runaway that they knew of their slaves' involvement with slaves on other plantations. Ads often mentioned the names of a male runaway's "wives" on other estates as clues to his whereabouts. One advertisement in the *Barbados Mercury* on 3 May 1783, for example, noted that a runaway named Grigg had "a wife at Mrs. Ann Walker's called Binah, and another at the Pool Plantation of Mr. Graemes."[43]

By the early eighteenth century on most Barbadian sugar estates there was some continuity in slave life. Generations were born, raised, and died on the same plantation. This "allowed for the emergence of grandmothers and great-grandmothers as matriarchal figures on estates, empowered with tremendous moral and social authority in the slave yards."[44] It also meant that black Barbadians could know their family lineages and traditions. Toward the end of slavery some planters also promoted Christian marriages; unions sanctified by the Anglican Church were, of course, meant to be monogamous. Many whites opposed blacks being married in the church, since Christian marriage would mean that the couple could no longer be regarded as "heathen," thereby removing part of the planters' justification for enslaving them.

The lives of slaves were controlled by "slave codes," a series of acts passed by the Barbados Legislature. The legislature was composed of the owners of large plantations and merchants, whose main concern was to protect the economic and political interests of their class. The first comprehensive code, established in 1661, called "Act for the better ordering and governing of Negroes,"formed the legal basis of slave-planter relations and sought to structure the social order of the plantation. The preamble to the act gives some idea of how planters perceived slaves, whom they described as "heathenish," "brutish," and a "dangerous kind of people" whose "wicked instincts" needed to be repressed. The codes tried to legislate many aspects of the slaves' existence, from prohibiting the beating of drums and blowing of horns to restricting travel off the plantation, which in early years was to be allowed only if the slaves possessed a pass or written testimonial from the planter. The code even went so far as to require that every slave be "diligently searched . . . once every week," presumably to prevent theft and plans of rebellion. Slaves were legally defined as "real estate" and therefore could not own property. Yet what the codes required and what was actually done in everyday life often differed considerably.

The codes gave planters the right to punish slaves in almost any way they deemed fit—branding, whipping, splitting their noses, or removing a limb. Under a later revision of the slave code a master could willfully kill his slave with no sanction other than a fine of fifteen pounds; there would be no fine at all if the slave died in the course of being punished without the planter's intent to kill. Slaves who stole property or struck or threatened a white person could be put to death, and many were. They received no protection from the courts, and it was not until the early nineteenth century that they were even allowed to give testimony against whites.

The slave codes did, at least, require owners to provide for some basic needs. The 1688 law, for example, ordered that slaves "shall have clothes once every year . . . drawers and caps for men, and petticoats and caps for women."[45] But there was no specification of how much food slaves were to receive. Although there was probably much variation between plantations, many slaves were underfed and suffered lifelong malnutrition, particularly during the early years of slavery, when planters believed that they should receive a diet reflecting their inferior social status. In this era, particularly, there was little understanding of the importance of diet in relation to health and work productivity. By the late 1700s, however, a better notion of what constituted an adequate diet had developed, and at least on some plantations slaves were given a weekly allowance of 28 pounds of yams or potatoes, 10 pints of corn, ½ pound of fish, ¼ pound of salt, and 1½ pints of molasses.[46]

Much of the English Caribbean patterned its slave codes after those of Barbados, which had demonstrated that it "not only [knew] how to manage profitable sugar plantations but also how to legally control their slaves."[47] Over time Barbados' codes were tempered. Planters relaxed rules against travel, for example, allowing their slaves to freely attend dances and markets and to visit friends and lovers on other estates without having to obtain passes (many slaves had long been doing this secretly anyway). Planters on other islands sometimes ridiculed the leniency of slave discipline and the privileges granted in Barbados. These were freedoms that were thought to be perilous to security if granted on their own islands.

Resistance to Slavery

Just as Africans resisted capture, slaves also resisted enslavement. One way in which they resisted their loss of freedom and the arbitrary authority of their owners was to run away. Running away, or "maroonage," was a fairly common individual response. Slaves sometimes left the plantation to protest the ill treatment of an abusive driver or overseer or when the general hardship of their lives had become intolerable. Others ran away to join lovers and children on other estates. Some ran away with the intention of permanently escaping, while others needed temporary respite and left with the knowledge that they would be recaptured. Notices in Barbadian newspapers seeking information on missing slaves suggest that running away was a common form of resistance. The following is a fairly typical advertisement, published in the *Barbados Mercury* on 3 March 1783:

> Runaway from Ashton Hall, St. Peter, one Negro wench, Sarah Clarke. Has been seen in B'town several times with a tray of clothes on her head, she is working as a washer woman . . . reward for her return.[48]

Gad Heuman's analysis of runaways listed in the *Barbados Mercury* found that 63 percent were male and that the great majority were under thirty years of age.[49] Slaves could escape to plantations where they had spouses or friends who would conceal and look after them. Chances were good, however, that they would eventually be discovered. On other islands runaway slaves could more easily hide in the mountainous interior. In Jamaica the regions of John Crow and Cockpit provided permanent havens for "maroons," or runaway slaves. Barbados' gentle terrain and limited forest cover provided fewer places to hide. Some slaves ran to Bridgetown and tried to "disappear" in the crowds. Men were more likely to run to the towns, while females favored the country, presumably seeking refuge in the slave villages of other plantations. Their chances of permanently escaping slavery were greatest if they had some skill, which would make them employable. A third, but more difficult, runaway option was to flee to another island aboard one of the inter-island boats.

Some whites in Bridgetown knowingly hired runaway women as domestics. If the runaway dressed well and spoke "good" English, he or she might pass as a "freedman." Ads placed by planters in the *Barbados Mercury* often mentioned the linguistic ability of runaway slaves. One public notice placed by Benjamin Pemberton for a runaway "wench" noted that she "speaks very good english" and was likely to pass as free.[50] Conversely, an advertisement for an African-born runaway informed the public that she could "speak little or no english, having been purchased from a Guinea ship about ten months ago."[51] She enjoyed two months of freedom before being captured.

Some blacks and mulattoes of mixed African and European ancestry had been freed since the early years of plantation society. Many were former slaves who had been set free by their owners; others had been born free. In either case they were never numerous. In 1748 there were little more than one hundred free blacks and mulattoes in Barbados; by the end of slavery they constituted only about 6 percent of the total population. Moreover, most free blacks lived in Bridgetown and its immediate environs.[52] There would have been very few in St. Lucy or other distant parishes.

Over 80 percent of all runaways, as suggested earlier, were eventually recaptured, most within three months. The captives were taken to Bridgetown and placed in "cages"—prisons especially constructed for runaways—until they were picked up by their owners. While in prison, they were sometimes sexually and physically abused by poor white guards. Despite the high rate of return and the floggings and brandings they received upon their recapture, some slaves chose to run away repeatedly. That one in every five runaways managed to avoid detection and escape permanently is testimony to the solidarity and support networks that must have existed in the black population. Their success also gave hope to others.[53]

Resistance also took the form of acts of violence against whites, although it occurred much less frequently than maroonage. A slave woman was convicted and executed in 1768 for trying to take the life of her master, with whom she had had a sexual relationship. There are other accounts of household slaves poisoning or attempting to poison their masters. Resistance to slavery also involved sabotage and the destruction of plantation property. In 1815, for example, Betty Phillis, a domestic slave, "set fire to the bed and curtains" of the great house on the Griffith estate, with the intention of burning the house to the ground. While slaves sometimes set fire to cane fields, the most common acts of defiance were feigning sickness to avoid work or stealing plantation property, which was then sold at weekend markets and on street corners in town.

Organized Slave Revolts

In the first half-century of slavery at least five organized rebellions by slaves (in 1675, 1686, 1692, and 1702) were uncovered and the insurrections aborted. In 1675, for example, some African slaves plotted to overthrow the plantocracy and seize control of the island. The rebels included slaves on several estates across the island who had been planning their revolt for three years. Just eight days before the insurrection was to begin, however, a few whispered words were overheard by a house servant, who reported the scheme to her master. An inquiry was organized leading to the arrest and eventual execution of one hundred people for their participation in the conspiracy. During the next twenty-five years three more plots were exposed and the ringleaders executed. After the aborted plot of 1702, however, the nature of black protest changed, and there were no conspiracies to revolt for more than a century, until 1816.

The reason some scholars give for the relative lack of organized resistance during this period was the strength of the military system, which included local militia regiments. Every plantation was required to employ one white tenant to serve in the militia for every twenty black slaves it owned.[54] Another deterrent to slave rebellion were the frequent visits of both the British imperial army and navy to the island. Yet another factor was the good network of roads leading to every corner of the island and a settlement pattern in which plantations were spread fairly evenly across the landscape, each within view of another. This arrangement made mustering and moving the militia across the island easier, if and when needed.

Factors internal to the slave community, notably improvements in living conditions, may have also lessened the urgency of revolt. William Dickson, a reasonably impartial observer, was fascinated by the refusal or inability of slaves to organize violent rebellions during the eighteenth century. He gave eleven reasons for slave quiescence, the first being the greater patience of island-born slaves, who outnumbered "imported slaves." He also believed the large white female population (much larger than on the other islands), "who are on the whole more lenient than men," produced a more civilized treatment of slaves and a more contented population.[55]

Black Barbadians were certainly not happy with their lot during the eighteenth century, but they were relatively better off than in previous generations. They no longer viewed violent revolt as a viable means of attaining freedom. They adapted to slavery as best they could while extracting concessions and freedoms from their masters whenever possible. They fought the system in a variety of ways but did so individually rather than collectively. The reduced threat of violence was welcomed by whites, who no longer felt the same acute fear—"the corporal dread of blacks"—that had been a part of planter-slave relations in Barbados in the earlier era.[56]

Life Outside of Work and African Survivals

Although the daily routine and much of the behavior of slaves was dictated by law and the requirements of the plantation, they did manage to have lives of their own. Music and dance were two essential aspects of life in the Negro yard. As the early codes that banned the playing of drums and horns were eased or lapsed, slaves arranged dances, especially on Saturday and Sunday evenings and on holidays. Other diversions became possible as planters realized that their slaves worked better after entertainment; as one contemporary account notes, "They went through work with greater cheerfulness without expression of any weariness than if they had rested all night long in their huts."[57]

Not surprisingly, many features of slave culture reflected African traditions. Often noted examples include the veneration of ancestors, particular mortuary rites, witchcraft and sorcery, religious rituals used in healing, and some basic beliefs about the afterlife and the way the world functions phenomenologically.[58] Also, slave dancing was very similar to West African dance in its explosive nature and physical expressiveness, involving body contractions and pelvic movements which mimic sexual intercourse. Barbadian slave culture, however, was no more wholly African than white planter culture was wholly English.[59] The beliefs and practices of slaves were largely syncretic. That is, they combined and blended elements from the different African traditions from which the slaves came, from the creolized slave plantation community, along with elements from the creolized English planter society which controlled their lives.

The shift from a population with a majority of Africans to a Creole population in which Barbadian-born and raised slaves were predominant, occurred earlier in Barbados than it did in most other islands. By 1817 only 7 percent of Barbadian slaves had been born in Africa; the comparable proportion was 36 percent in Jamaica and 44 percent in Trinidad. A likely result is that Afro-Barbadians acculturated into European cultural norms quicker than Afro-Jamaicans or Afro-Trinidadians. Two examples often cited are the smaller proportion of African words in the Barbadian vocabulary and the absence of

African religions such as Haitian voodoo and Trinidadian *shango*. With fewer slaves from Africa, black Barbadians were also more likely to have succumbed to pressures to adopt European traits, such as standard English, which offered a chance to gain their owners' favor and better themselves. The Anglican Church also discouraged blacks from following practices that were alien to Europeans or that appeared pagan. Blacks selected for higher-status jobs in plantation houses and for training in a skill undoubtedly came from the ranks of those who were most outwardly acculturated to European customs.

Emancipation

After years of agitation by British humanitarians, with latter support from some economists who argued that slavery was inefficient and wasteful, the British Parliament passed a law in 1833 calling for the freeing of all slaves in the West Indies. Slave resistance, culminating in open revolts in several islands, including a rebellion in Barbados in 1816, also played a role in convincing legislators that the time for emancipation had come. The revolt in Barbados began at 8:30 P.M. Easter Sunday, when cane fields were set afire on a plantation in the southeastern parish of St. Philip. The insurrection quickly spread to other parishes, with the rebels attacking the economic basis of the plantocracy—torching cane fields and eventually destroying one-fifth of the crop. The rebels were outgunned by the local militia and imperial troops, however, who in a joint counteroffensive quashed the rebellion in three days. Only 1 white miltiaman was killed in battle, compared to at least 100 slaves; another 214 slaves were later executed or transported (exiled).[60] While the organized uprising failed in Barbados, a successful revolt in Haiti (1791–1804) had shown that a slave rebellion could succeed, and it proved to be a significant force toward emancipation.

How the transition to freedom was to take place was left up to each colonial legislature. The Barbadian legislature, not surprisingly, opposed the British Parliament's plan to free all slaves. Slavery was still profitable, and white planters feared that they would be bankrupted if they no longer had slaves to operate their estates. As a result, a compromise was reached with Parliament in which slaves would become "apprentices" for a period of time, during which they would continue to work on their plantations for three-quarters of the workweek. During the remainder of the week they were free to work for wages. The compromise produced widespread discontent on both sides. Some planters drove their former slaves harder than ever, giving them inadequate food rations, since they were no longer concerned about their long-term health. Many owners refused to support children under age six, since they had been granted immediate freedom under the emancipation act and owed no labor to the plantations. Slaves, it was said, became insolent, insubordinate, and slack in their attitudes toward work. Recognizing the problems of apprenticeship, the Barbados' House of Assembly, in May 1838, agreed that all apprentices should be declared free. In August seventy thousand Barbadians of African descent celebrated the end of slavery. As the lyrics of a then popular folk song attest: "Licks" (whippings) and "lock-up" (jailings) were "done wid," "jin-jin" (the young Queen Victoria) had "set we free."

It might be expected that, once granted their freedom, the former slaves would have scattered and sought work far away from their former plantations. But fifty years after the end of slavery most black Barbadians still lived on plantations and worked in agriculture. Their choices were very limited. All the arable land on the island in 1838 was owned by white planters, and jobs in Bridgetown were scarce. Emigration was an option for some, but it was fraught with uncertainties and meant separation from community and kin who remained in Barbados. As a result, most blacks were forced to stay on the same plantations they had worked on as slaves. Usually, they received a small wage and a house spot in a "tenantry" (a collection of houses) on marginal land in exchange for their labor. These tenantries evolved into the present-day villages of rural Barbados.

Chapter 3

From Sugar to Tourism

Until the 1970s most residents of St. Lucy worked in agriculture on nearby plantations while also cultivating small plots of sugarcane and vegetables at home. This pattern began to change as tourism expanded and the economy diversified. Today fewer than one in six people in St. Lucy work in agriculture; many young people disdain all agricultural work. This chapter takes a macro-level look at sugarcane production and its decline and the rise of tourism, before examining the economy at the local level in St Lucy.

Sugarcane

Sugarcane is a giant perennial grass, first domesticated in southern Asia.[1] Today it is grown in many parts of the world for sugar,[2] and, together with sugar beet, supplies "every inhabitant of the globe . . . with more than 50 grams of sucrose per day," equivalent to about 8 percent of each individual's total food energy intake.[3] In Barbados sugar is grown on plantations, which average about 250 to 300 acres in size, and on tiny plots, many less than 1 acre, which are owned by several thousand small farmers who also grow vegetables for home use and sale in the domestic market.[4] With sugarcane, however, small farmers have a guaranteed market, since the island's factories buy all the cane that is produced. Vegetables may bring a higher return if the quality is good, but finding a market is not guaranteed.[5] Sugarcane has the additional advantages of requiring less labor and expertise than other cash crops.

The agricultural year is divided into two seasons, "crop" and "out of crop" (often called "hard times"). Crop time is the period when sugar cane is reaped, usually beginning in February and extending through May or early June. This is also the dry season. During the out of crop season there is little work on most plantations, which employ

Cane cutter at work. (Photo by Ellen Frankenstein.)

half as many people as in crop time. The seasonality of agricultural unemployment has been somewhat reduced by plantations devoting part of their acreage to producing vegetables (notably, carrots, cassava, sweet potatoes, yams, green beans, cucumbers, squash, and okra) that grow best during hard times, the wet season.

The sugarcane harvest officially begins when the island's three sugar factories notify growers that they are ready to receive cane. The timing is based on laboratory analysis of the sucrose content of cane samples taken from the fields of each plantation. The starting date can vary by several weeks from one year to the next, depending upon rainfall. A wet growing season means an earlier starting date. When the fields are ready, the factories start up and run round-the-clock until the harvest is completed several months later.[6]

Sugarcane can be harvested with machines, and the trend is toward more mechanization.[7] But many of Barbados' fields are still harvested manually and in a fashion that has not changed much over the centuries. Manual cutting has one advantage over the machines: it yields more cane per acre, since machines waste some of the crop by not always cutting the stalks low enough to the ground. Mechanical harvesters, which weigh between 6 and 10 tons, also compact the soil, which can reduce future yields.

Cutting cane is hot, sweaty, and onerous work. In spite of the heat, fieldworkers typically wear gloves, long-sleeved shirts, and long pants with the cuffs tucked into their socks to protect them from "prickers" (cow itch) and the sharp edges of the cane leaves. Cane cutters use a machete-like knife called a "collins," or "bill," to clear away the dead leaves, or "trash," along the sides of the stalk, to cut the stalk off at the bottom with one swift blow, and then to lop off the leafy top. For energy and liquids field hands suck on chunks of sugarcane as they work. Nevertheless, most cutters are exhausted during the first few weeks of crop season until their bodies become accustomed to the exertion.[8]

Traditionally, only men cut cane, and, while this generally remains the pattern, some women also cut.[9] Most of the fieldworkers who stack the cane into piles or tie the cane in bundles are women.[10] Once enough cane has been stacked in piles about 10 feet apart, a "loader" (a tractor with a mechanical arm) drives through the fields to pick up the piles and load them into trucks or "carts" pulled by a tractor. Before the load leaves the field, workers remove some of the trash that has gotten mixed in with the canes and secure the load to prevent too much cane from falling out on the way to the factory. Some loss is inevitable, however, and during crop time the roads are littered with crushed stalks.

Cutters are paid according to the tonnage they cut.[11] An average worker can cut about half a truckload (about 3 to 4 tons) of cane per day. In 1996 cane cutters earned anywhere from $300 BDS to $600 BDS per week. Often a group of men, seldom more than five, will work together as a "gang" and divide the profits. The problem that all gangs face is ensuring that all members do a somewhat equal amount of work. When an individual does not keep up, takes longer breaks, or does not return promptly from lunch, there is friction, and the gang often dissolves. "You don't really make that much money in a group," explained Junior Brathwaite. "People might just be a body, and not really work hard. It's not easy out there in the hot sun, and some people can't handle it. Then what happens is that the ones that work hard carry the ones that don't work hard, and you make less money."

At the factory trucks and tractor-drawn carts bulging with canes drive onto a scale to be weighed. Next, the load is lifted off by an overhead crane. The canes eventually make their way onto a conveyor belt that carries them inside the mill. Although Barbadians speak of "sugar factories," what actually takes place is not so much a manufacturing process as a conversion process, in which canes are crushed to produce a liquid, which is then converted to a solid (sugar).[12] The process yields sugar, molasses, and two by-products, dried cane fibers ("bagasse"), which fuel the factory's boilers,[13] and "mud" (foreign matter), which is returned to the fields as fertilizer. The yellowish sugar is loaded into tank trucks and, just as in colonial times, taken to the port for export to Britain and North America for further processing. Molasses is transported in tank trucks to rum refineries, where it becomes the raw material for making Barbados' famous rums (e.g., Mt. Gay and Cockspur). Molasses is also used in cattle feed and to make industrial alcohol.

The Decline of Sugar

In 1961 there were 244 sugar plantations in Barbados and nearly twenty-eight thousand small farmers,[14] about 90 percent of whom grew sugarcane. As anthropologist Jerome Handler has noted, small

Unloading cane in the factory yard of the Port Vale sugar factory. (Photo by George Gmelch.)

Hogsheads (barrels) of molasses at the wharf in Bridgetown ready for export (ca. 1900). (Photo by W. G. Cooper, courtesy of Mary Kerr.)

farmers formed a "relatively important element in the national economy and [were] a significant variable affecting the nature of rural life."[15] Sugar was the primary means by which many rural Barbadians earned cash and improved their living standard. Today the picture is very different. All the statistical measures show a decline in the role and importance of sugarcane cultivation in the Barbadian economy. The number of plantations has shrunk to 100; the land in sugarcane production has dropped by half, from a peak of 52,000 acres in the late 1960s to 26,000 acres in 1990; the output of sugar has decreased by two-thirds.[16] Most dramatic of all, the number of small farmers growing cane has dropped tenfold, to about twenty-eight hundred people.

On several occasions when standing with older men in Josey Hill, where there is a panoramic view of the coastal plain below, they have swept their arms from west to east and spoken of how just twenty years ago all the land within view was in sugarcane. Today part of it is in cotton, pasture, or sits idle and is reverting to bush. Throughout Barbados, arable land is being taken out of production every day, with about 10 percent being developed for housing and tourism, while the remaining 90 percent sits idle.

Young Barbadians today view agricultural work as degrading. "Working on the land is now considered beneath young people," said a disgruntled sixty-year-old villager. "They dream of landing a job in New York city." Reflecting on his youth, Marcus O'Neale said:

> Back then, there used to be more workers than work. Now there is more work than workers. The young just don't want to work in the fields. In my day that was all you could do. The only choice you had was which plantation you were going to find work on. You couldn't get further away than you could walk, because there was no way to get there other than on foot or bicycle. There was no other opportunities for employment, no stores, no restaurants, and no hotels like there are now.

Twenty-year-old Rudolph Hinds, cutting cane for his first season, explained why he had no plans of ever doing it again. "People think that cane cutters are stupid. . . .You can come onto a girl, talk to her in a deep voice, and tell her nice things, then you tell her what you do, that you cut cane, and suddenly she ain't interested no more. People have no respect for you." Today many young villagers would rather be unemployed than work in the fields (though some welcome the opportunity to cut cane in Florida, where the wages are higher and they will not be seen). While Barbados' official unemployment rate has hovered in the 20 to 25 percent range for some years, the country has had to import workers from other Caribbean islands and from Guyana to harvest its crop.[17]

Why has Barbados lessened its dependence on sugar? Both economic and social factors play a role. The profitability of sugar production began to decline in the mid-1960s, which one expert refers to as "the era of cane fires."[18] Most of the fires were intentionally set at night by cane cutters in order to make the harvesting easier. But fire also hastens the loss of sucrose and destroys the cane trash, which acts as mulch, protecting the soil from erosion and moisture loss. In short, fires reduce both the present and future yields of the fields.[19] By 1981 many estates were losing money due both to declining crop yields and rising costs.[20] In the 1990s, although sugar has again become profitable, growers fear that foreign prices for sugar will decline and that sugar producers will lose their guaranteed markets abroad.[21] The fickleness of overseas markets continues to make the profitability of sugar production insecure.[22] In the 1980s, for example, the Reagan administration, without warning, decided to phase out its sugar program and abruptly reduced Barbados' allocation. Three years later, after a severe cold spell in the southern United States caused domestic sugar production to slump, the Bush administration raised Barbados' allocation.[23] Producers also worry that artificial sweeteners like Nutrasweet and saccharine will eventually lower the prices offered for sugar. At present, however, the increasing consumption of sugar in many developing countries has kept demand fairly high. Recently, cane fires—now set by vandals rather than workers—have also troubled many growers. Although fire towers have been erected in some places for early detection, so far the government has been powerless to prevent fires.

Some planters are accused of using a variety of excuses in order to justify selling their land to developers, at a considerable profit. Indeed, a number of former plantations are today golf courses and housing developments.

For small farmers there have been other reasons to get out of sugar. Much needed wage increases for cane workers demanded by the Barbados' Workers Union have increased the cost of production.

Plantations could mechanize, thus reducing their dependence on hired workers, but small farmers were left in the lurch. No longer able to hire help and still make a profit, many small farmers abandoned sugar cultivation, switching to livestock or vegetables, selling their land to developers, or leaving it idle.

Education and the Decline of Sugar

The expansion of educational opportunities to all Barbadians beginning in the 1960s has also contributed to the decline of sugar. Since independence from Britain in 1966, successive Barbadian governments, regardless of the party in power, have emphasized the importance of education.[24] This commitment is reflected in government expenditures: Barbados spends more than 20 percent of annual revenues on schooling, an extraordinarily high figure even by the standards of the industrialized world.[25] The United States and Britain, for example, spend less than 5 percent of their annual revenues on education. During the 1960s and 1970s a number of new secondary schools were built along with a new campus of the University of West Indies (1963), a community college (1969), and a polytechnic (1970), allowing a whole generation of rural Barbadians to obtain an education beyond primary school.

Rural Barbadians attending secondary schools became exposed to a curriculum and values that were antithetical to agriculture. The schools did not teach agricultural science, although this was partially corrected in the 1970s with a new syllabus. But then agriculture was not treated as a field of serious study, and teachers seldom conveyed the notion that an occupation in agriculture might be respectable. Newspaper editorials still complain about the neglect of agriculture in the schools,[26] yet the problem goes beyond teachers and curriculum. The aim of education in the minds of rural parents is to provide their children with a means of avoiding the toil, low wages, and, now, stigma associated with agricultural work. Secondary education is seen as the opportunity for children to rise above agriculture and get into better-paying and more rewarding occupations. "In the old days colored people had to do agriculture work," explained a middle-aged villager. "They toiled hard for low wages. . . . After a man pass down that road, he don't want his children to pass that road too." Errol Barrow, who led Barbados to independence and became the country's first prime minister, contributed to the changing attitudes toward sugar. In a May Day speech in King George Park in the parish of St. Philip, he told the crowd that he hoped to see the day when he could look from the park all the way to the St. Lucy lighthouse (metaphorically, the entire length of Barbados) and not see a single cane blade. He later tried to retract his statement, saying that he had been misunderstood, but the damage had been done. His sentiments were taken by many to mean that the country's future would be in tourism, which then was new and booming.

Negative attitudes toward agriculture, to some degree, have been around as long as slavery. Jerome Handler, writing about freed slaves in the eighteenth century, noted that they shunned agricultural work because it was the "hallmark" of slave status. In the words of one eighteenth-century observer, "In no instance will [parents] entertain the idea of agriculture as a pursuit for their free children, the thought appears humiliating to them."[27] The association between agriculture and slavery was highlighted in the post-independence era, when the history taught in Barbadian schools became less Eurocentric and began dealing more with the Caribbean. As teachers devoted more time to colonialism and slavery, agriculture's relationship to plantation work became even more apparent. "It has reached the point," explained a shopkeeper, "that kids are embarrassed if their parents were farmers. Some kids today won't even eat yams and potatoes because they think it's slave food, food that slaves grew and ate."

The stigma now attached to agricultural work is such that villagers are often reluctant to admit that they work in the fields or once did. A student of ours wrote about the attitude he encountered when asking people in his village their occupation as part of a survey he was conducting:

> When I asked about their previous forms of employment I found that almost no one would volunteer that they had cut cane. However, when I asked directly, "Did you ever cut cane?" many people admitted that they had and told me something like it was so long ago that I needn't write it down. . . . It was part of their past that they weren't proud of or, at least, didn't want me to record.

Such negative attitudes are also evident each time villagers learn that we plan to have our students work in the fields cutting cane for a day as part of their anthropology experience. Their first reaction upon hearing this is usually a chuckle of disbelief, astonishment that middle-class American university students and their professors could get any benefit from cutting cane. This turning away from the land would not have been possible had there not been alternative forms of employment. Beginning in the 1960s many jobs were created in the new tourism "industry" and in the related construction and service sectors of the economy.

Tourism

During the 1960s the construction of hotels boomed and unemployment dropped as the Barbados government began to promote tourism as a major sector of the economy. By 1968 the number of tourists visiting the island had grown to 111,000. Six years later the number had doubled and tourism surpassed sugar as the main earner of foreign exchange. Today over 420,000 tourists stay on the island each year, and another 480,000 visit briefly aboard cruise ships.[28]

Other islands in the eastern Caribbean have also experienced a boom in travel arrivals but not on the same scale as Barbados. As a coral island, Barbados is endowed with miles of excellent white sand beaches. Other islands in the eastern Caribbean, such as St. Lucia, St. Vincent, Dominica, and Grenada, are volcanic and have few such beaches. Barbados' low relief also allows nearly constant trade winds to produce a delightful climate and cloudless skies during much of the year. There is also a high level of basic services—water, power, telephones, and television—which are important to many tourists, who want to travel to an "exotic" place without losing the comforts of home. Barbados' extensive road network also makes its plantation houses, gardens, historic places, and other sites accessible to more adventurous visitors.

Tourism has had an enormous affect on the island, including the people of St. Lucy. On the positive side it has contributed markedly to the country's gross domestic product (GDP) and has become a significant earner of foreign exchange. Although the growth of tourism has slowed in recent years, tourist expenditure is still considered the most important growth-inducing factor in the economy. As the major source of foreign exchange it helps to maintain the national income in the face of oscillations in sugar sales abroad. As a labor-intensive industry, it has created a significant amount of new employment, at the rate of about one job for every hotel bed on the island.[29] Many of the Barbadians who work as maids, waiters, gardeners, watchmen, and kitchen staff were lured away from agriculture by better wages and work conditions in tourism.

Proponents of tourism like to point out that it stimulates other sectors of the economy and that its impact extends well beyond the hotel belt. In assessing the economics of tourism, analysts talk about the "multiplier effect," referring to the outward ripple of tourist dollars, which foster demand for goods and services in other sectors of the economy. Farmers, fishers, and merchants benefit because, to feed the large number of visitors, they must supply more food—fish, meat, poultry, eggs, vegetables, and fruit. Likewise, the tourists' desire for curios and souvenirs generates work for local artists and artisans. In the 1960s the largest ripple effect from tourism was in construction. Hotels, guest houses, restaurants, and other services had to be built for the expanding number of visitors. It has been estimated that by the mid-1960s over half of all the construction on the island was associated with tourism.[30]

Although there are no tourist hotels within the parish of St. Lucy, many villagers work in tourism. A survey of the occupations in four St. Lucy villages in 1994 found that 15 percent of all employed adults worked in tourism as maids, waiters, gardeners, security men, cooks, beach vendors, desk clerks, and hotel activities staff.[31] Other people work in affiliated occupations such as taxi driving and construction. The nearest hotel employing people from the parish is the 288-room Almond Beach Resort, located in nearby Speightstown. Other villagers travel further south to work in one of the many hotels and private vacation homes that line the west coast. Given the sheer number of tourists who visit the island, even people who do not work in tourism frequently come into contact with tourists on the street, beach, or in a bank or store. The myriad social impacts of tourism will be discussed in more detail in chapter 8.

Tourism has not been the only new influence changing Barbados' economy. Since the 1960s governments of both parties have encouraged foreign companies to set up shop on the island in an attempt to diversify the economy, reduce the island's dependence upon sugar, and earn foreign exchange. Through a package of financial incentives, successive governments have succeeded in attracting a number of "offshore" operations, which assemble electronic components, manufacture garments, and process information. Wacoal is a Japanese-owned corporation headquartered in the United States that has a factory in St. Lucy. In a large cinder block building constructed at government expense, 160 local women sit at sewing machines stitching women's undergarments for the U.S. market (40 more employees supervise, inspect, and maintain the factory's physical plant). The garments are sold under the Wacoal label but also under designer names such as Donna Karan. The seamstresses earn between $3 and $4.50 BDS ($1.50 and $2.25 U.S.) per hour. For a forty-hour week the women earn not much more than what one of the high-end bras they stitch retails for ($53 U.S.) at Macy's or Bloomingdales. While the women earn less than American seamstresses or women employed at the company's plant in Puerto Rico, they earn more than twice the wages of workers at Wacoal's third plant in the Dominican Republic. Local management worries that the parent company may move its operation to another country should the St. Lucy plant's reputation for high quality slip or wages rise much more.

State-of-the-art satellite technology, allowing cheap transmission of information between "offices" all over the world, has allowed data processing operations like those of Delta Airlines to employ Barbadians to enter data on computers. Barbadians now handle foreign insurance claims, airline ticket reservations, consumer warranty cards, and magazine subscriptions. Some companies, like Offshore Keyboarding Corporation based in California, enter manuscripts written by North American authors into computers.

For Barbados the attraction of the offshore companies has been job creation and much needed foreign exchange. The attraction for foreign corporations is freedom from the stricter environmental and labor regulations of North America and Western Europe, low wages relative to the metropolitan countries in which the corporations are based, English-language literacy and proficiency, a well-educated and adaptable labor force, political stability, and proximity to the U.S. market. In the last decade, however, there has been increasing competition from lower-waged Caribbean territories, including the Dominican Republic, St. Lucia, St. Vincent, and Jamaica as well as from less-developed countries in Asia and Central and South America, where, as anthropologist Carla Freeman notes, the strikingly high accuracy rates (for keyboard operators) and still lower wages will likely attract business away from

Barbados.[32] Yet, so far in the 1990s, the offshore business sector has been growing faster than any other sector of the economy.

Work and the Local Economy

The most salient characteristic of work in rural St. Lucy is the extent to which people rely on several sources of income to make a living. Anthropologist Lambros Comitas coined the term *occupational multiplicity* to describe this phenomenon in the Jamaican village he studied in the 1960s.[33] Since then the concept has been used to describe similar economic patterns in other Caribbean communities.[34] Our field students are always struck by this phenomenon because it differs from the middle- and upper-middle-class American homes they come from, in which one or both parents have a single occupation. A student from Boston, whose father is an engineer and whose mother is a school-teacher, found himself living with a family in Pie Corner in which her host father is a postman as well as a Pentecostal preacher and part-time farmer, while her host mother runs the family's mini-mart and looks after their many pigs, chickens, and sheep.

Having multiple skills and multiple sources of income is the means by which most villagers earn enough money to live comfortably. It also offers villagers a measure of economic security. When one job fails or is no longer very remunerative, they can turn to something else. This is amply illustrated in the household profile of Judy and Roosevelt Griffith in the next chapter. When Judy was laid off from her government job as a cleaner, she expanded her baking, which she had previously done on a casual basis, into a business. One of our students was living with the Griffiths at the time. She was surprised at how calmly Judy accepted the loss of her job, describing her as "unruffled." She tried to imagine how her own mother in Wellesley, Massachusetts, would have reacted to the same news: "She'd have freaked out," she concluded. Over the next few days the student discovered that Judy's calmness was not only due to her "easygoing nature" or even to a certain fatalism that many villagers share but, instead, to the fact that she had economic alternatives, including baking, growing vegetables, and raising pigs.

Esther Cumberbatch provides an example of how even middle-class villagers in comparatively secure positions may learn additional work skills in order to have greater economic security. Esther was promoted to a top-level administrative position. Nonetheless, she took time out to learn a new trade.

> When I got the promotion, lots of people [at work] were jealous. Some of them wanted to know why I had been promoted when I was working there only a short time. They didn't say anything to me directly, but I heard the gossip. They talked down about me, and the least little thing I do somebody complain. I was afraid that some of their talk might get to my bosses and they might start believing it. So I decided to have a back-up, and I started a course with this hairdresser, which normally takes three months if you go everyday. But I am working and can only go every Saturday, so it took me two years. Now I am finally finished. I've got it if I need it, and I can do the hairdressing on the side when I need extra money to pay a bill or want to buy something for Sandra [her daughter].

The person we rent our car from is a schoolteacher who supplements his teaching salary running a small fleet of rental cars.

The economic uncertainty that villagers feel is largely due to the island's dependence on an external economy. The fortunes of Barbados for most of its colonial and postcolonial history were determined by world demand and prices for sugar. Today it is also foreign tourism and offshore services. The number of tourists who visit the island and the amount of money they can spend is greatly influenced by the health of the economies of the countries from which they come. The ebb and flow of the economies of the metropoles ripple out to produce boom and bust, good times and bad, in places like Barbados and in other, distant nations. So, when Esther Cumberbatch learns a second trade and devotes a quarter-acre of her yard to a kitchen garden, she is, besides earning a little extra income, cushioning herself from a future recession in North America.

Such occupational pluralism means many villagers work long hours. Our neighbor, who drives a taxi ten to twelve hours per day, gets up earlier than he would if that were his only job in order to water and stake out his sheep before leaving for work. A student wrote about the daily routines of the men and women he had gotten to know in the village of Pie Corner: "No one here comes home from work, pours himself a Scotch and puts up his feet and watches the news like at home. First, there are crops to look after and animals to bring in from pasture."

Although their hours are long, many Bajans approach work differently than most Americans. As in most tropical environments, the pace is slower than in northern climates. "When it comes to getting a job done, Bajans like to take their sweet, sweet time about it," complained a returned migrant who had spent two decades in England. Characteristic of small-scale societies in which workers know many of the people they come into contact with, Bajans often combine conversation and socializing with work. Urban Americans, in contrast, tend to separate work from play, treating them as exclusive activities.[35]

Village Work and Economy

Table 1 lists the occupations of 202 adults living in four St. Lucy villages who were part of a household survey conducted in 1994.[36] We have sorted their occupations by economic sector to give an approximate idea of the underlying basis of the local economy.[37] The sample may be slightly skewed, however. This can occur, for example, when an individual encourages and smooths the way for his or her relatives and neighbors to find work in the same field. Pie Corner is said to have a disproportionate number of policemen for this reason.[38] With this limitation in mind, let us look at what table 1 can tell us about the village economy. One of the most obvious facts is that villagers are engaged in a wide variety of work, from maids to social workers, masons to mechanics, bakers to barmen, cotton pickers to schoolteachers, civil servants to carpenters.

This range in occupations represents an enormous change from just one generation ago, when, as noted earlier, nearly every adult in the villages worked in the fields of nearby plantations or in sugar factories. A generation ago nearly everyone walked to work; today more than 80 percent of the population commutes, leaving the parish each morning by bus or car. The self-employed—shopkeepers, bakers, seamstresses, tailors, and the like—most of whom work at home in the village, constitute less than 15 percent of the labor force.

Although agricultural work has declined steadily for Barbadians since the 1970s, nearly 17 percent of the adults surveyed continue to work in this sector.[39] Of these, 12 percent farm (many farmers have

TABLE 1. Village Occupations Grouped by Economic Sector (N 196)

Occupation	N	Occupation	N
Agriculture[a]		Manufacturing	
Farmers	24	Machine operator	7
Cotton pickers	5	Factory (misc.)	3
Vegetable sellers / hawkers	3	Mechanic / "engineer"	2
Cane cutters	1	total	12
total	33	General Services	
Tourism (hotels)		Shop keeper	9
Maid	11	Store clerk / cashier	9
Other hotel workers	6	Bank teller	9
Waiter / waitress	3	Baker	7
Gardener	2	Hairdresser	7
Cook	1	Butcher	4
Security guard	1	Seamstress / tailor	3
total	24	Barman	1
Government		Pharmacist	1
Police	8	Secretary	2
Nurse	7	Bus driver (private)	1
School teacher	6	Data entry	1
Civil servant	6	Taxi driver	1
Postal service	4	Auto mechanic	1
Road worker	3	Store manager	1
Telephone	3	Other	3
Military	2	total	60
Social worker	2	Construction	
Bus driver / conductor	1	Carpenter	13
Customs officer	1	Mason	9
Engineer	1	Electrician	2
total	44	Plumber	1
		Other	6
		total	31

[a]The absence of any fishermen in this table is due to the fact that none of the surveyed villages is a fishing community; only two of St. Lucy's approximately thirty communities are fishing villages.

other jobs as well), and 5 percent are either agricultural laborers who harvest someone else's crop or are vegetable wholesalers and hawkers who buy crops from small farmers for resale. One woman we know buys vegetables, herbs, and eggs from farmers in St. Lucy and delivers them to customers in the parishes of St. James and St. Michael; she also raises pigs, which she sells to hotels and supermarkets. Most hawkers are also women. Some village women sell fruit and vegetables on the streets of Speightstown or Bridgetown. Hawking is attractive to rural

The grounds of a former plantation, with the land now in pasture. Note the remains of the windmill; such millwalls are a common feature of the Barbadian landscape today. A former tenantry lies at the end of the road. (Photo by George Gmelch.)

women because of their access to vegetables and fruit and the flexibility of its hours, which makes it compatible with childcare. It is also preferable to the grueling labor of plantation "fieldwork" and the low pay and long hours of domestic or factory work. In a few cases hawking is a family tradition—something grandmother, mother, daughter, and granddaughter have done.

Many other people grow crops on small plots of land for home consumption, selling or giving away their surplus to neighbors. Nearly half of the households surveyed grow vegetables in backyard "kitchen gardens."[40] Many villagers also tend "tree crops," notably coconuts, bananas, papaw (papaya), mango, sugar apple, and breadfruit (a green, starchy fruit that is used as a vegetable).[41] Which crops are grown varies somewhat from village to village depending upon microclimate, soil, and tradition. One of our students, for example, who lived in a village with many breadfruit trees, was served breadfruit (boiled, steamed, roasted, and baked) on sixteen of his first seventeen days there, while fellow students in other parts of the parish had not yet tasted it.

One-third of village households raise livestock, with chickens, black-bellied sheep, and pigs being the most common animals kept, followed by cows and goats. Generally, men tend the animals, although chickens, which are kept in the yard, are often looked after by women. With the exception of one dairy and one chicken farm in St. Lucy, no one makes a living solely from animal husbandry. Rather, having a few pigs, sheep, and cows supplements other sources of household income; eating them saves money, and they can be quickly converted to cash in a financial pinch. Some people compare raising cows and sheep to putting money in the bank. As Rudolph Griffith says: "I keep them in case of an emergency. If the economy presses down on me, I can turn around and sell a sheep or a cow and be back on top again."

When an animal has grown to full size, its owner lets friends and others know that he or she will soon be butchering. He then takes down orders, keeping track of how much meat has been requested. Normally, all the meat is sold in this way, providing villagers with fresh meat at a low price and giving the owner extra cash. Occasionally, however, animals are sold on the hoof to a butcher, supermarket, or hotel; some locally raised sheep and goats are also purchased by itinerant East Indian merchants who regularly visit the villages.[42]

Nearly 12 percent of the surveyed adults work in the tourist sector, mostly in hotels as maids, waiters and waitresses, bartenders, gardeners, and security guards. This figure is comparable to the national average,[43] but it is higher than one would expect for a parish that has no hotels or restaurants and only one commercial tourist attraction (Animal Flower Cave). (St. Lucy's other tourist sites are scenic views.) Many of the 31 percent of villagers who work in the service sector are employed in jobs that cater to tourists. For example, nearly all of the fares of a Josey Hill taxi driver are tourists. Similarly, most of the sewing that seamstress Aileen Allman (profiled in chap. 4) does is for tourism—making uniforms for hotel staff.

Only 5 percent of the men and women in the village surveys hold jobs in the manufacturing sector. This is about half the figure for Barbados as a whole and reflects the relative absence of factories in St. Lucy and adjoining parishes. Most industry on the island is located in the industrial estates around Bridgetown, a considerable commute away.

If we group occupations by skill and status, we find that roughly 9 percent of villagers hold white-collar managerial or professional jobs—teachers, social workers, civil servants, a store manager, and a pharmacist. Seventy-five percent work in skilled or semiskilled jobs, as bakers, masons, mechanics, cooks, and postal workers. The remaining 16 percent labor at unskilled jobs, as road workers, security guards, construction workers, and hawkers.

Women and Work

Women in the Caribbean have long had dual work roles, performing both domestic labor and work outside the home. During slavery all women except elites worked. After emancipation most black women had little choice but to continue working, since the elite ideal of man as breadwinner remained "unattainable and unrealistic" for them.[44] It was not until the twentieth century that the notion that women should confine themselves to domestic tasks and not engage in wage labor began to take hold among the black population. Some feminist scholars believe that the West Indian Royal Commission of Inquiry, or Moyne Commission, of the late 1930s played a role in this change.[45] The British commissioners who came to investigate social conditions in the Caribbean and propose reforms following a series of riots brought their biases with them, including a paternalistic and protective view of women. Caribbean women, the commissioners believed, should be trained for marriage and should only work outside the home when necessary and then at "suitable" careers such as teaching, nursing, and social work. Women's work should be supplemental to that of the male household head. It was following the Moyne Commission report that the idea that women's place is in the home began to take hold.

Although many parish women work today, the kinds of jobs they typically do are those considered appropriate for women. In blue-collar work women are usually found in domestic jobs, such as sewing, cooking, and cleaning. In St. Lucy's Wacoal garment factory, for example, all 160 of the sewers are women. The only male employees are managers and the mechanics who maintain the sewing machines. Likewise, in the parish's Superchick processing plant the vast majority of the poultry workers are women. Managers at both plants said that few men would consider applying for jobs that women do. Career women are likewise found predominantly in the "caring" professions of nursing and teaching. All but one of the 13 nurses and teachers in the household survey are women. Today, however, younger and better-educated St. Lucy women are moving into a wider range of jobs and careers, contributing to a growing gap in the experience and standard of living of older and younger women in the parish.

The least well-off village women make do by pooling resources from their own economic activities and the help they receive from other household members and "boyfriends." (Although most women receive support from male partners at some point in their lives, the amount is often small and unreliable.) Many women, like Uzil Holder, who is profiled in chapter 4, work in the informal economy, selling home-made bread, chicken, fish cakes, or rotis.

Unemployment

Although we do not have reliable statistics on unemployment in St. Lucy, the official jobless rate islandwide in the mid-1990s stood between 20 and 25 percent of the work force.[46] Unemployment among young people, aged fifteen to twenty-four, was over 40 percent. Unemployment in St. Lucy is at least as high. Many youths, upon leaving secondary school, are disappointed with the type of work and wages available to them and choose not to work. While waiting for something better to come along, they live at home with their parents, helping out in small ways around the house, in the garden, and with the livestock. Some go without employment for months or years before surrendering their aspirations and accepting a job they once considered beneath them. Other youths eventually find "acceptable" work, while still others emigrate to further their education, get special training, or find a job overseas.

Village elders frequently complain about the large number of young adults—primarily males—who seem to have nothing better to do than hang out, or "lime" (which literally means to watch the lime trees grow). Older adults like to remind them of how hard they worked when they were young and of the fact that they had no choice in what they did: "It was work in the fields or don't eat." One of us was sitting at Esther Cumberbatch's kitchen table one morning when she chupsed (sucked air through her teeth) and, with an attitude of disgust, pointed down the road to a derelict house in which a half-dozen young men were playing cards and gambling, while immediately next door a middle-aged woman and two older men cut cane in a small field.

> The young people will not even take a job for the moment, like cutting cane or pickin' cotton, and put a few dollars into their pocket. No, they will not do that. They sit on the road all day, and they interferes with the young girls passing on the road in an abusive way. The only time they go into the cane field is to take cane for themselves to chew. Just look at the road, and you'll see all the peelings from the cane they've taken from the field, and the field is not theirs. . . . You won't ever see them asking for work in the fields. It's so bad that the plantations now have to get workers from St. Lucia and St. Vincent because these boys here don't want to work.

In the words of sixty-year-old Michael Hinds: "The pay [cutting cane] is good, but the kids today don't want to do the work. They come out of school with fancy degrees and think they are too good for this kind of work. They would rather sit home and do nothing than go out and work in the fields." Trevor Hind, twenty-three years old and unemployed, responds to the criticisms of older people, expressing the sentiments of many youth:

It's hard to find work now. . . . The old people say that we all just lazy, that we don't want to do no work. When they were young, there was work for all. They worked in the fields because they didn't know no better. . . . There is still some jobs cutting cane, but I didn't go to school all these years to cut cane. If there be real jobs, I'd be working.

Most Bajans believe that unemployment is a factor in the increasing incidence of crime. Yet, otherwise, joblessness in Barbados—which statistically approaches that of the United States during the Great Depression—has not produced social turmoil or strife. The reasons, which are complex and not easily disentangled from one another, relate to points discussed earlier. First, most young unemployed adults are able to live in reasonable comfort at home. Extended households are common, and kitchen gardens and a variety of food-producing trees throughout the year make it possible to eat cheaply. There are also fish to be taken from the sea. "In Barbados, you don't need money to live," explained one villager. The profile of Eric O'Neale in the next chapter, which describes the accommodations one young man has made to unemployment, is instructive. Second, as fairly devout Christians, Barbadians are charitable and quick to help out those in need. In almost every village people willingly share food, whether from the tree, garden, or pot. Third, unlike the northern United States, Barbados' tropical climate—in which temperatures seldom fall below 70 F and fluctuate little during the year—means that clothing requirements are minimal (and there is no need for heat in the winter). Fourth, the jobless can entertain themselves at little or no cost in street corner groups, playing dominoes, cards, road tennis, fishing, and village-organized football (soccer), cricket, and basketball. Competitive village team sports, in particular, siphon off pent-up energy and engage males in a socially valued activity. And there is always talk. Finally, there is still a certain optimism among the unemployed that if they just wait long enough a decent job will eventually come.

Employment opportunities for Barbadians, however, are not expected to improve in the near future. Two former outlets for job seekers have withered. In post-independence Barbados much of the island's surplus labor was siphoned off by an expanding public sector—government jobs—and by emigration. The energy shocks of the 1970s and the economic recession and balance of payment difficulties of the 1990s has changed that. The latter forced the government to turn to the International Monetary Fund for help, which in turn required Barbados to undergo a major "structural readjustment." The economic reforms included downsizing the government. Three thousand government employees were lost; those who managed to keep their jobs took an 8 percent salary cut. At the same time, fewer new jobs are being generated by tourism, as growth in this sector has leveled off. Meanwhile, Barbados' secondary schools continue to turn out graduates with skills and high aspirations. New agricultural enterprises could absorb some of these new school leavers, but as previously indicated, few youths are willing to work the land.

Chapter 4

Farmer, Fisher, Baker, Maid

The six profiles in this chapter will personalize the economic patterns we have just discussed. They also introduce some of the people behind the ethnographic descriptions that follow. Selwyn and Barbara Greaves farm but also work for wages, Selwyn as a truck driver and Barbara formerly as keyboard operator. Sandra Broomes works in tourism as a hotel maid. Judy and Roosevelt Griffith operate a home bakery. Eric O'Neale fishes and is intermittently employed as a mason. Aileen Allman is a seamstress, and her husband, Siebert, has worked at a variety of jobs, both in Barbados and as a migrant. Uzil Holder, a Guyanese immigrant of Barbadian descent, sells rotis and picks cotton. In these sketches Barbadians' ties to the global economy become apparent—in their reliance upon immigrant remittances, labor migration, tourism, and employment in offshore international businesses.

SELWYN AND BARBARA GREAVES
Small Farmers

Selwyn and Barbara Greaves are farmers, although Selwyn also drives a truck. They are in their mid-thirties. Both are tall and lean, with bodies like marathon runners. Selwyn wears aviator-style wire-rimmed glasses and has large sideburns. Barbara has a slender face with fine features. They live with their two children, Damian and Richelle, and Barbara's eighty-year-old grandmother, May Hinds, in Peterses, a neighborhood consisting of a single long road adjoining the village of Josey Hill. The neighborhood has an isolated feeling to it: few residents own cars, and probably no more than a dozen vehicles pass by on even a busy day. The only sounds are those of farm animals, mostly chickens, the wind rustling the trees, and, occasionally, the radio coming from the open window of a neighbor's home.

The Greaves live in a modest, four-room wall house. A color tele-

Selwyn and Barbara Greaves. (Photo by George Gmelch.)

vision sits prominently on a table between the small kitchen and the living area; it can be watched from either room, while one is cooking or relaxing. They also have Nintendo, which eleven-year-old Damian plays after school. Barbara was born in Leicester, England, where her mother had migrated at age eighteen in 1950 to study nursing. She became pregnant with Barbara in 1958, and when Barbara was just five months old she sent her back to Barbados to live with her grandmother. Barbara's mother returned home three years later, "fed up with the cold," while Barbara's father remained in England. Although Barbara has never seen her father, he occasionally calls on the telephone, and once a year he writes her a letter. She does not expect to meet him in person, since he has never expressed any interest in visiting Barbados, and she does not wish to spend her savings on airfare to England.

Barbara and Selwyn are devout Seventh Day Adventists. Selwyn is a deacon, and both sing in the choir of the Chance Hall Seventh Day Adventist Church, a twenty-minute walk from their home. They spend Saturday morning in church attending Sabbath school and the worship service; they are back again on Wednesday for an evening service and on Thursday for choir practice. As conscientious Adventists, they try hard to adhere to the church's teachings, by not working on the Sabbath (from sundown Friday to sundown Saturday), not drinking alcohol or caffeinated drinks, and not eating pork and other meat. The church also discourages its members from eating chicken and fish, which Barbara and Selwyn have not yet managed to give up fully.

After leaving St. Clements Senior School at age sixteen, Selwyn learned carpentry by working with his father, but he didn't like it and soon took a job as a gardener at a complex of private guest houses on the coast in St. James. Three years later he was offered a new job in St. Lucy, less than a ten-minute walk from his home, milking cows on a former sugar plantation that had converted to dairy farming. For the past eight years Selwyn has been employed as a truck driver, delivering cement, lumber, sand, and stone to building sites. But his chief interest is farming. When asked about farming, Selwyn's eyes brighten, and his voice and manner exhibit an enthusiasm that he doesn't have when talking about driving a truck or his earlier occupations.

Selwyn and Barbara are typical of the half-dozen larger-scale farmers in Josey Hill. They grow vegetables on a half-acre of land behind their house and are currently looking for an acre plot to rent so they can expand their farm. Beans, sweet peppers, and cucumbers are their major crops, but they also grow okra, cabbage, and carrots. Around the perimeter of the field Barbara's grandmother grows pigeon peas; she also keeps sixty chickens in the yard. Her hens produce about twenty-five eggs each day, which she sells to a baker in the village. To determine which crops to plant and how much space to allot to each, Barbara and Selwyn talk to their wholesaler and to other farmers and examine the wholesale prices being offered for different crops that are listed each week in the island's two newspapers. Their chief strategy is to plant crops that are yielding low prices at the moment, because, explains Barbara, "By the time the price has risen back up, your crop will be ready, and you'll get a good price for it." Until this year they did everything by hand, including the heavy work of "forking" (turning over the top soil with a pitchfork). They now hire a "contract plow," that is, an individual who brings his tractor to prepare their land—plow, furrow, and "rotivate." The government also has a plowing service for small farmers, and Barbara says they could save a few dollars using it but don't because "it doesn't always come when you need it."

They have been fortunate in not losing much of their crop to monkeys, as many small farmers in St. Lucy do. They attribute this to the farms on either side of their land that produce ground nuts and potatoes, crops that monkeys prefer. Both neighboring farms lose a sizable percentage of their crop to monkeys, despite their owners' efforts to keep them away by spreading newspaper in the furrows and tying plastic bags to sticks in the ground with the hope that the noise they make in the wind will scare off the monkeys.

Both Barbara and Selwyn farm six days a week, only taking Saturdays off, their Sabbath. On most days Barbara is in the field pulling weeds, loosening the soil, and watering and tending her plants from 8:00 A.M. until noon, when the sun is overhead. She then comes inside to get lunch and does housework until mid-afternoon, when she returns to the field until "night closes in," around 6:00 P.M. Selwyn does not get into the field until he returns home from his truck driving job around mid-afternoon. But on most days he is able to work several hours until dusk; he is also in the field on Sunday. Together they put about sixty hours a week into their farm.

For Barbara farming is more profitable than the clerical job she once held, and, since the garden is near home, it allows her to be close to her family. Although the work is tiring and both Barbara and Selwyn are usually exhausted by the end of the day, they find it satisfying. "The beautiful part," says Barbara, "is watching the crops grow. Sometimes you just have to stand up and admire them." Selwyn likens gardening more to a "hobby" than to a job. "With farming you always have something to do. It keeps your mind occupied, and it keeps you out of mischief. And at the end of the day you get a good bath, and you go to sleep in a hurry."

Barbara and Selwyn sell their produce to a wholesaler in the village of Bishops on the coastal plain below Josey Hill, who in turn supplies hotels. Selwyn calls the wholesaler a week before the crop is ready to be "reaped." There is no haggling, since the wholesaler always pays the price listed in the newspaper or better. The Greaves keep some of their crop for the family freezer, and, occasionally, they give or sell vegetables to neighbors.

May Hinds, Barbara's grandmother, picks, shells, bags, and sells the pigeon peas that grow on bushes bordering the field. They are a staple of Barbadian cooking, a necessary ingredient in rice and peas. She loads them in a large sack and takes them by bus to Bridgetown, where she "hawks" them, sitting on Swan Street in a place where the congestion causes pedestrians to slow down and take more notice of the hawkers' produce. On a good day May can sell 25 pints of peas at five dollars per pint and even more around Christmas, when demand is greatest. Altogether, farming yields about one-third of the family's income.

From January to May Barbara earns extra income picking cotton on nearby Lamberts Plantation.[1] Usually starting at dawn, she and a group of four or five neighbors walk to the "cotton ground" at the top of the village. They are joined in the fields by other women and some children to pick the fine sea island cotton, which is exported to Japan, where the high-quality fibers are spun into cloth used in expensive garments. The women work steadily, plucking the chest high cotton pods, or bolls, and placing them in a "crocus" (burlap) bag, which they trail with them as they move down each row. The women rarely talk while picking, except when the cotton is thin. "When the cotton is good," says Barbara, "you don't want to form a conversation because then you lose concentration on what you're doing and you pick less.

And, if you pick less, you make less money. But when it's thin you crack a joke and laugh with one another." When the cotton is plentiful the women may stay in the fields all day, not returning home until dusk. At home Barbara separates the cotton from the pod, usually while watching television, or saves it for a rainy day.

Barbara earns a dollar per pound. "Fast pickers" can pick 50 to 60 pounds a day, while "slow pickers" come home with 25 to 30 pounds. They take the cotton home with them and store it until Wednesdays, when the plantation truck comes to each picker's home to collect and weigh the cotton. The truck carries the cotton back to the plantation "barn" and then to the "ginnery" in another parish, where the seeds are removed from the soft fibers, before it is loaded onto a ship destined for Japan.

In the field Barbara works steadily until lunch, stopping only briefly for a sip of the "frozen water" she brings with her. At noon she and neighbors sit down together to eat rice and peas, macaroni pie, and bread or biscuits. Their meals are always high in carbohydrates, since they "keep you heavy so you can work for a long time." They drink homemade lemonade or *mauby* (a refreshing beverage made from the bark of a small, shrubby tree).

Barbara laughs at the stigma attached to fieldwork and jokes that her nonagricultural neighbors call her "Queen of the Crop." Most villagers, she admits, are "ashamed to be seen on the cotton ground, even though they'd like to have the money." Barbara could find work outside of agriculture if she wished. She completed two years at the Barbados Polytechnic, having taken courses in typing, bookkeeping, and commerce. She also took a three-month training program to be a receptionist. And in 1989 she worked for a year in an offshore data entry house, as a "keyer"—or, in the company's vernacular, a "text operator." Barbara was one of one hundred young women and one man who, grouped into clusters of four at different work stations scattered throughout a large "open office," typed manuscripts from North America—reference books, dictionaries, medical texts, and scientific journal articles—into computers. Barbara remembers becoming adept at glancing at a line of text, committing it to memory, and then typing it in without having to look back at the page. All the keyers worked fast, since "incentives" were paid if their average hourly productivity exceeded a certain number of keystrokes.

Her employer at that time, Offshore Keyboarding Corporation, is a California-based company that also has overseas operations in Sri Lanka and Grenada. Like other offshore companies, it operates in Barbados to take advantage of low labor costs. Anthropologist Carla Freeman, who studied Barbados' off-shore pink-collar sector, describes the work setting:

> Their fingers fly, and the frenetic clicking of keys fills the vast and chilly room [air conditioned, for the computer technology] as Walkman-clad women work . . . at video display terminals—constantly monitored for productivity and accuracy—typing to the latest dub, calypso, or easy-listening station. The muffled clatter of keys creates a sort of white noise, and the green glow of a sea of computer screens lends a sort of Orwellian aura to the tropical setting outside.

Barbara earned only twenty-four dollars for a seven and a half hour shift (or about $1.60 U.S. per hour); the trip from Peterses to the company's plant near the deepwater harbor in Bridgetown took at least an hour each way. Only by working overtime could Barbara make the job worthwhile; she routinely worked an extra half-shift (four hours) and occasionally double shifts, in which case, after fifteen hours of typing, she would take the midnight bus home, getting to bed at 1:00 A.M. only to rise four hours later to start a new workday all over again. When Barbara first applied for the job, she was excited, and it still looked appealing when she first started—the workplace was tidy and air-conditioned and the corporate offices were plush and gave the workers pride in being employed by a "corporation" and an American-owned one at that. Her workmates were neatly dressed and looked "middle-class" in appearance (a company requirement). But what appeared to be a good "clerical job" in the beginning was, in reality, a repetitive, semiskilled, and low-paying job only marginally better than traditional factory jobs or working in the garment industry. Before the year was out the glare from the video display terminal caused eyestrain; she had difficulty focusing, and her eyes were tearing.[2]

Barbara is content with her life at present but hopes that in the future she will "have to work less hard and be able to relax." She also hopes that her children will have things "a little bit easier."

SANDRA BROOMES
Maid

Sandra is short and slender with a coffee-colored complexion and a broad, frequent smile. She has been cleaning the rooms of North American and European visitors for most of her life and seems sincerely to enjoy meeting tourists. At thirty-one she is the mother of two teenage girls, Fontaine and Kareen, and has never married. Never having been able to save enough money to buy a house of her own, she and her daughters live with an aunt and her sister's two sons in a humble, three-room board house on the edge of the village of Half Moon Fort. They do not have electricity. The land the house sits on is rented and is located fifty yards back from the road and the electric lines. It would cost them a thousand dollars to have a "pole" put in, which they cannot afford and have little motivation to do, since the land is not theirs. An unusual feature of Sandra's house, especially considering its small size and the absence of electricity, is a bookshelf overflowing with children's books. "I didn't get much schooling," Sandra explained. "I say that what I didn't have my children must get, and that was learning. So from the time they able to read, whenever they have a birthday or Christmas, I always buy them books."

Sandra went to school until age fourteen. She began work when she was twelve, weighing produce and packing bags in a grocery store. During crop time she helped her mother work in the sugarcane fields "tieing canes" (tieing cane stalks into bundles before loading on trucks for transport to the sugar factory). She wishes she could have stayed in school longer, but her mother needed help to support her thirteen children. Sandra's father was absent much of the time and contributed little to the support of the family, eventually developing a relationship with another woman. Having seen the hardship her mother endured, with little support from a man, combined with her own disappointments with men has made Sandra skeptical about marriage or becoming permanently involved. The father of her first child went to the United States and never came back. Despite promises to the contrary, he has never written or sent money. The father of her second child comes by the house sometimes to visit their daughter: "He comes to the curb and blows the horn, and she goes out to him." He doesn't contribute to her support. As she puts it: "You got too many men here in Barbados who only want you for being their maid, to do their dirty

Sandra Broomes. (Photo by George Gmelch.)

work, and for their bed. I don't want my life to be so. I saw how tough my mother had it, and it ain't for me."

Sandra began working as a maid at age sixteen, in a guest house on the west coast. She stayed only a year and a half because the guest house was hidden in the trees and was always being broken into, and after a time she didn't feel safe there. She then became a maid at Heywoods Holiday Village (now Almond Beach Resort), a 288-room hotel complex spread over thirty acres of beach front property in nearby St. Peter, which was once a sugar plantation. For the first five years Sandra worked full-time as a maid, being responsible for twelve rooms.

> You always make up the bed first, then you do bathroom—the sink and faucet, tub and toilet—the tub is sometimes not so good when people don't drain it and you have to put your hand down into their dirty water to open the stopper. Then you sweep the floor, pull the drapes, spray scent, leave, and close the door. If anything bad happens in your rooms, like the light or the froster [air conditioner] not work, then the management call you to the desk and you have to answer for it.

The only part of the job that really bothers Sandra is "having to pick up peoples' dirty what-nots. Some people leave their things lying all about; even their dirty sanitary pads. That makes me very uneasy." There is also the occasional tourist who misplaces a camera, cash, or jewelry and reports it stolen at the front desk. She is certain that some of the claims are fraudulent, that some guests do it to make an insurance claim and collect money. She likes most of the guests she deals with, however, but adds that some women can be very difficult: "I don't know what it is, but nothing is ever right for them." She recounts how some female guests will claim that the sheets aren't clean and request that they be changed, when Sandra knows she changed them that very day: "In the morning, before you come in to do their room, they put a mark on the sheet with a pencil, so they can know if the sheets do be changed. I don't know what their problem be, but they can annoy you so. But I try not to let it enter my mind. It's better if you don't let them bother you."

Sandra takes pride in doing her job well. At the present time she mainly works in the poolside towel room issuing towels to guests.

Most days for Sandra start at 5:30 A.M. She gets up to prepare breakfast, pack a lunch for her daughters and nephews, and get them ready for school and then catches the bus down the coast three miles to Heywoods. After "clocking in," she changes into her uniform. All hotel staff are issued three uniforms, which are washed and pressed each night so they always looks neat for the guests. Once changed, Sandra reports to her "station," the towel room, where she issues and collects from one hundred to two hundred towels a day. Although the guests are only entitled to one beach towel per day, some always want two. Sandra can see no reason why anyone would need two beach towels, but rather than argue, she gives in, but with a warning that they must return both or be charged. There is much free time in the towel room, and Sandra fends off boredom by doing crossword puzzles, by reading *In and Out* (a newspaper for tourists) and religious pamphlets, and by talking to the guests. She tells them interesting places to visit, things to do at the hotel, and where not to walk at night.

She gets off work at 6:00 P.M. and goes directly home to prepare dinner for her kids. Often she sits on the back steps for awhile and helps her aunt clean and bone flying fish, which bring in a small amount of cash during the flying fish season (December through June). Dinner is usually rice and peas and steamed flying fish. Canned corned beef substitutes for flying fish when the fishing season ends. Like most Bajan households, the family does not sit down to eat together, except on Sunday; rather, the food is left on the stove, and each person eats when he or she is ready. Without electricity they have no refrigeration and no way to preserve leftovers, so Sandra tries to prepare no more than what the family will eat in one sitting. After dinner the children often go two houses away to the home of a relative to watch television; her aunt goes off to her sister's, while Sandra reads by a kerosene light or lies down on her bed to rest and say her prayers.

On her days off—Wednesday and Sunday—Sandra walks across the road to the sea for a "seabath." She goes either early in the morning or late in the day to avoid the midday heat. Unlike many villagers, she can swim; she likes the feeling of the water on her skin and thinks it's healthy for her body.

Sandra's household has only her paycheck as income. She earns about twenty-five dollars (U.S.) per day but takes home much less after taxes and other deductions. What little money is left after paying for food, daily bus fares to and from school, and clothing and shoes for her daughters goes into maintaining the house. Over a period of five years Sandra had saved enough money for the airfare to New York to visit her sister in Brooklyn: "I heard so much about America from the guests that I really wanted to go see it, and to see my sister." Her two daughters were able to travel to Florida to see Disney World with their school class, but Sandra was twice denied a travel visa by the U.S. Embassy in Bridgetown and is now losing hope of ever seeing the States. Being denied a visa was a "major upset." She cannot fathom why Americans are able to come to Barbados so easily, with nothing more than a driver's license or birth certificate, while she is unable to travel to their country, even with a passport. Curious about why she had been denied a visa and thinking that we might be able to help, we inquired on her behalf at the U.S. Embassy. We were told that Sandra was probably turned down because she didn't have a bank account or own land in Barbados and, therefore, "didn't have sufficient ties to the country" to convince the official that she would return to Barbados.

Otherwise, Sandra Broomes is satisfied with her life and says she will work at the hotel as long as there is a job for her. "My mother used to tell us," Sandra recalls, "never hang your hat higher than you can reach, because you could fall. If I'd tried to go too high, I might get into situations that I can't handle. And I don't want to fall." The only other kind of work that Sandra has ever considered was as a telephone operator. Her attitude, which ambitious middle-class Americans or Bajans might dismiss as fatalistic, is in fact quite realistic. With her limited formal education in an environment in which so many Bajans now have a secondary education, Sandra would have difficulty obtaining a job above her present level. Unfortunately, the low pay she receives will make it difficult for her ever to save enough money to buy a house of her own, and, financially, as she readily recognizes, life will continue to be "tough." But she genuinely enjoys going to work, where she has many friends, and she likes her job, which she asserts is more than most people can claim in Barbados or the United States.

ERIC O'NEALE
Mason, Fisherman, Unemployed

Eric O'Neale, age twenty-six, fishes and works as a mason when he can find work, which isn't often. He is of medium stature, with an athletic build and a quiet disposition. As a schoolboy, Eric never had any particular career ambition, although, he says, "For a time I fancied

Eric O'Neale. (Photo by George Gmelch.)

being in the army or the police. But, as I grew older, I learned the things they did to other people just from a simple order, and I thought it wasn't for me."

After leaving St. Lucy Secondary school at age sixteen, Eric learned masonry by working with his older brothers, Timothy and Malcolm. They built houses, although the work was never steady. He shared an apartment in Bridgetown with one brother and some friends. At night he would sometimes hang out in the nightclubs and pick up or be picked up by a female tourist. Most of the women he left with were German, many allegedly having come to Barbados in hopes of a romantic relationship with a black male. He sometimes moved in with them for the duration of their two- or three-week stay. "But I stopped that after awhile," he said, "because of the emotions. Even though these are short-term relationships, you get into peoples' lives. You develop feelings for them and them for you, and then they have to go home. It can be hard to separate. For some guys it's an ego thing—how many women they can sleep with. Some guys do it for the money, but I never got into that."

Having grown up in rural St. Lucy, Eric had difficulty adjusting to the city and has vowed never to live in Bridgetown again.

> The streets are dirty, there's pollution, there is theft, and people can be selfish. They don't know one another, and they don't care about anyone but themselves. In the morning, when you are trying to sleep, people will drive up and beep their horn. I consider that selfish. And then there is all the break-ins and theft. You couldn't pay me money to live in Bridgetown today.

With long stretches between jobs, Eric returned home to St. Lucy to live with his parents.

> Renting an apartment was very expensive, you have to pay around six hundred dollars (BDS) a month, and, with what I was making, I didn't have much left over for anything else. My parents were getting older, and they could use someone to help them out around the house and in the kitchen garden with things they can't do so easily anymore like forking [turning over the soil].

At home Eric doesn't pay rent, but he does help out with the family's bills.

Today Eric does home maintenance and looks for work as a mason, mainly building house extensions such as bedrooms and washrooms. He earns about seventy-five dollars (BDS) a day, but it is often months between jobs. His passion, and a supplemental source of income, is fishing. He fishes from the cliffs, a mile from his home, beginning at dusk and not returning home until sunrise. With a large shank hook baited with a moray eel, 200-pound test line, and a steel leader, he goes after shark ("smooth skin" and nurse shark) and coevally. On most nights he will get at least one shark (50 to 80 lbs.). At low tide or when the sea is calm regardless of the tide, he spear fishes on the reef just offshore. With snorkel and mask, a four-foot Champion speargun, and a float from which he suspends a mesh bag, he swims out from one of the small bays that dot St. Lucy's rugged, precipitous coastline. Ever mindful of the treacherous currents and undertow, which keeps most villagers from ever going into the sea along the north coast, Eric hunts for fish in "white holes"—large holes, or breaks, in the reef with white sand bottoms that reflect the light and contrast with the surrounding dark-colored reef. His prey are porgies, blue barbers, chubs, and coevallys, generically known as "pot fish" because they are more commonly caught in fish traps, or "pots." Aiming for the head and firing his spear gun within ten to fifteen feet of his quarry, Eric hits his target two times out of three. He avoids the much larger and stronger tarpon or albacore, which are able to swim off with gear, unless he is very close to shore and confident of a head shot. On a good day Eric may spear 30 pounds of fish. He sells most of his catch to local families, some of whom have placed orders with him in advance.

> I sell some for six dollars [BDS] per pound, but some I sell cheaper to older people who don't have the money. I always give some to two kids who do favors for me and whose moms are unemployed [and fathers are absent].

With his free time Eric hangs out with friends near a coral stone wall in the village. There he and his age-mates listen to music (dub, reggae, calypso), play dominoes and cards (harps, rummy, cricket), drink beer, and talk. Frequent topics of conversation are money (who has it and how it's spent or invested), women (who looks good, differences between local and tourist women), sport (cricket and football, depending on the season), family (behaviors and characteristics of village families, family problems), and jobs (who has them and how good are they). They may also watch the Pie Corner or another parish team play football (soccer) or cricket on the nearby field. And they play road tennis (a sport developed in Barbados and played with a homemade wooden paddle and a tennis ball on a small court marked out on the street). The game is halted, and the net—a plank—is removed whenever a vehicle passes. Like streetcorner groups in all villages, Eric and his friends also have "cookouts."

> The guys will say, "Let's cook out tomorrow." We might go over to Patrick's house and everyone brings something. I'll catch some fish; Jefferson will bring some breadfruit. We roast the fish and breadfruit over the fire and throw everything else into a saucepan and stir it together. When you're hanging out, you are trying to find things to occupy your mind, so you do little things to get your mind away from what you are not doing—working.

Eric says he is seldom bored. And, while he is able to live comfortably, although simply, at home, he prefers to be working and earning money. "When I am working and the day comes to an end, I feel better because I have done something, achieved something. It makes me feel more independent, too."

Eric says he has never had a "craving" for money, but he does dream of someday being able to save enough to own a fishing boat.

> If I had my own fishing boat, I could make up to a thousand dollars a day. Most fishermen in Barbados are very lazy. Some fish to buy luxury, but lots fish just for enough money to buy rum or their other dirty habits. In other parts of the world people catch fish by the ton; here we catch fish by the pound. If I had a boat, I'd be making real money.

His ambition suffered a set back in 1994, when his savings were wiped out by an ill-fated trip to London with his Bajan girlfriend.

> When we got off the plane [at Gatwick Airport] the English immigration man asked where I was from, why I was coming to England, and how much money I had. I tell him all the answers. It seemed okay, but then this other immigration guy came over and took charge. He asked all the same questions, all over again. Then

he asked me to come to this room. I sat there for three hours—it was really cold. Then he came back and asked me all the same questions all over again. I told him all the answers—that I was with my girlfriend, who lived in London, and that I on holiday with her—but he say he didn't believe me, and he left the room again. Maybe an hour later he came back, and I said, "Listen, if you are going to send me back, send me back now, but don't keep me in this room." He said, "Okay, I am sending you back." The trip cost me $2,100 [BDS], and I never saw England . . . except the airport.

Eric also hasn't seen his girlfriend since, though they did talk on the phone on Valentine's Day.

JUDY AND ROOSEVELT GRIFFITH
Bakers

Judy and Roosevelt Griffith make and sell baked goods, raise vegetables, and tend a few livestock. Until recently Judy also had a part-time job cleaning a community center in a neighboring parish. They are in their mid-forties and have been together since she was sixteen years old and he was twenty-two. They have raised two sons and a daughter. The eldest, Trevor, is a constable in the police force; the second child, Shernell, lives in New York, where she is a caregiver to several elderly women; and the youngest, Donny, drives a van that picks up vegetables from small farmers and transports them to hotels and stores.

Judy is a large-boned, strong woman with a soft voice and a gentle manner. Though serious and somewhat shy, she is quick to see the humor in things and likes to laugh, despite having endured a good deal of hardship. Her father died when she was four and her mother when she was seven. Before their deaths the family had been prosperous, living in the first wall house in Josey Hill, which her grandfather had built with "Panama Money," savings from the years he spent working on the Panama Canal. After the loss of her parents, Judy was raised by her eldest sister, who today owns a rum shop at the top of the hill. But the loss of both parents, both breadwinners, impoverished the family.

Judy is one of several women of her generation in the community who take it upon themselves to help elderly neighbors who are in

Judy and Roosevelt Griffith. (Photo by George Gmelch.)

need. She frequently stops by the homes of several old widows and a widower, to visit and offer assistance. She may bathe them, run errands or shop for them when she goes to town, and, if repairs are needed on their homes, she will arrange for a tradesman to come. At Christmas she brings them each a little present, and she helps the elderly widower with his wash. "When I passing in the road," she explains, "some people just shout me, call me, and ask me to do things for them. Things they can't do for themselves." People like Judy who selflessly give their time to look after people who are unrelated to them, say other villagers, are a vanishing breed. Judy and those like her are a vestige of a time when the village was a close-knit community, when people worked on the same plantations or at least at the same jobs, socialized together, and, to varying degrees, looked out for one another's welfare.

Roosevelt, better known as "Griff," has an open, friendly disposition and a fondness for greeting others with "Yeah man, how you doing? That good, good, good." He has a handsome face, with gray hair at the temples. He is missing two teeth on the right side of his mouth from an auto accident, which occurred at night near the Mt. Gay plantation. His passenger was killed, and, although the accident was not Griff's fault, friends and relatives of the deceased are still bitter toward him. The memory of the accident has caused Griff to avoid that road, even though the alternative is a longer route to town.

Griff was raised in the village of Cave Hill. Like many village boys, his ambition was to drive a bus or a truck, because, as he says, "as young boys that was mostly the only kind of work you saw outside of plantation work. You didn't know nothing else, so that's what you wanted to be." After completing secondary school, however, Griff went to the Barbados Technical Institute to study engineering and, after earning his City and Guilds certificate in 1972, found work with a Bridgetown manufacturer, Barbados Packers and Canners. There he serviced and repaired machinery and rose to the position of chief engineer before a dispute with his superior resulted in his dismissal in 1985. For the next two years he worked at home raising thirty-five pigs, tending a large garden, and taking people to town in his car.

When the Arawak Cement Plant on St. Lucy's western coast was completed, Griff found a job there doing maintenance. At the cement plant Griff met a fellow worker who had recently returned from a job on a Shell oil tanker. "I didn't see much opportunity to progress at the cement plant . . . there was a bottleneck [barrier]; you had to be in a certain clique to move ahead," explained Griff, "so I made inquiries about going to sea. I thought the experience would be good for me and that I'd see some of the world too." Griff applied at Shell's recruiting office in Bridgetown and, after passing the medical exam, was offered an eight-month contract on a VLCC (very large crude carrier). A week later he was on a plane to Spain and then to Gibraltar, to meet his ship, the SS *Leona*, which was hauling oil from Iran and Iraq to the West. The thirty-five-man crew was composed of about a dozen English officers and twenty-plus Barbadian seamen—cooks, stewards, pump room mechanics, greaser, deckhands, and the like. As a pump room mechanic, Griff's work station was the engine room, where in the Middle East the temperatures could reach 130 F. The ear protectors all crewmen were required to wear only partially muffled the noise of the engines. The work was hot and dirty, and the hours were long, as Griff worked all the available overtime. It was not uncommon for the crewmen to put in twelve- to fourteen-hour days. Between overtime and working on his "off-days," Griff earned about a thousand pounds a month, or three times what he had been making at the cement plant in St. Lucy. And with nothing to spend his money on during the long stretches at sea, and his food provided for, he was able to save 80 percent of his earnings. "I had a vision," he says, "that I could save enough money to finish the house." He and Judy had begun construction five years before on a wall house that was still unfinished for lack of funds. They were anxious to get it far enough along to be able to move in. The house sits on the shoulder of the hill with a panoramic view of the northern coast of St. Lucy, from the Caribbean sea on the west all the way around to the Atlantic Ocean on the east.

Griff's hopes to see the countries he sailed to were frustrated by few opportunities to get ashore. Unlike freighters, which usually dock in port cities, large oil tankers, having twice the draft, must take on and discharge their cargo in deep water. "In the Gulf of Mexico," explained Griff, "the jetty is so far out to sea that you can't even see land." In many places the distance to shore, the red tape in getting a shore pass to clear immigration and a refinery pass to get back onto the vessel, and the cost of a taxi from the terminal to town made it impractical for Griff and his sea mates to go ashore. Before starting his first "contract," or voyage, however, he had a week in London on his own and was able to visit many of the places—Buckingham Palace, 10 Downing

Street, St. Paul's Cathedral—that he had learned about in the British-based school curriculum that was taught in Barbadian schools during his youth. During the two years he spent at sea on Shell tankers, he was also able to spend a few days in Singapore, Rotterdam, Dubai, the Bahamas, and several cities in Malaysia and the United States.

It was during his third trip that Griff saw an advertisement in an English magazine, *Exchange and Marts,* for a home securities business, etching identification numbers on personal possessions. Interested in the idea of having his own business, of being his own boss, and growing weary of life at sea, he wrote to his sister-in-law in England and asked her to buy the equipment he would need—an air compressor and a small sand blasting gun that could etch ID numbers on TVs, cameras, VCRs, automobile windshields, and the like. He called his new business Arline Security Systems and placed ads in Barbados newspapers and on radio and television. With crime on the increase, especially burglaries, he reasoned there would be considerable demand for his services. But the timing was wrong, as Barbados was entering a recession. "People seemed excited about it," Griff says, "but there was very little business. Very little." After a year Griff stored his equipment away, never having recouped his investment. He thought he might start up his business again once the economy picked up, but since then an East Indian in Bridgetown has started a similar business, and Griff believes he would have a hard time competing against him: "In Barbados if you see a Bajan and a foreign guy both start business, more people will go to the foreign guy. We still have a small island mentality that the big country guy is better . . . and Bajans don't like to see one another get ahead." The end to Griff's hopes of restarting his business came when the Barbados police began to offer a similar identification marking service to all residents for free.

While Griff's business was failing, Judy was laid off from her cleaning job at the Belleplaine Community Center. Like most rural households, the Griffiths had always depended upon several sources of income. To make up for the loss of one income it is often possible to expand into another area, just as Griff had done by raising pigs and increasing the size of his garden after being dismissed by Barbados Packers and Canners. They considered several options. At one time Judy had made handicrafts—table and doormats from *khus khus* grass and baskets and table mats from cane lilies—and sewed women's hats and bags, which she sold in a handicraft store in Speightstown. But the demand for them was seasonal, as many of her goods were bought by tourists during the winter months, and, besides, the store was not doing well. Judy had always made a little extra money by baking, selling her breads to the local rum shop and some villagers. She has a knack for baking, and people especially like her salt bread. So she and Griff decided to try baking on a large scale and selling beyond the village.

Working together, they have now been baking for four years. On Tuesdays and Fridays they bake all day, while on Wednesdays and Saturdays Griff sells the baked goods from the back of his hand-painted orange Toyota van. The hours are long; on baking days Griff is up at four in the morning mixing the ingredients (flour, sugar, butter, eggs, lard, essence, spice, baking power, yeast). Judy gets up an hour later to begin shaping the dough and placing it in their homemade oven. All through the day they load and unload the oven.

Once the baked goods cool, they put them into plastic bags and load them into the van. By 3:00 P.M. Griff is ready to start out on his regular circuit which takes him through most of the villages of the parish—Crab Hill, Grape Hall, Pie Corner, Rock Hall, Allendale, and more. Over the next six to seven hours he cruises slowly through each community honking his horn, pausing longer in front of houses of regular customers, always waiting a "reasonable amount of time," he says, to see if they appear. By ten at night Griff's route has brought him full circle back to Josey Hill. Usually, he will have sold all of the hundred turnovers, seventy salt bread packages, eighty small coconut breads, and the several dozen cassava pone, rock cakes, and light sweets that he started out with. The surplus, if there is any, is used at home, fed to the pigs, or shared with children who pass by the house on their way to school.

Like many Josey Hill residents, Judy and Griff also have a garden and raise a few cows, pigs, and goats. They graze their cows and goats on pasture land on the coastal plain below the village. Like most livestock, they are staked out, tethered with a long rope to keep them from wandering off. Each morning Griff goes down the hill to move them to fresh grass and give them water. When the cows and pigs grow to full size, Griff has them butchered, earning upward of a thousand dollars per cow and five hundred dollars per pig. They may keep some of the meat for home use, but they usually sell the bulk of it. Sometimes they sell the animals on the hoof, before they have been butchered, all except the goats, which, as Griff says, "you get so little money (seventy-five dollars per goat) that it's not worth you sellin' them. You do better to eat them yourself." Griff and Judy grow peas, cassava, pumpkin, potato, seasoning, thyme, and peppers. The crops are mostly grown for home consumption, but they give away any surplus to neighbors. If they have a sufficiently large harvest, they will sell it to a wholesaler.

Judy and Griff hope to expand their baking into some unfinished space at the side of their house, to hire help, and to buy an electric mixer. They are proud of having gotten the business off the ground, and they like being independent, but, Griff adds, "baking is not my love, not 100 percent. If someone tell me a year ago that I'd be selling bread today, I'd have laughed. No, I'd rather be doing engineering, working with machines."

SIEBERT AND AILEEN ALLMAN
Emigrant and Seamstress

Siebert and Aileen Allman are in their late fifties with five grown children. They live in a large house in Sutherland on St. Lucy's western coast. Siebert is a modest, private man who prefers his own company and television to the rum shop or a social gathering. Some neighbors have mistaken his reserve for snobbery. Aileen is loquacious and buoyant. They come from humble origins. Siebert, for example, lost his father when he was six; his mother supported him and his sister by working as a maid in the Blackrock mental asylum. Emigration and years of hard work and saving have enabled them to enter the ranks of the middle class. Indeed, they own one of the nicest homes in the village of Sutherland.

Like many Barbadians, Siebert sought to get ahead in life by emigrating. When he was twenty-five he left his work as a cabinet maker and went to England. "I thought there would be more opportunities there," he explained. "With all the people here going to England, you had to think it must be good. . . . In those days you could just buy a ticket and go, since we were a colony belonging to Britain." Like most migrants of the time, he left his family behind until he saw what the conditions were like and determined whether they would all benefit by being there. Soon after arriving, he obtained a job as a bus conductor with London Transport, a major employer of West Indian immigrants.

Aileen and Siebert Allman. (Photo by George Gmelch.)

Siebert worked Route 134 from Victoria Station and Route 43 to Londonbridge, each route extending about fifteen kilometers out before retracing its journey back into the city. Taking fares on double-decker buses, he remembers, was very tiring. "It was up stairs and down stairs all the time . . . [and] you'd have to deal with people who didn't like you just because you were colored. I remember this one lady who put her fare on the seat. She wouldn't hand it to me because she didn't want me, being a colored person, to touch her hands." Siebert learned to ignore such racist acts, reminding himself that there were similarly narrow-minded people back home in Barbados. The "teddy boys" and punks, however, who got on his bus late at night after drinking were more menacing. Some liked to intimidate immigrant conductors. After one Barbadian conductor was badly beaten by teddy boys, Siebert did his best to avoid them, even to the point of sometimes not asking for their bus fare. While in England, Siebert worked all the overtime he could get, as his sole purpose in emigrating had been to earn money and improve his family's standard of living at home. With overtime he could make thirty pounds per week; he kept ten pounds for his own meals and lodging and sent the rest home. While the money was better than what he had been making in Barbados, he sorely missed the company of his family. "To put away the loneliness, I used to travel on the bus after I finished work," he recalls.

> I'd go to Trafalgar Square, Hyde Park, and places like that—anything to distract me. When I was tired I'd go home, just to lay down and sleep. Otherwise, it was too lonely. Some of my friends got involved with other women and started families in England, but that wasn't for me.

The loneliness caused him, after two years in England, to return home to Barbados. He wasn't home long, however, when London Transport's recruiting office in Barbados asked him to go on the radio and speak about working in England, to help them recruit Barbadians. To set an example, and concerned that Siebert being home in Barbados might create the wrong impression, they encouraged Siebert to return to England, offering him free airfare, his old job, and other incentives. By then (1963), however, an economic recession and rising unemployment was creating resentment in England toward immigrants. That the British government and some private corporations had actively recruited tens of thousands of Siebert Allmans to fill the jobs needed to get postwar Britain back on its feet seemed unimportant to the British working-class men and women, who believed they were in competition with West Indians, Pakistanis, Indians, and other "colored" immigrants. "Things had really deteriorated for colored people in England," recalls Siebert. Some of his bus passengers were now openly hostile, and he began to overhear people call him derogatory names, including "nigger." This hostility, and loneliness for his family, caused him to return home after just one year. At home he returned to making cabinets, with limited prospects for growth in his business in a stagnant Barbadian economy.

Five years later, in 1968, Siebert and Aileen together applied to the Canadian High Commission to emigrate to Montreal. They had been encouraged by newspaper advertisements for artisans that Barbadian friends in Montreal had sent. Siebert, a skilled cabinet maker, and Aileen, a seamstress, decided they would earn more money in Canada, and, besides, Siebert said, "Aileen had never traveled before, and I wanted her to see how the other side of the world lives." They arranged for neighbors to look after their four children until they got settled and could send for them.

When they arrived in Montreal, neither of them were able to find skilled work. Instead of making cabinets, Siebert ended up working on a conveyor line inspecting desks for scratches; instead of making clothes, as she had done in Barbados, Aileen now merely sewed pockets on shirts. They worked all the overtime available and sent most of their salaries home for deposit in their Barbadian account at the Canadian Imperial Bank of Commerce branch in Speightstown. With the money out of reach, they reasoned, there would be no temptation to spend it. They saved for the day they would return home and build a new house. Aileen recalls that Siebert complained a lot about the cold. Every evening at six o'clock, she remembers: "He'd turn on the TV to see what the weather was in Barbados. He'd say, 'What am I doing here? If I was home now I could go to the beach . . . .' He used to annoy me so."

But the high wages, at least relative to what they had been earning in Barbados, kept them in Montreal. It wasn't until they returned to Barbados on a holiday in 1974 that Siebert decided it was time to come home for good. They had brought along a French-Canadian friend of theirs, recalls Siebert. "When she came here and saw our home and all our family, she said, 'What are you living in Montreal for?'" She loved the climate here, the sea bathing, and all the different foods. She'd say, "What are you trying to achieve? You have everything here." Well, hearing that made you think different. It was then that we decided to really come home."

For three years they planned their return. Aileen wanted to stay in Montreal, but Siebert was determined that the entire family should come home together, and in the end he prevailed. They had saved enough to build a large wall house, the ambition of every migrant Barbadian. Their four-bedroom house with a veranda is perched on a bluff overlooking the quiet fishing village of Half Moon Fort and the Caribbean Sea. Like a beacon, it signals to the community below the Allmans' success as migrants. Inside the house the kitchen accessories, wall-to-wall carpeting, drapes, and sliding glass doors are pure North American. With the money they saved the Allmans have also sent all five children to college; two have done graduate work, and their son, Hugh, making use of the French he learned in Quebec's public schools, worked in Barbados' embassy in Belgium as a foreign service officer until moving back to the Caribbean.

Like many successful migrants who resettle in their home villages, they have encountered people who were jealous of their new wealth. Aileen says: "When you have traveled, people think you're rich, and they try to see how much they can get out of you. They don't know how hard you worked for your money." Malicious rumors circulated that the Allmans had won the lottery or that they gained their wealth illegally.

Siebert and Aileen opened a small general store near their home, but they had few customers, because, says Aileen: "They thought we were already too rich . . . we had a big house and two cars." After two break-ins, and with their insurance company refusing to cover their losses, they closed the shop. Aileen returned to sewing full-time, just as she had done in the years before they went to Canada. Siebert had several different jobs in Bridgetown, eventually becoming a supervisor with Rayside, a large construction firm.

Today Aileen is still at home making hotel uniforms for the door-men, bellmen, and maids at Sandy Lane, Barbados' most exclusive resort. She also sews other apparel, such as wedding dresses, for individual customers. Inured to hard work, she still rises before dawn to begin sewing, and, when deadlines approach, she will work late into the night. She uses some of her earnings to visit three children who are still living abroad, one in Manchester, England, and two on the island of Tortola.

UZIL HOLDER
Roti Maker

Uzil Holder, forty-eight, is a single mother of three children. She has a wide, pleasant face and an open, friendly disposition. She is an immigrant from Guyana, one of over twenty-five hundred Guyanese living in Barbados, 60 percent of whom are women.[3] There are six Guyanese households in the Josey Hill area, four of them headed by Uzil's siblings. Barbados and the former British colony of Guyana have been linked since the nineteenth century, when British Guiana became one of the first destinations of freed slaves in the decades following emancipation. Uzil's story is intimately tied to her immigration to Barbados and her struggle to forge a new life there.

Both Uzil's mother and paternal grandfather were Barbadian. They had migrated to Guyana in 1921, when, explains Uzil: "Things were better there than in Barbados. There were jobs in the gold fields, in bauxite [aluminum ore], in cutting cane, and there was lots of land for farming." Uzil's mother had ten children, all of whom were raised in the district of Uitvlugt (pronounced "Eyeflot"), an area of many small villages whose inhabitants rented their house plots from a single sugar plantation, the second largest in the country—"a plantation," says Uzil proudly, "half the size of Barbados."

> When we were growing up [in Guyana] all us kids were aware that our mother was Barbadian and our father's father too. We didn't have no connections with relatives in Guyana, and like all kids we wanted to know our family. The only grandparents we had, and nearly all our aunts and uncles and cousins as well, were in Barbados, so naturally you are curious about them . . . every kid wants to know his grandma and grandpa. But we were a happy family in Guyana, and as time went by my father, who was a logger, and my mother, who worked washing and ironing other people's clothes and doing home baking, improved our lives to a comfortable middle-class style with a two-storied house.

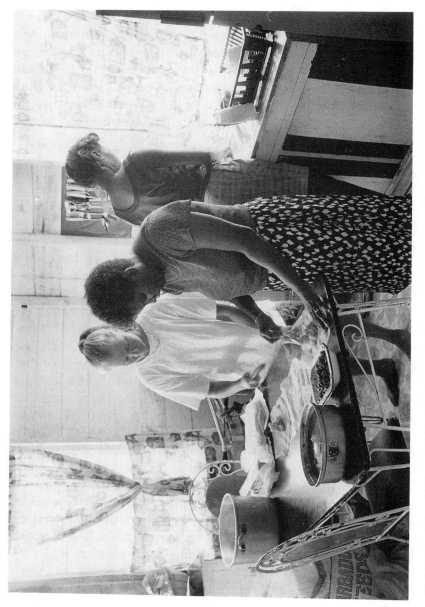

Uzil Holder in her kitchen with her daughter, Yolanda, and student Chantal Von Saher. (Photo by George Gmelch.)

After Uzil left school at sixteen, she did needlework and made baskets and Sunday hats for people in the district. But it wasn't enough:

> The money was too slow in affording me my dreams of what I wanted to achieve in life. So I got my mother to purchase me a sewing machine on hire purchase [installments], and I started cutting patterns for clothing on old newspaper. I made a skirt suit which made me the envy of so many. Friends came from other districts to get me to cut patterns for them. What I earned by dress making afforded me the fee to attend evening classes in the city [Georgetown] in accounts.

After the course ended, Uzil obtained a job with the Booker Sugar Company as a telephonist and payroll clerk on the same plantation where she had grown up. She had a relationship with a supervisor at Bookers, and they had a child, Yolanda. They were together for six years before Uzil left him. "He didn't have a settled mind or a future that would be secure. When he joined the Defense Force, I thought it would be a lifestyle—partying, getting involved with other women—that I wouldn't like, so I broke it off."

Uzil's job at Bookers allowed her the income to make several trips to Barbados to get to know her grandmother and relatives and "to see the place where my mother had come from." Every five years each employee of the sugar company was given free passage to any destination in the region, and Uzil used hers to come to Barbados. But Uzil never expected that she would settle there. Like so many emigration decisions, her moving to Barbados resulted from a series of unforeseen circumstances. It began in 1959, when her mother returned to Barbados for the first time. Uzil went along and stayed for six months, getting to know her relatives. In 1977 her mother was asked by family members to return to Barbados to look after Uzil's grandmother, who was now ill and bedridden. As Uzil remembers: "There was no one there to look after her as all the other sisters were working in the fields, and the grandchildren who were living with her were all males. There were no female children around, so they asked my mother to come. She left us, her husband, and a good house in Guyana to go to Barbados. It was a big sacrifice for her, which I don't think the relatives in Barbados ever understood."

At home in Guyana, Uzil, then thirty-three and with a three-year-old daughter, was trying to get out of an unhappy relationship:

> We had broken up, but he wouldn't stay away; he wouldn't leave me alone. He tormented me. I thought my temper might get the better of me and that I might do something to him that I'd regret for the rest of my life. I had Yolanda to look after. I thought the best thing was for me to get away. I thought maybe I will meet someone who will cut me out of this bad luck. I was young, and when you're young a little change can be great.

Uzil planned to stop in Barbados for a while to visit her mother, and to leave Yolanda with her, and then go on to New York. In New York she hoped to get a job as a domestic and to save enough money to do a course in cosmetology and, if that wasn't possible, to continue her training in accounting. In Guyana she had begun a correspondence course at the Rapid Results College in "accounts and commerce," but a shortage of funds and spare time had prevented her from completing it. If things worked out in New York, she would send for Yolanda. Uzil never got further than Barbados, however.

Once in Barbados her cousins persuaded her that she could do just as well there as in New York and that she wouldn't have to deal with winter. They said she would be among family. So Uzil decided try it for awhile and see how things worked out. She saw an opportunity to start a small village shop. The house in which she was living with a cousin was an ideal location for a shop—a spot where the bus turned around before heading back toward town. The bus usually stayed there for a while; its passengers would have a few minutes to come into the shop to buy something to drink or eat. Moreover, there were no other shops in the village of Rock Hall at the time. Uzil and her cousin started the business together, building a wall addition onto the house. While the cousin owned the property and put up most of the capital to get it started, Uzil ran the shop. It was an instant success, and they soon expanded their inventory. Their "cake shop" soon became a small mini-mart, selling dry goods as well as baked goods and soda. As Uzil explains:

> The money we made was more than my cousin ever imagined, and that was the start of the trouble. She began to think that, with

all the money coming in, maybe I was holding back some for myself—that I was cheating her. One day she tells me that she wants me to record every little sale in a book, right down to five-cent candies that the children buy. Everything has to go into a book. Now I had twelve years experience working in an office in Guyana, while my cousin had worked in the fields. I told her we could do stocktaking every month, but she didn't know anything about running a shop. She didn't want to hear it.

Tensions increased between them, Uzil resenting her cousin's suspicions and her attempts to exert more control and intervene more in the running of the shop. "She started calling me up at all hours to check and see if the shop was open," recalls Uzil. "She'd call at ten o'clock in the evening to ask if the shop still open, and then she'd call early in the morning to see if the shop be open yet." When her cousin brought several pigs and chickens for Uzil to look after in the yard behind the shop, Uzil had had enough. "Because I was an immigrant from Guyana, even though I was a relation, she thought she could boss me around, that she could have me do whatever she wanted and that I wouldn't mind, that I would be grateful for being able to live in Barbados." Uzil believes her Barbadian relatives assumed that, because she had left her home in Guyana, that her living conditions there must have been bad and that she should be grateful for anything they did for her. When in fact, she says, "In Guyana we lived in an upstairs house with electricity and running water that was superior to some of my relatives' homes in Barbados. In Barbados you had to walk down the road to the standpipe to get water, and the light was a kerosene lamp. My relations had never come to visit us in Guyana, and they didn't know what we had there."

At about this time Uzil's cousin from New York city returned to Barbados, dashing any plans Uzil had of emigrating. "Even if I was to go, I now had no one to stay with," she explained. "I started looking for a job as a clerk in town." In 1980 Uzil's grandmother, who Uzil's mother had been looking after since her return to Barbados three years earlier, died. No one told Uzil's mother when the will was to be read. Only weeks later did they learn of its contents, that they—the Guyanese side of the family—had largely been left out. The house, in which Uzil, her daughter, and mother were living, had been left to a relative who had been living in England for nearly twenty years and

never once returned. She came back to claim her inheritance, nevertheless, and asked her Guyanese kin to vacate the house immediately. Her
attitude toward Uzil's mother and family was, recalls Uzil: "You were
asked to come to Barbados to do a job, and, now that you've done it,
you should all go back to Guyana where you belong": "What really
bothered me, too, was that she didn't acknowledge my mother as a
Barbadian. When my grandmother died, we discovered that my family
didn't mean anything to our Barbadian relatives." When Uzil, her
daughter, and mother didn't immediately leave, their English-Barba-
dian cousin got a court order to have them removed from the house.
She was concerned that, if her relatives were allowed to remain, they
might have a legal claim to the property. The suspicious circumstances
surrounding the will made Uzil determined to stay in Barbados to
make inquiries and also to help support her mother. The process
dragged on for months. In the end Uzil was rebuffed by the lawyer and
by the person who had signed the will as a witness. But in the meantime she had found a new job as a clerk in the shoe department of N. E.
Wilson and Company, a general store in Bridgetown, and was gradually settling in.

Several of Uzil's siblings also moved to Barbados in search of better
economic circumstances. "Things were getting tight [in Guyana]," explained Uzil. "The economy was going bad, and the cost of living was
getting out of hand. So we grouped together and helped pay the passage
of my brothers and sisters." Together the family rented a three-bedroom
house in Peterses, not far from Barbara and Selwyn Greaves. The arrival
of her brothers and sisters contributed to Uzil's decision to stay in
Barbados.

For the past fourteen years Uzil's main source of income has come
from making and selling rotis (curried potato and beef or chicken
wrapped in a tortilla-like shell), which was introduced into Barbados
by East Indians. Much like the circumstances that led Roosevelt and
Judy Griffith into baking, making rotis was not something that Uzil
had planned to do. It began when she was working as a clerk in the
shoe department of N. E. Wilson:

> My wages, fifty-nine dollars per week, were so small that I began
> to make pastries, jam and pineapple tarts, coconut tarts, and
> cheese tarts to take into work to sell to some of the other girls
> [employees] and to the people who worked in the stores nearby.

> Then I started making up lunch packets. I'd take orders from the store and prepare the lunches [pastries and cakes] before coming to work in the morning, and then during my lunch break I'd go around delivering the lunch packets. I was making more money doing that than I was from my job, so I quit the store.

She decided to specialize in making rotis, largely because there was less waste: "People can be destructive. They squeeze pastries and ruin them, so you have a lot of loss. But not with roti." Today Uzil sells her rotis to restaurants, mini-marts, and a few individuals in the village. Both her daughters, Yolanda and Abigail, help out. Every evening Yolanda—twenty, tall, thin, and pretty—cuts up and cooks the meat, while Abigail, fourteen, prepares the potatoes, and Uzil makes the roti skins. Starting at 6:00 A.M. the next morning, Uzil mixes the meat and potatoes and spices and rolls up the mixture in the skins and then wraps the finished rotis in wax paper. Abigail takes some by bus each morning to the mini-mart across from her school. Yolanda delivers rotis to two restaurants in Holetown. On an average day Uzil makes about thirty-five rotis, for which she receives three dollars each for the meat and potato and two dollars each for the plain potato. Her business has recently declined by half, however, because of the recession and the increase in the number of people on the road who sell home-made baked goods. A couple of her best customers have also gone out of business.

During the cotton season, from January to May, Uzil earns extra cash by picking cotton in her spare time. Uzil likes to be active, or, as she says: "I don't like to sit; I like to keep moving forward." The cotton ground is less than a five-minute walk from her house, so, whenever she has free time, she goes there to pick. Later she will sit with her sister Pauline and her sister-in-law Daphne, who also pick cotton, and separate the white fibers from the pods while chatting and watching TV.

Uzil also receives some money each week from her "boyfriend," John, who is the father of her youngest child. John is a self-employed auto body repairman who Uzil has been dating for twelve years. "He helps financially, depending on what he makes," explains Uzil. "I try to be content with whatever he can give me." The fathers of her other two children do not contribute any financial support, and Uzil has not heard from them in years. Uzil saves her money through a meeting turn (an informal credit group described in chap. 6). There are two meeting turns in Josey Hill. The one Uzil organized has eight members, about half of whom are Guyanese. The average "hand," or weekly deposit, is $50; Uzil tries to put in three hands ($150) per week, which entitles her to draw her "turn" once a month. The money she draws each month, about $600, enables her to pay her bills and mortgage on the small house and land she bought a few years ago, which she rents out.

All nine of Uzil's siblings came to Barbados. Seven have stayed in the country, with four living in the Josey Hill area. Uzil had an idea of starting a community center where young people could meet, instead of hanging out on the road, a place where they could learn crafts and cooking and play games—dominoes, chinese checkers, and draughts. She planned to volunteer her time to teach needlework, basketry, knitting, and pastry making. But, after discussing the idea with a number of the villagers, says Uzil, "it got back to me that people were saying: 'What is this foreigner wanting to teach us Barbadians. What does she know?' So I dropped the idea. I didn't want to start something and have people getting abusive, calling you all sorts of names."

When asked about the future, Uzil talks about hoping "to become more settled" than she has been. Although she owns the wood frame house her family lives in, it is on rented land. She would like to purchase the land, which would enable her to fix the house's foundation and cement steps leading to the front door. She is reluctant, as a renter, to invest much money in making permanent improvements that she cannot take with her. Ideally, she would like to open her own restaurant or "snackette." The rents for business places, however, are too high at the moment, and there is little prospect of them becoming more affordable in the future. Uzil wants a better life for her children. Even though her youngest child, Michael, is being groomed by his father to follow him into the auto body repair business, Uzil believes it is important that all her children get good educations.

Epilogue

In the two years since these household profiles were written there have been some changes. In 1996 Barbara Greaves and Uzil Holder were no longer picking cotton. Competition from Mexico, Guatemala, Antigua, Grenada, Montserrat, and Nevis, among others, had driven down cotton prices. Without markets fewer Barbadian farmers were planting cotton (in 1996 a mere 175 acres were being reaped vs. 750 acres the year before). Barbara has expanded her farming. Uzil opened a snackette in Speightstown; she advertises with a hand-painted sandwich sign on the curb: "Uzil's Snackette for your great taste in rotis—beef and potato, chicken, lamb and vegetable—and *dhal-puri.*" Judy and Roosevelt Griffith expanded their baking business by adding an extension onto the house and hiring help. They have their own label: "J & R Bakery—Quality Is All We Bake." Heywoods Holiday Resort, where Sandra Broomes worked in the towel room, was sold to Barbados Shipping and Trading Company. After major remodeling, it was reopened as an all-inclusive resort (the current trend in upscale tourism) under the name "Almond Beach Resort." Sandra was kept on and has returned to being a maid. She was finally granted a visa to visit her aunt in Brooklyn but has not yet made the trip. Eric O'Neale, unemployed at the time the crop (cane harvest) started, decided to join two friends cutting cane at the nearby Spring Hall plantation. But, being new cutters, they were assigned the worst fields and couldn't cut enough tonnage to make the job worthwhile. Moreover, a work slowdown at the sugar factory meant that the canes they had cut sat in the fields for days, drying out in the hot sun and losing weight (workers are paid by the ton). Earning less than forty dollars (BDS) per day for arduous, sweaty work, they quit. Eric returned to fishing and looking for small masonry jobs.

Chapter 5

Gender and the Lifecycle

People in every culture make the same journey through life. But every culture signposts the route somewhat differently and assigns different meanings to the markers along the way. Gender relations, too, vary from one society to the next, although men and women in every culture share the same basic survival and emotional needs. In this chapter we describe in broad strokes the major stages in the lives of men and women in St. Lucy—birth, childhood, adulthood, old age, and death. What is each stage in the life cycle like? Do men and women share the same experiences, and how do they relate to one another?

Men, Women, and Sex

For most men and women, although relationships with the opposite sex are eagerly sought, they are also antagonistic.[1] Many village men regard women with suspicion, claiming they are materialistic and devious. Most women, in turn, believe that men are fixated on sex and are fundamentally untrustworthy. These opinions reinforce one another, of course, shaping expectations and behavior toward the opposite gender. Boyfriends and girlfriends often adopt a utilitarian approach to their relationships, each one calculating the benefits to be gained from their partner. One of our students was surprised, for example, when she was advised by a village friend to try to get more out of her boyfriend after she returned home. "You never know how long men are going to be around, so you want to get something out of the relationship", she was informed. "I mean, I'm a great girlfriend. I give Stuart [boyfriend] what he wants and I cook for him. All I have to do is ask him for something, and he'll give it to me. I got him to buy me a wardrobe. You should really try to get something out of Jim [the student's boyfriend] while you can."

On the streets casual gender interaction frequently includes sexual taunting. Virtually any woman who is not elderly who walks by a group of men can expect to be hissed at, have her body appraised, and sometimes be given lewd sexual suggestions.[2] Anthropologists Constance Sutton and Susan Makiesky-Barrow, who worked in another part of the island, found that "Stylized sexual banter between men and women occurs in public and private settings and is enjoyed by both sexes."[3] While many women undoubtedly enjoy engaging in sexual banter, the remarks many receive on the street, to the outsider at least, constitute harassment. Most village women ignore these, walking by without speaking; their attitude seems to be that this is just "something men do." But some women make an effort to avoid such encounters when they can. One young woman we know, for example, waits inside her house any night she plans to go out until she sees the bus coming. Then she walks quickly to the bus stop to avoid giving the men who hang out nearby the opportunity to make remarks.

Among working-class village men—for whom "respect" and reputation among their peers, rather than income, establishes status—manhood is achieved largely through sexual conquests.[4] The cross-cultural encounter our female students have had the most difficulty dealing with over the years has been local men's persistent and overt interest in having sex. They feel bombarded by sexual comments and requests, from younger village men and even from some of the professionals such as policemen, teachers, and reporters whom they have met for formal interviews. Likewise, our male students are encouraged by village age-mates "to score." The following description from a student's field notes reveals much, not only about his experience but also about young men's attitudes toward women:

> The conversation last night among the men was preoccupied with sex. Every man wanted to know how many Bajan women I had scored with. They said they were going to hook me up because if I don't, my Barbados experience will not be complete. They all seemed to regard themselves as great lovers. They told many a creative story of their exploits, such as how they met this lady in a bar and she turned out to be a wild animal. They all told me I should not be shy because I would be surprised what I can get away with. They said if Bajan women think I have money, I will have no problem picking them up. Another recommendation they gave me is to lie and say that I'm a famous actor from the States here on vacation.

A female student described a similar conversation she had with a male friend:

> Basically, what X told me is that the guys think my host brother is crazy because I am living under the same roof with him and he hasn't "wocked" me yet. . . . When they see white women, the first thing that comes to their minds is sex. When I asked about that, he said that's because white women are more bold than Bajan women. For example, it would be uncommon for a Bajan woman to approach a few Bajan men and say, "Hello. How are you?" So when they see me acting that way it sends them some sort of message. He asked me if I've had the urge to have sex since I've been in Barbados. I told him no and that I have a boyfriend back home. He tends to get really annoyed when I say I have a boyfriend, because to the Bajan man that means nothing. The common attitude is, "Your boyfriend back home, and you in Barbados now." I told X that he has a one-track mind, and he said, no, that he just wants me to become his "close, personal friend." I asked him why he couldn't just be my friend and what was wrong with talking. He said that the other guys would say that he should be "wocking" me right now. Then he said, "Personally, I think I should be wocking you, too." I explained to him that in America it's common for men and women to be close friends but not in a sexual way.

Years ago most village men and women began serious relationships formally. A young man wrote a woman's parents to ask permission to meet them and court their daughter. On the appointed day he arrived, and, after a suitable period of conversation and a thorough looking over, he left. If her parents approved, the two were allowed to see each other. The rest of the time parents kept a close watch on their daughters. Grace Walker, a woman in her fifties, recalls her father's attitude toward her suitors and the onset of her sexual maturity:

> I had a very good childhood until I got to be a woman. But after I become a woman, my father feel that he don't want me to leave the house. So everybody [young men] that say they like me, he chased them off. My father was very strict. He said I mustn't run around with friends. You know, mustn't run about, going from house to house. No. No. I couldn't do that. I had to stay at home

and do what I have to do—wash and cook and keep the house. From home to school and back home, and do what I have to do. Sundays we go to church and then back home, and then back to Sunday School and then back home again. . . . Two young boys write in for me, but he wouldn't permit it.

Most parents in the parish still keep their daughters reined. This may be the main reason so few young women are seen outdoors in the villages, especially at night.

Opportunities for young men and women to meet are actually quite limited in the parish, especially once they leave school. Only a few villages have community centers, and these are rarely open at night. Before streetlights were introduced in St. Lucy, lovers are said to have checked the calendar for full moons and arranged to meet in a pasture or cane field at night. Courting today largely takes place over the telephone. Couples make plans to rendezvous at a concert or night-club, in town, or at the beach on the weekend. Those who attend the same church have more opportunities to meet, since church activities are frequent. Church, in fact, provides one of the few socially sanc-tioned places for young village women to mix with men. Members of the same church or village, however, may avoid going out with one another because of the gossip ("everybody know everybody") that will arise. And, as one young woman put it, "You don't want to have a relationship with someone you've known your whole life." Local foot-ball and cricket matches provide an opportunity for villagers to meet young men and women from other communities.

At night young adults who can afford it travel into Bridgetown or the south coast tourist belt to attend concerts, nightclubs, and parties. Others attend local "field parties," which are usually held to celebrate holidays such as Errol Barrow Day or special events like the return of an immigrant to the community.[5] Here families and young people mix outdoors, dance to loud music, and eat fried chicken and "pudding and souse."[6] Other youths attend private "house parties," which they learn of through friends or from newspaper ads or posted handbills. These are typically held in homes or rented halls—schools and com-munity centers—and have disc jockeys and sometimes live music. There is always a bar and a cover charge to help organizers recoup the cost of food and make a profit; many are fund-raisers for a specific purpose, such as sending someone off the island to school.

Partygoers are disproportionately men, most of whom stand together drinking while watching others dance with the relatively few women present. Some parties are so dominated by men that young women jokingly refer to them as "male boxes"—an apt pun, since any woman attending is soon boxed in by overly attentive males coaxing her to dance or asking for her telephone number. When dancing, Bajans' uninhibited attitudes toward sex are apparent. Our students are always startled, and the women intimidated, by the first dancing they see. One student described it as "sex with your clothes on, but sex like I've never seen!" Bajan dancing is graphic and uninhibited. Sexual desire is accepted as natural, and Bajans do not avoid expressing it. Without a word or even eye contact, one or more men come up behind a woman to "grind" or "do the dog" to the music's pulsating beat. Although it initially takes some coaxing to get women onto the dance floor, by the end of the evening both men and women have abandoned themselves to the music. Dancing is one of the few opportunities young women have to express their sexuality openly.

Sociologist Graham Dann reports that most Bajan men have their first sexual experiences between the ages of fifteen and seventeen, girls slightly younger.[7] Despite the watchfulness of village parents, many young girls end up going out with men several years older. One village girl we know, referred to by some as a "little force ripe" because of her precocious behavior and body, is only thirteen but has a boyfriend who is twenty. By dating at such an early age, it is not surprising that many young girls also have sex at any early age. Although birth control is widely available, the responsibility for its use falls heavily on women. "I don't believe in it myself," explained a seventeen-year-old boy. "Some girls use it [birth control] nowadays, but it doesn't really concern me." Even in the age of AIDS many young village men do not use condoms.[8] According to a woman we know who works as a clerk in a convenience store, "They are ashamed to buy a condom, but they're not ashamed to have sex. Guys come into the store where I work and try to hide them from other customers, and even from me!" But young men also resist using condoms for other reasons. Having sex while wearing one was likened to "washing your foot with a sock on." Indeed, most men find having sex "bareback" (without a condom) more pleasurable. Consequently, birth control pills are the most widely used form of contraception, although some young village women believe they cause serious side effects: blocked arteries, "damage to your insides," and even birth defects once they are stopped.

For girls who become pregnant, especially if they are still in school, abortion can become de facto birth control. Legalized in 1983, it is estimated that 20 percent of pregnancies in Barbados end in abortion, the rate being higher in urban than in rural areas like St. Lucy. Young women claim that it is often their boyfriends who are most in favor of abortion because they do not want the responsibility of parenthood. "Some women don't want the abortion," explained a village friend, "but the men say to them, 'Well, I can't afford to have a child.' So they listen and have one. They love the man so bad that they don't want the friendship to break up." Most women who decide on an abortion go to a doctor, but some employ their own remedies. One villager remembers trying to terminate her first pregnancy at age fifteen: "I went to the gully and jumped from a tree, but nothing happened." Other women have drunk concoctions like coconut oil and epsom salts. Many villagers, however, are strongly opposed to abortion on religious and moral grounds.[9] They view it as "murder" and "a sin." A woman who had an abortion was once referred to as a "graveyard."

Young people's early initiation into sex and lax attitudes toward birth control result in many out-of-wedlock births. Nationally, the Child Care Board estimates that 75 percent of Barbadian births are out of wedlock. One reason is that many young women do not understand their own physiology, and few parents explain sex to their children. Twenty-two-year-old Marcia Springer remembers being too "scared" to ask her mother a single question about her changing body or sex:

> I could never ask a question. Do you know that, when I first got my period, I was over at Shirley's [an aunt] house, and I didn't even know what it was? I never told my mother; it was Shirley that told her. Then one day my mother said, "Now that you got it [menstruation], you just keep away from boys!" That's all she ever said to me about sex.

Despite many village parents' reluctance to talk about sex and reproduction with their children, cultural euphemisms for bodily functions like menstruation are positive: "Did you see your flower yet?" and "Did your ripe tomato burst?"

Peer pressure plays a role in early pregnancy and out of wedlock births. By having sex with a boyfriend and becoming a mother, many young girls believe that they are demonstrating their maturity. Motherhood is the defining rite of passage into "womanhood" in Barbados—

so much so that women who were unable to conceive were once cruelly called "mules." If a young girl is dating someone older, she may be especially eager to demonstrate her womanhood, and is too young to think about what becoming a mother may mean for her future. Having a child out of wedlock is not strongly condemned in the villages, unless a woman comes from a very religious home or is still very young and in school. Her pregnancy will cause comment but will not severely damage her reputation (and fatherhood is likely to enhance her boyfriend's status). If she cannot raise her child, there are always mothers, sisters, aunts, and even grandmothers willing to assume the responsibility. Such informal adoptions are common in Barbados and the Caribbean.[10]

Birth and "Marriage"

As recently as the 1970s, most expectant mothers in the parish gave birth at home assisted by a local midwife. As "Nurse Phillips," a ninety-three-year-old retired midwife says about the village of Pie Corner, "Anybody over fifty years old is surely one of my babies." Today, however, virtually all women go to the hospital, and only a few folk beliefs about birth remain. Underlying most of these is the "law of similarity" (to use anthropologist Edward Tylor's early formulation): the idea that like produces like. Eating okra (which becomes slimy when cooked), for example, will help the baby slide out. Eating too much pepper will give it speckled skin. Most women still keep their child's umbilical cord, however. In what was undoubtedly originally an African practice—although it is also found in many other parts of the world—the umbilical cord and placenta were once buried near the home, symbolically connecting a child to its birthplace. The question "Where you nabel [navel] string bury?" is still asked by the elderly, meaning "Where are you from?" The Mighty Gabby's calypso song "Jack" (a critique of tourism and the closing of beaches to locals) includes the line, "Tourists nabel string not buried here." Reflecting the other part of Barbados' heritage, infants are sometimes given silver coins for luck, a custom known as "handseling" in the British Isles.

With the birth of a child several things can happen. The new mother may remain with her parents, or she may move out and establish a household of her own, with or without the child's father.[11] For most women the birth of a child is a good reason for a couple to live together or marry; for many men, however, it can be a reason to part. According to research by anthropologist Christine Barrow, Bajan men regard attachments to women warily:

> Their general opinion is that women will try to find out their level of earnings, demand more than they can give, accuse them of supporting "outside women" and use "tricks" . . . to satisfy their greed. Women who "pull together with a man to build a home" or remain with him through lean times are said to be rare exceptions.[12]

Economic factors play a role in the decision of whether or not couples live together. Not all of them can afford to establish a new household. Consequently, many couples continue to live apart after their child's birth, usually maintaining a "visiting" relationship in which the boyfriend regularly visits his child and girlfriend at her parent's house or, if she is older, in her own home. She provides him with domestic labor (cooking, cleaning, and child care) in exchange for a degree of financial support. Economic considerations also shape attitudes toward marriage. Many committed couples delay marrying until they can afford to own a house. Those living together in common-law unions often defer marriage until they can afford to have a proper wedding ceremony. Bajan weddings are elaborate affairs with custom-tailored clothes, a full complement of attendants, rented reception hall, and huge amounts of food. For many village couples marriage ends up being the celebratory capstone to a long relationship and occurs after children have been born.

Religion also shapes a couple's attitude toward marriage. Many churchgoing couples of even modest means marry because they are good Christians. The following comments of Arlette Holder, a woman in her early forties, are revealing:

> I had never given marriage much thought, because my mother and none of my sisters are married. But the older I get, the more important it becomes. Looking back on my children's fathers, I'm glad I didn't marry either of them. But I want to lead a Christian life, and the Church teach that you have to be married or cut out the boyfriends altogether. My boyfriend and I have talked about living together, but I will not unless we get married, which I hope will be soon.

Marriage is thus supported by religion and is a cultural ideal—the "proper" thing to do—even though many people remain unmarried for a variety of reasons.

Household composition in St. Lucy, as in the rest of the country, is often complex. Single-parent, female-headed households are common among poor and working-class villagers. Fully 44 percent of parish households are headed by single women, many of whom have never married. The figure is the same nationally.[13] Some of these households are composed of only a mother and her children, but more often they consist of extended families that span three generations and include an assortment of kin. The norm for middle-class and upwardly mobile villagers, in contrast, is for two-parent nuclear family households.

Many men, including those who are married or in long-term common-law unions, have lovers, "outside women," and father "outside children." In some cases their wives and long-term girlfriends know and accept the situation. This arrangement resembles in some respects the polygynous household structure found in many West African societies and other cultures. In Barbados it reflects a cultural ethos that still measures manhood largely by sexual prowess. Some village men are critical of this attitude, however, as the following remarks of a twenty-six-year-old show:

> It's a big thing in certain communities. Mr. Holder thinks he's a dude because he's got ten children from all these different women in the village. My friend Leonard comes up to me yesterday all proud and says, "Hey Malcolm, I got a son. When you gonna get one?" Like I gotta have one to be a man. All most men want from a woman is house tidy when you come home. Food when you want it. Clothes clean. Clothes off.

Those women who knowingly pursue sexual relationships with men who are living with or married to another woman share responsibility for these attitudes.

The work of maintaining the household and caring for children falls largely on village women. They manage most of the activities required to sustain a home: shopping, cooking, laundering, cleaning, as well as nurturing children and preparing them for school. Women who do not have male partners in the home control all household finances and decision making. When couples live together, decision making is shared. According to one study, the nature of the couple's union influences their perceptions of their household roles.[14] Couples who are married generally consider the man to be the "head" of household, while one-quarter of the women in common-law unions described themselves as the household head. The patriarchal religious teachings surrounding marriage legitimize male authority.

Most village men define their household and familial roles as narrowly restricted to financial support. Those who live separately from their "girlfriend" and children usually contribute money to the household if they wish to maintain the relationship. Men who share a household with their partner and children usually work hard to provide materially for their family. The work profiles of Selwyn and Barbara Greaves, Roosevelt and Judy Griffith, and Siebert and Aileen Allman in chapter 4 attest to this. Nevertheless, public service announcements aired on CBC television often reveal what Bajan society regards as problem areas; recent ads have encouraged men to talk to their children and spend time with them, in other words, to broaden their familial role to include emotional as well as financial support.

To a large extent even couples who live together lead separate lives. Not only are they apart during the workday; they also do much of their socializing separately. Village women become involved in church activities, visit female relatives, and talk to friends over the telephone. Men tend to spend their free time working in the yard or socializing at the rum shop, a sporting event, or favored spot. "Most husbands and wives in Barbados," asserted one villager, "are not friends. They not really friends. There's not much social life between them." Likewise, when a student of ours referred to a married man and woman she knew as a "couple," she received a surprised reaction and was informed that the word "couple" refers to people who are dating and enjoying each other's company, while "husbands and wives do not."

Many men and women who live together also keep their money and property separate. "I just buy the small things for the house like decorations. He buys the furniture," one woman explained. "I buy the soap for the laundry and the food. He buys the equipment for fixin' up the house. But if you don't have an ambitious man, you have to go ahead and buy the big things yourself." Most couples have separate savings accounts because, in the words of one woman, "men and women spend their money different." Most women also value their independence ("so he doesn't know everything I do") and feel it is

Youths in a rum shop. (Photo by Ellen Frankenstein.)

important to have their own savings as insurance in case the relationship fails.

Women without a partner are proud of being able to support their children and household without a man, although they must often rely on others for help. When a woman leaves for work, for example, a large part of her parenting and domestic responsibilities falls to other women. "Leaving de child at Granny—dat is my culture," lyrics from the Mighty Gabby's calypso hit "Culture," captures the important role of the grandmother in Bajan society. Sandra Broomes, introduced in chapter 4, has three children by two boyfriends, neither of whom contributes to her household financially. Instead, Sandra relies entirely on her income as a maid and on the help of her aunt. Some women become so used to managing households on their own that with the passage of time they lose interest in marrying or ever living with a man. "I used to think about getting married," commented one forty-five-year-old woman. "Doesn't everybody? But today I feel different. I'm too old and set in my ways. My friend has his own house, and I'm happy this way. I can run things any way I want."

Today village women want fewer children than in the past. Most recognize that they will be able to achieve a better standard of living with fewer mouths to feed. "Times are hard, and to have a lot of children is expensive," explained one eighteen-year-old. "It used to be that the woman would stay home, keep house, and take care of the baby. But now we want jobs; we have education. We want to do the jobs that the men do." In most cases women have also seen their own mother, grandparents, and other relatives struggle to survive and want a different life for themselves. "I want to give my children a good home and a good education," commented Sandra Broomes, "a better life than I had." A majority of Barbadian men now also favor small families, mainly for economic reasons.[15]

Childhood and Discipline

In St. Lucy the focus of child rearing is on teaching children to be obedient and respectful. In the past village children were taught never to speak back to an adult, to say "excuse me" when entering a conversation, to address their elders as Mr. and Mrs., to say "good morning" and "good evening" when passing adults in the street, to offer to carry heavy parcels and run errands for the elderly, and to give them their

The Husbands family. (Photo by George Gmelch.)

seat on the bus. Although the older generation regularly complains about today's youth and about the breakdown in social order, many parents still teach their children such manners. In addition, most children are taught early to help around the house. Even four- and five-year-olds may be asked to do small tasks such as water a plant, take their cup to the sink, or place empty soda bottles into a crate. By about age eight or nine children are expected to do daily chores. Here a gender division emerges, with girls doing numerous indoor chores such as making beds, folding laundry, ironing, "picking rice" (removing extraneous material), cooking, washing dishes, and minding younger siblings. Boys are more likely to be responsible for outdoor chores: taking out the garbage, weeding, tending animals, and sweeping the yard. Many boys in St. Lucy, however, also learn how to cook and do dishes, to wash and iron their clothes, and to sew, so that they will be able to take care of themselves later. The difference is that boys usually do not have to do these tasks regularly.

During the schoolyear children get up early to do their chores and prepare for school. After age eleven some begin attending secondary schools outside the parish and must rise as early as 5:00 A.M. to bathe, iron their uniforms, make and eat breakfast, pack a lunch, and catch the bus.[16] If their parent or parents have already left for work, they may also have to help younger brothers and sisters get ready. When primary school children return from school, most eat a snack and go outside to play. Those in secondary school are more likely to watch television (especially if they have cable) or begin their homework, although many boys still go outside to play. As evening approaches, most children disappear indoors; few are allowed back outside after dark. This prohibition was once reinforced with the legend of the "heartman," who was alleged to roam the countryside at night ready to rip out the hearts of any children he found.

With respect to children the village still functions as an extended family. People tend to watch out for the community's children, going outside to check when they hear a suspicious sound and comforting one another's children when they are injured. Any adult standing near village children who are still playing outside after 6 P.M. is likely to tell them to "go on home." Parents also report on one another's children when they think it is important. One mother we know, for example, did not hesitate to telephone her neighbor to report that she had just seen her daughter walk into the bushes with a boy.

All children, but especially boys, are regarded as naturally unruly, as "hard ears" in need of firm discipline and control. "Spare the rod and spoil the child" is a belief shared by many villagers. Even older children threaten younger siblings with "licks" (hits): "You better watch out, girl, and leave me be, or you'll have licks." Virtually every adult in St. Lucy can recall the "floggings" and "lashings" they received as youngsters. According to one person, "If you sneeze too hard, you got a lash." "I had quite a few floggings by my uncle," remembered a middle-aged man:

> One time I was out on the jetty with my sister and some boys around seven [P.M.], and my uncle came down, "What are you doing down here at this time of night!" He had a twig behind his back, and we didn't see it. My sister was faster than I was, and she didn't catch any of it, but I got a good one. You just hope that when you get home he didn't tell your mother because you'd get it again.

Teachers also used corporal punishment, administering lashes to children who were disrespectful or disobedient, who spoke when not spoken to, who lied, who arrived at school late, and who had not done their homework. One woman remembers hiding to avoid lashes at school:

> When we were going to school, if you were going to be late, you would leave your house and hide in the gully, go home to lunch, and then back to the gully until school was over. We didn't love school as such; it wasn't a place of comfort but more like a correction center.

Today lashes can only be administered by the headmaster or head teacher, and they are given less often and, generally, more lightly than in the past.[17] Still, being struck several times with a leather strap or wooden switch across the buttocks, back, legs, or the palm of the hand is no laughing matter.

Attitudes about corporal punishment are changing. People are beginning to question its wisdom, even if they still believe in its effectiveness. Some teachers are convinced that lashing is psychologically harmful but still think children learn more if they are lashed when they need discipline. As one primary school teacher explained: "When we were young, we got lashes, and we learned. We memorized things, because, if we didn't, we'd know we'd get lashes." Today many younger and better-educated parents object to lashing and are punishing their children, instead, by taking privileges away. A twenty-seven-year-old male agrees with the changing attitudes:

I went through some hard years. Boy, I got a good few licks—like a person fighting in a ring. I'd get smashed and slapped. Some people get strong by the more licks they get, but some get to not be bothered by them, and then they go and fight or lick others. Instead of licking, parents should turn off the television: "Okay, you're going to bed early." Or, if the child like sports, they shouldn't let him play a while. I don't believe in licks. I feel that talk should be the way. That changes things, not licks.

Older villagers, however, complain about the boldness of children today and blame it on the lack of discipline: "Children are big talkers now. They'll say, 'You can't tell me what to do; my mother doesn't even tell me what to do.'" According to one elderly woman: "The young people today are very wicked. They will curse you! Cursing older ones! When I was young, you'd get lashed for sure, for sure. Children today got no culture." Although villagers still watch out for one another's children, gone are the days when they felt free to give any child who was misbehaving a good smack. They are no longer sure the child's parents will back them up.

Growing up in St. Lucy is not all hard work and punishment, nor was it so in the past. Country children, especially boys, have always enjoyed freedom and adventure.[18] Roy Campbell fondly remembers his childhood near Rockfield in the 1960s:

What I like about growing up in St. Lucy was the outdoor life. It was the country with wide open spaces, and the sea was near. You could do a lot of running around, and there was nothing that could get you into trouble. You looked forward to the change of seasons. During Easter season, from the beginning of Ash Wednesday, we started flying kites and we'd do that until the crop finished. On Sunday we'd be off to the sea to go fishing. We couldn't afford to buy hooks, so we'd use common pins and a nylon cord.

You'd take fish home and roast them in the fire. And when the sea egg [sea urchin] season was in you'd get them from the fishermen. They'd give you two or three. Sometimes the sea eggs were in pretty close to shore so you could get them yourself.[19]

Opinions about when the transition to adulthood occurs vary. Some people regard age sixteen, because it is the legal age of consent and also the time when most Barbadians leave school, as the age at which adolescents become adults. Others think that adulthood begins at eighteen: "You adult when the government make you responsible for yourself and you can cast a vote." Still other people say that being an adult is less a matter of age than of how mature a person acts: "A nineteen-year-old who gets on the bus and laughs or snickers and mixes with little fellows," explained one woman, "is no adult." Independence is another criteria. Children become adults, many Bajans say, when they can "turn their own key."

Economic realities often defer true independence for many years. Only some young adults in St. Lucy find jobs upon leaving school and are financially able to move out of their parents' homes; most continue to live at home for a number of years in order to save money to buy a car, land, and a house of their own. Eric O'Neale, profiled in chapter 4, lives with his parents and works at part-time jobs. Other young adults attend a polytechnic school or enroll in a hotel training or other specialized course hoping to make themselves more marketable. Those with higher career aspirations and some financial help attend the Barbados Community College or the University of the West Indies at Cave Hill. Those from better-off families or who win scholarships often go abroad to universities in the United States, Europe, Britain, Canada, and other Commonwealth countries, which offer more advanced training and a broader range of graduate work than is available at home. The daughter of our immediate neighbor in Josey Hill studied biotechnology in the Netherlands, then went to New Zealand to complete her Ph.D. degree.

Old Age and Death

Old age in St. Lucy is linked more to fitness than to years. An eighty-year-old who is vigorous may not be considered as "old" as someone in his or her early sixties who is in poor health. Most elderly villagers

Three village teenagers at the Holetown Festival. (Photo by Ellen Frankenstein.)

remain active after they retire, raising a few animals and working a small plot of land on which they grow "provisions" such as potatoes, *eddoes,* and yams. Some men raise and harvest small plots of sugarcane or ground nuts to sell; women often sell homemade baked goods and sweet drinks from their kitchen door. Men with skills such as tailoring, upholstery, and carpentry often continue to work but at a slower pace. George Fitzpatrick, a seventy-two-year-old neighbor, who sewed two pairs of pants a day in his prime, in retirement slowed down to one. Many elderly women are kept busy watching grandchildren while their daughters and sons are at work. The combination of healthy diet and work means that many rural elderly are not only fit and active but also strong. A twenty-one-year-old joked: "Have you seen the way the old people shove to get on the buses? They strong! That's because they eat a lot of ground provisions instead of hamburgers and stuff." One of our students described the strenuous daily routine of his seventy-year-old neighbor:

> Mrs. J., who I see quite often, works long, hard days without complaint. She usually begins to work at 7:00 in the morning and works in the field behind her house until about 11:00 or until "the sun begin to scorch" her. She is either picking crops, weeding the garden, or feeding and tending animals. She hardly ever takes a ten-minute break but, instead, opts to work continuously. She feels that it is her job to do her part "so the Lord will provide." After lunch she heads back to finish her work, and she might be in the fields until four or five in the evening. The night is occupied with fixing dinner and doing household chores. She is usually in bed by 10:00 and sets her alarm to get up by 5:00 the next morning.

"Since I was little," explained an eighty-three-year-old woman, "my momma told me to keep the faith and stay humble and never worry about things that you can't get."

Many elderly live in extended households and have daughters and grandchildren around. Those who live on their own usually have children nearby who visit them each day to make sure their needs are met. Older villagers who do not have relatives in the village are looked after by neighbors and visited by church groups, who come to read the Bible and offer companionship and aid. The government also provides basic support and services: small old-age pensions, free medical treatment and bus travel, and reduced rates for water and electricity.

In the past, when storytelling was a part of village life and the outside world was more distant, the elderly were valued for what they had to say. Today they complain that young people "don't like to listen." "If they were by chance to listen, and they hear an older person talking," observes Marcus O'Neale, "they amazed. They say, 'That happen in your day?' They amazed to hear we once worked for a penny a day. But they embarrassed, too. They don't like to hear how bad things was—about the chiggers and lice."[20] Elderly villagers recount cleaning their teeth with salt and ashes from the kitchen fire, having head lice, walking barefoot to school, and sleeping on flour bag mattresses stuffed with grass. Stories like these do not interest many young people today, and even some adults hesitate to tell them. Perhaps this past is still too recent and painful.

Until the 1960s when a villager died, a wake was held in their home for family and close friends who gathered by the corpse to drink rum and cocoa and sing through the night. Before the funeral a viewing was held, after which friends and neighbors accompanied the coffin to the church. In the recent past, the procession was led by the "family car" in which the nearest kin rode, followed by the hearse, and then the "walkers"—neighbors, friends, and more distant kin who walked behind, two abreast, the women dressed in white, the men in black. They were followed by other mourners in cars. Today the deceased is taken straight to a funeral home and, on the day of internment, transferred to the church. Most funerals begin around 4 P.M. and follow a set ritual that starts with the mourners filing past the open casket on their way in. Photographs of the deceased are usually taken; many families later put together an album of the funeral. After about an hour the coffin is closed and wheeled further into the church for the service, which typically consists of prayers, hymns, an address by the officiating minister, and a eulogy by a friend or family member. Pallbearers then carry the coffin to the cemetery. After the ceremony is over people retire to the family's home or a rented hall to socialize and eat.

Funerals are major social events, which draw large numbers of mourners and spectators, especially if the deceased person was well-known or the death occurred under tragic or questionable circumstances. Attendance is facilitated by the daily obituaries and funeral announcements that are read over the radio each morning. Modern funerals, villagers say, are less somber than in the past. There are fewer open displays of grief; some people now wear colored clothing to the service rather than dress in only black or white; and the atmosphere afterward can seem surprisingly light. The death of a young person, however, causes great anguish. After the tragic death of an eighteen-year-old girl in one village, for example, most mourners wept, and four young men claimed to have seen "duppies" (spirits) in front of her home. The death of an elderly person is accepted more readily; a strong, shared belief in the hereafter allows the living to let go more easily.

The Griffith family, Coles Cave. (Photo by George Gmelch.)

Chapter 6

Community: Past and Present

Not that long ago St. Lucy's villages were largely self-contained. People could obtain almost everything they needed within the village or else nearby. Village specialists like the midwife, tailor, joiner, and tinsmith supplied essential goods and services. Families grew most of their own food, purchasing the rest from hawkers or the local rum shop or plantation store, which stocked basic supplies: rice, salt fish, and kerosene. Some communities had a corn grinding mill for flour and a public oven.[1] Families and neighbors shared what they had—ground nuts, yams, sweet potatoes, and breadfruit—to be repaid later with a loaf of freshly baked cassava bread, ripe mangos, or a papaya. Neighbors also helped one another in other ways: looking after children, clearing brush, moving a house. People depended upon one another and cared: "We was all one big family." Of all the parishes St. Lucy especially was known for its hospitality, as a place where even outsiders were welcome. Its isolation in the era before paved roads and public transportation, reinforced its cohesiveness.

In recent decades economic development—including the introduction of modern amenities like piped water, electricity, and bus service—has dramatically altered rural life. So much so that Barbadians who return after living abroad sometimes have difficulty believing the changes that have taken place while they were away. To what extent do villagers feel that a fundamental transformation in community life has taken place? Are St. Lucy's villages still cohesive communities despite the change? And, if not, what do people think about it?

Modernization and Change

The standard of living for most people in the parish began noticeably to improve in the late 1950s and 1960s, as new technology and services filtered in. Until then few families besides "the great"—local elites such as the plantation manager, school master, and rector—had more than anyone else. Those who did were villagers with extra ambition and luck who had worked hard and managed to save or else families with "Panama money"—money earned by relatives who had worked on the Panama Canal and returned home to buy land and upgrade their homes. Everyone else lived similar and modest lives.

Until the late 1950s most people in St. Lucy cooked outside over wood fires built in "rock kitchens"—simple coral or rock hearths sheltered from wind and rain by low walls and roofs made of branches or galvanized metal.[2] The fires required careful tending and a steady supply of wood, which was cut from the nearest gully. When wood was unavailable, dried coconut husks and cane stalks that had spoiled in the fields or fallen from the plantation truck were used and sometimes cow dung. At meal times smoke from the outdoor fires curled over the villages like signal fires, coating houses and yards in soot. At night people placed potatoes and breadfruit in the coals of the fire to roast overnight.

The poorest families ate from platters that were little more than cross-sections of wood and from bowls and cups they fashioned from the gourds or dried fruit of the calabash tree. The "calabash" was a common measure: "Put three calabash of water in to boil the peas," mothers directed their daughters. "Give a calabash of soup for de small ones, two for de big ones, and three for de men that working," other mothers instructed, "and leave a calabash in de pot, case anyone pass by and need food or de bus break down by de door." Other utensils and containers such as buckets, graters for cassava and potatoes, and "tots" (tin mugs), were bought from the local tinsmith. In the 1950s mass-produced enamelware plates and utensils began to replace calabashes and tin. Like any new and "expensive" item, however, it was at first a status symbol. To own enamelware showed not only that a family had the money to buy it but also a degree of refinement, since it probably meant they no longer had to eat with their hands.

Piped water was one of the earliest public services to change village life. Before it became available, people collected rainwater, used natural springs like those at Spring Garden, River Bay, and Cove Bay, and washed and bathed in natural ponds.[3] After the devastating cholera epidemic of 1854, which killed one person in seven on the island and more than a thousand people in St. Lucy, the government worked to extend clean water to the farthest reaches of the island. Eventually, four hundred roadside spigots called "stand pipes" (short for "standard pipe") were installed, bringing pure water to the rural population. Forty-nine were erected in St. Lucy; most were placed near plantations.[4] Even with stand pipes many villagers still had to carry water home from a considerable distance away. Virtually every villager over the age of forty today remembers having to "head" water—that is, balance a heavy bucket on his or her head with only a cloth pad for cushioning and a palm frond or leafy branch on top to keep the water from sloshing out. "Carrying water was hard, hard," remembers fifty-nine-year-old Arnold Griffith with a grimace. "After getting home from walking through de hills, your head and neck would ache bad, bad. But after a while you become numb to it." During crop season plantation mills and, later, sugar factories used such large amounts of water that the stand pipes often ran dry. Heavily loaded cane trucks sometimes drove over the pipes on their way to the factory and broke them. Then people took turns walking to the stand pipe to check; when the water came back on, they filled every container they had.

Eventually, people could pay to have pipes extended to their homes. Valenza Griffith from Coles Cave remembers her father's pride at being able to have piped water put in: "He always used to remind us how he spent all his savings to put water in. You know what it cost? Seven dollars." When the village stand pipe ran dry, Valenza's mother opened the gate to their yard to let their neighbors in. Although some people in St. Lucy acquired piped water in the early 1950s, most villagers did not get it until the 1960s. In some areas water mains were not extended to all parts of the village until the 1970s. Having water piped into the yard or house, of course, greatly simplified many household chores.

It also simplified bathing. In the view of one elderly villager: "Young children today living the king's life and the queen's life. Get up, go to the bath, and turn on the shower." Before water was piped to individual homes, however, many adults bathed only in preparation for church, carrying a water bucket and bar of blue soap into a stand of canes or trees at the back of the house. Only a few villages had public bathhouses. Working men typically rinsed off at the stand pipe on their way home from work; children often stripped to wash in the rain. Most women sought some privacy, but they did not feel overly self-conscious if seen bathing. "In the past you would see grown women with

A roadside bath (ca. 1960). (Photo by E. Fitzpatrick, courtesy of The Barbados National Trust.)

their breasts bared bathing at the backs of the houses," remembers Velma O'Neale, "and nobody bat an eye. Today men would be peeping at you." When piped water arrived, most people built private bathing sheds and showers in their yards. One consequence is that villagers today are more conscious of nudity.

Today almost all village homes have piped water, and over two-thirds have indoor plumbing.[5] More affluent families also have small, rooftop solar water heaters. Initially, having piped water, like owning enamelware, was a status symbol, a sign that a family had moved up in the world. In *Growing Up Stupid under the Union Jack*, author Austin Clarke recalls his childhood embarrassment at having to collect water at the stand pipe when other families in his community had "in pipes." Status distinctions within the village were once made on the basis of such differences: "We don't have to bring water," "We don't have to pick up wood," "We have electricity," the children of better-off families would smugly say.

Although stand pipes are still used by some people in the parish (and by many people when there is a problem with the water supply), they are no longer at the heart of village life. Children no longer meet their friends to walk to the stand pipe together. Adults no longer "queue up to catch water," exchanging jokes and news while waiting in line. When older villagers are asked what they miss about the past, many immediately mention the "pipe." For, despite the hard work of carrying water and the fights that sometimes broke out when water ran low or someone jumped the queue, the stand pipe has come to signify "community" and all that was good about the past.

Before piped water and indoor plumbing villagers retreated to the cane field or gully to relieve themselves during the day and used a chamber pot at night. Some families dug "pit wells" (outdoor toilets) in the yard. Coals and ash from the kitchen fire or a land turtle which lived in the pit helped keep the stench down. Occasionally, sewage from the shallow wells leaked out, however, flooding yards. "Every once in a while the air would be spoiled from the wells in the village," remembers a resident of Josey Hill, "and it would practically kill you." Today 70 percent of parish homes have indoor toilets.

Laundering is the one household task that has not changed dramatically over the years for most people. Fewer than half of St. Lucy's households today have washing machines. Most women continue to wash clothes in a bucket or tub in the yard, vigorously rubbing the

A village hair braiding session. (Photo by Ellen Frankenstein.)

fabric over itself and against their wrist or on a wooden "jooking," or "jukking board" (washboard). In the past imported salt meat drums purchased from the local rum shop were cut in half to create washtubs, which were set up in the yard or near a stand pipe. In a few villages women walked to a nearby pond to wash, spreading their clothes on the grass and bushes to dry. Saturday washing in the "pasture" was an important social event for these women and their older daughters. Most households also had a "bleach rock," a rock bed on which they spread wet clothing that had been soaked in blue soap to bleach in the sun. When women left the house, they often asked a neighbor to sprinkle their clothes for them so that they would continue to bleach. Laundering today is easier, even without a washing machine, because of piped water and commercial cleaning products, which have replaced items like homemade cassava starch.[6] But people also own more clothing, change them more often, and create more laundry.

In the 1950s kerosene stoves began to replace cooking with wood and coal. Kerosene made cooking easier and cleaner, but, because the stoves lacked ovens, women still baked sweetbread and cassava pone in coal pots (dutch ovens) or in ovens built over the rock hearth. Most people also continued to roast breadfruit and flying fish over a wood fire, preferring its smoky flavor. In the 1960s, with the introduction of clean-burning "gas" (propane) stoves with ovens, cooking for most people moved completely indoors. "Now everything so easy," observes Malcolm Hinds. "You turn the switch, you cook." Although women still prepare most family meals, with gas (and, more recently, electric stoves) anyone can easily heat or cook food.

Electricity reached St. Lucy in the 1960s, bringing with it a host of changes. Before electricity people used candles and "snuff lamps"— glass bottles filled with kerosene and a rag wick—for light. Others used tin lamps made by the local tinsmith, or if they could afford one, a glass chimney lamp with a metal reflector. With electricity daylight was extended into the night, filling "de whole room with light." This gave villagers more time to finish chores before retiring to bed. Streetlights also made socializing outdoors easier. Men, for example, now played *warri*, dominoes, and cards on makeshift tables under the streetlight.[7] Previously, they had assembled at the rum shop and played under an oil lamp or else waited until a bright moonlit night. Before streetlights the only time most people stayed outdoors at night was during a full moon. Then children and adults played games to-

An important match, Barbados

Village cricket in times past (ca. 1900). (Courtesy of Mary Kerr.)

gether: "every single house wud be empty. Even de little babies wud be wrap up in towels and pass from han' to han', so dat de mudders got a chance to play."[8] Because all villagers participated in the play, such games knit people together and represented a celebration of community. Today nearly 90 percent of parish homes have electricity.[9]

Electricity dramatically changed the quality of village life in many ways. "After we got electricity, everything went modern," declared one woman. Electricity made refrigeration possible, and for many people that was as important as light. Previously, few foods could be kept without spoiling in the tropical heat; only the wealthy could afford blocks of imported ice. Most people ate salt fish (dried cod from Newfoundland) and flying fish, which they ate fresh or else dried on the roofs of their homes for later use. Others salted pork and "jerked" (canned) it in clay pots. With refrigeration a greater range of foods could be kept. Refrigeration also simplified food preparation. No longer did every meal have to be made from scratch and eaten on the same day; instead, leftovers could be stored in the refrigerator to be reheated as the need arose. At first, however, many of the elderly resisted, believing that eating leftovers was an unhealthy thing to do; some claimed it would cause cancer.

Electricity simplified ironing as well. No longer did villagers have to use heavy, cast-iron flatirons, which had to be heated in the coals of the kitchen fire or over the kerosene stove, wiped with a leaf, and then polished with a cloth to remove all traces of soot before use. Few people besides the tailor owned a gas iron, which was fueled by kerosene and lit with methylated spirits. When electric irons arrived, ironing became cleaner, easier, and faster, although it remains a time-consuming household task, since most villagers are fastidious about their dress.

Electricity made television possible. First introduced to Barbados in 1964, television began to appear in parish homes in the late 1960s and early 1970s.[10] It was an instant success, quickly making the mobile movie van obsolete. The movie van had driven into larger villages, such as Checker Hall, set up an outdoor screen, and shown short documentaries followed by comedies like Abbott and Costello. Today, when villagers talk about the importance of different amenities in their lives, they almost always rank television first. Neil Rock remembers what happened when his family acquired the first television in their village. "My dad bought a television in 1973. Everyone in the village would come over to watch it at night. It became annoying after a while because the house was always full. But soon everyone bought TVs, and the village scattered, and people stopped coming around to visit. Everyone was busy watching their set." Television has meant that villagers spend more time inside their homes than outside, where they once socialized with neighbors. The evening games and stories that brought people together—adults and children alike—have all but disappeared. Other innovations that have come with electricity such as refrigeration have similarly weakened community. "Before the refrigerator," says Velma O'Neale, "people always running over to borrow, and I be going over to get something. With the fridge no need to do that."

Telephones arrived in the parish about the same time as television. The first private household to have one is said to have been St. Lucy's representative in Parliament. Before the telephone, information and news had to be relayed by mail or in person, often at great inconvenience. When someone needed a doctor, a neighbor or family member had to walk or ride a bike to the Crab Hill police station to summon the police van. When someone died, people walked or pedaled from community to community to pass the news and fetch the undertaker. "Even if the sun was blazing, people need that message, and you got to go," remembers Velma O'Neale. Now emergencies can be handled more easily. The telephone may also make obtaining jobs easier. Successful applicants can be contacted by telephone, whereas before they could only be reached by mail, which, villagers claim, could take two weeks. By making communication easy, the telephone also allows friends and family members, including those living overseas, to stay in regular contact. By increasing the independence of individual households, however, it works to weaken community.

Prior to nationalization of the bus service in the 1970s, many villages in the parish were quite isolated. The private bus concessionaires in business had few routes, and their service was infrequent. Today the number of government "transport" buses as well as privately owned minivans, known as "ZRs" or "route taxis," has dramatically increased, and so has their frequency of operation. Moreover, all major roads are paved, which greatly increases the ease with which people can leave the parish to work, attend school, and shop. Many St. Lucyians work in Bridgetown or on the west coast hotel strip; some people spend as much as three hours each day on or waiting for buses. This amounts to fifteen hours a week, or a month each year spent in transit.

The first bus arrives in Josey Hill, the village we live in, at 5:30 A.M., about a half-hour before dawn; throughout the day government buses are scheduled to arrive every hour. Transportation on the government-run buses is the topic of much conversation and grumbling in village homes and rum shops. Some buses are driven recklessly; stretches of road are potholed, making for a rattling and bumpy ride; and, not infrequently, the buses do not arrive on schedule.

Today the nearest approximation to the pipe in creating community is the bus. Most villagers in St. Lucy ride government buses or privately owned mini-vans five or six days a week to work and to shop in town. Their reliance on buses was apparent when we visited two of the parish's main industries—a chicken processing plant and garment assembly plant, each with more than 150 employees—and were struck by the virtual absence of cars (four or five at most). Riding the bus, like collecting water at the stand pipe in the past, is a shared, daily experience with a component of hardship built in. Most rural roads are narrow; many follow the cart and footpaths first established in the seventeenth century. For the outsider riding a government bus can be a frightening experience as it careens around blind corners, barely missing approaching cars. For villagers, riding the buses is more often an exercise in frustration. When a bus breaks down or a driver calls in sick, the transport board may not arrange for a replacement, leaving people stranded at bus stops all along the route. Occasionally drivers stop to conduct private business, leaving their passengers sitting in the heat. Like the standpipe, however, riding the buses also strengthens community bonds. While waiting at the bus stop, people exchange greetings, talk, and catch up on local news. Regular riders watch out for one another's interests, alerting neighbors when the bus is about to come and getting the driver to hesitate so that a friend can get on. People also take parcels home for one another and watch to see that young children get off at their stops. Someday villagers may look back nostalgically at the bus the same way many today fondly remember the stand pipe.

Interdependence and Community

Modern technology and services have clearly eliminated the most grueling aspects of daily life and greatly reduced the isolation of rural villages. They have also opened up new forms of entertainment and created opportunities for further education and outside work. Most villagers value these improvements and have no wish to return to the past. Those over fifty years of age clearly remember the poverty and hardships of their youth. Yet, for every convenience or comfort gained, something is lost. The dilemma of development and "progress" everywhere in the world is that it brings negative consequences along with the good. How have the changes just described affected people's sense of community—their identification with their village and feeling of shared fate?

The village today plays a smaller role in most people's lives. Although more than 80 percent of St. Lucy's residents were born within the parish (the highest figure of any parish), villagers are increasingly living independent lives. No longer do most people walk to the same plantation in the morning to work, nor do they socialize together at night. Most people now work outside the village in Speightstown or Bridgetown, in hotels scattered along the west coast, or in one of St. Lucy's four small industries, and spend many hours away each day. At night and on weekends those who can afford to, especially the young, typically leave the village to attend fetes, concerts, movies, nightclubs, and sporting and religious events elsewhere on the island. In some communities, outsiders are moving in, while the offspring of families who have long lived there are moving out in order to live nearer to their work and professional colleagues or to the stimulation of Bridgetown. Approximately one-quarter of village households are not related to any others.[11] Many people's friendships and support networks now extend well beyond the confines of the village and parish to include family, friends, coworkers, and church members living in other parts of the island. The village, for a growing number of people, is a community in only a physical sense; it is no longer the focal point of their lives nor the primary source of their support.

Nor do all villagers live at the same level as their neighbors, and the economic and educational disparities are growing. One of the first comments middle-aged and older villagers make when asked to compare the past to the present is the lack of "neighborliness" today. People, they claim, are not as friendly or as caring as they once were; instead, they have become materialistic and self-centered. According to one villager,

At one time we live good, but not now. People think they're independent now. It used to be that, when the man across the street kill the pig, he would bring over a piece for me and my family, and, when I kill my cow, I do the same thing, but not anymore.

In the past villagers' isolation and shared poverty and educational level created interdependence and contributed to an egalitarian ethos. "When everybody live together [the same], we learn to share," explains seventy-year-old Errol Sobers. "Everybody share. But today things develop. Now, one person feel he more up [is better] than the other." Meryl Cumberbatch, age fifty-two, concurs: "When I was young, if you don't have, and I do, then I share with you. But not today. Today is self only!" While most villagers today work at skilled, semi-skilled, and unskilled jobs, some are white-collar professionals and a sizeable minority is unemployed. Educational differences also exist. In the past the "11-plus exam" determined which select few among village children went on to secondary school. The protagonist in George Lamming's semiautobiographical novel *In the Castle of My Skin*, for example, experienced a sense of split identity being both a villager and a high school boy, so unique was the experience. Today most of the younger generation has completed secondary school, while most older villagers have completed only "seventh standard" (primary school).

Antagonism often exists between members of different generations, but it seems especially marked in St. Lucy's villages today. Many of the elderly accuse the youth of being "lazy," "wicked," "unmannerly," and "soft." They are dismayed by young people's materialism and apparent lack of interest in work. Ralph Cumberbatch, in his seventies, puts it this way:

> The young today have no idea how hard us old folks worked. We worked for nothing. The young today will buy things like stereos for seven hundred dollars. When we were young, we would buy calves or pigs with the small money we had or put it in the bank. The kids today don't think about raising animals. They like the sport life. They like to have fun. The old people don't understand why the young don't put their money in the bank and save it to buy a house or a piece of land.

Many parents, of course, have discouraged their sons and daughters from working the land and have struggled to put them through school so that they can have a "better life." High school graduates can hardly be expected to want to work the land.

Older people are also offended by the decline in manners and the disrespect they detect. Elders say that village youths "look you in de face and don't say nuttun' [fail to greet you]." The young, of course, do not know what village life used to be like and are far less critical of the present. They cannot remember the time when life events were everyone's business, when good and bad news was shared by all, and when the experiences of an individual became part of the village's collective consciousness. As a result of their mobility and education, and the influence of modern mass media (e.g. television, videos, and music lyrics), they are oriented toward the outside world and focused on their own pursuits. What the elderly regard as "neighborliness," the young consider nosiness and interference: "They've already lived their life, and now they want to tell us how to run ours." Many of the young would agree with the views of twenty-year-old Shirley Maycock, who believes, "Older people like to stick their mouth where it's not wanted. Boy, they stir up trouble."

Crime is another concern of villagers, especially the elderly, that is exaggerated by the weakening of community bonds. Today most people in St. Lucy keep their doors locked and their windows closed at night. Many of the elderly lock their doors whenever they leave the house, even if they remain nearby, and they avoid walking anywhere alone at night. "You used to be able to walk to Speightstown in the middle of the night with no problem, even a girl," remembers an elderly man from Cave Hill. "Now there's rape, murder, and robbery." Our students are surprised at the number of warnings they receive about their safety and are distressed at having to swelter in the heat because they are not allowed to keep their bedroom windows open. We have seen a dramatic increase over the last thirteen years in the precautions that host families take.

Although crime has risen on the island, especially in more populated tourist areas, few offenses have occurred yet in St. Lucy. Much of people's fear seems to stem from the frequent depiction of crime and violence in the news and on television and from the elderly's growing sense of unconnectedness and vulnerability. In some St. Lucy communities groups of young men seen liming during the day without work may increase their fears, although there are probably fewer idle young men in St. Lucy than in other parishes. Most keep busy in positive pursuits: during the harvest some work in the cane fields; others go fishing; still others, like Eric O'Neale (chap. 4), engage in reciprocal labor with neighbors and friends. St. Lucy is also dotted with tiny village parks decorated with painted rocks, ornamental plants, and hand-made sculptures, which have usually been created by young unemployed men. Nevertheless, in the view of many elderly, crime is on ·the rise because "The young generation today get wicked."

Despite many real changes and a definite weakening in the bonds that bind villagers together, there is still evidence of community in the parish. Many working women, for example, are only able to juggle their dual roles as mothers and workers because of the help they receive from family, neighbors, and friends. Most neighbors still share garden produce, loan tools, take messages for those without a telephone, and perform other favors for each other. The unemployed sometimes help friends and neighbors with major jobs such as putting on a new roof, building a house, and planting a garden. They know they can count on similar help someday and in the meantime, that they will always be welcome in that person's home. When disaster strikes villagers always pitch in; a community party was held in one village during our stay to raise money for a family whose house had burned down. Having said this, it is also true that many goods and services that were once given free are now likely to be sold. Today villagers who butcher animals let others know but usually to allow them to place an order. With modernization, generalized reciprocity is giving way to market exchange.

Several forms of credit still exist in many villages. Many rum shop owners, grocery store proprietors, and local bakers allow their regulars to "trus'" (trust)—that is, ·o buy goods on short-term credit. Such credit is especially important at certain times of the year, such as immediately following Christmas, when many villagers are financially pinched, having spent all their money on an elaborate meal and fixing up their homes with new paint and "blinds" (curtains). Another community-based form of support is the "meeting turn," an informal rotating credit association. Villagers, seldom more than ten or twelve, who feel confident of one another's trustworthiness "throw," or contribute, a specified amount of money each week into a common pool collected by the "meeting holder." Each week one member draws the entire sum, until everyone has drawn in turn. If someone has a special need, such as the final payment to make on a refrigerator or funeral expenses, they can usually arrange to take their turn early. As a form of compulsory savings and a simple way to acquire an interest-free loan, the meeting turn helps villagers meet their financial commitments and improve their standard of living.[12] Meeting turns also extend beyond the village and parish. One meeting holder in Josey Hill has members in the parishes of Christ Church and St. James. Other villagers belong to work-based meeting turns.[13]

Various community institutions also continue to bind villagers together. Of these, religion is the most important. As a member of a church, a villager belongs not only to a spiritual community but also to a social one. Most villages have at least one church or "meeting hall"; many have several. Weekend services, evening Bible study, and prayer meetings are attended regularly by women and children and by a smaller number of devout men. Most congregations also have youth clubs and service groups, like the Salvation Army's League of Mercy, which visits the sick to prepare meals, read the Bible, and clean their homes. Church members also provide one another with needed emotional and financial support, handling funeral arrangements for a distraught family, for example. Religion, of course, also inspires individuals to personal acts of Christian charity and generosity. Recall the charitable work of Judy Griffith, described in chapter 4, who visits several elderly people in Josey Hill to run errands, arrange for home repairs, and wash clothes.

The rum shop lies at the other end of the spiritual spectrum yet rivals the church in importance as an institution that binds a certain sector of the community together. Whereas the church is largely a female preserve, the rum shop is strictly a male one. In Barbados there is almost one rum shop for every three hundred people.[14] Josey Hill, a fairly typical community, has three. They serve as informal community centers in which men "stand rounds" (take turns buying one another drinks); talk about sports, politics, and women; play dominoes and cards; and pass the time. While men of all ages hang out at the rum shop, the regular clientele tends to be middle-aged and working-class. For regulars who have been unable to find steady employment or who have resigned themselves to the impossibility of advancement, the rum shop clientele forms a "fraternity of commiseration."[15] For men who are too old for sports or who are not attracted to other forms of relaxation and entertainment such as picnics, fetes, the cinema, or church-sponsored events, the rum shop is their primary social outlet.

For many younger villagers, especially men, village and parish-based sports teams are important in creating a sense of community. Any village with a flat piece of land nearby is likely to have a cricket

Cooperative house building. (Photo by Ellen Frankenstein.)

A village store and rum shop near Half Moon Fort owned by Davis Babb, who hosted student Chet Urban. (Photo by George Gmelch.)

A cricket match. (Photo by George Gmelch.)

and a football (soccer) team, sometimes several.[16] Typically, as many village teams are created as are needed to accommodate all the men who want to play.[17] During the cricket season, from May until early December, many men's weekends are filled with cricket play and talk. For important village matches large numbers of fans turn out. The football season, which lasts from January through April, is even more popular than cricket and draws more fans. Communities near St. Lucy's secondary school and its sports facilities also have basketball teams, which are organized into league play by the Barbados Amateur Basketball Federation. When people watch and root for their home team in games against other villages, they unknowingly affirm their pride in their community.

Public and religious holidays are also important occasions for celebrating community, providing opportunities for families, friends, and courting couples to get together. Picnics are a major form of working-class leisure in the parish, with women spending much of their time preparing food and socializing, while men play dominoes or sports.[18] St. Lucy's bays and beaches (Cove Bay, River Bay, and Archer's Bay) are favored not only by locals but also by people from other parts of the island. Errol Barrow Day, which honors St. Lucy's most prominent son and Barbados' first prime minister, has special importance in the parish. It usually spawns village-based field parties at which people gather to enjoy music, dancing, and food. Religious holidays—Christmas, Easter, and Palm Sunday, for example—and special church services such as harvest celebrations and children's days are also well attended, reasserting shared values and community.

Chapter 7

From Anglican to Pentecostal

Religion is a cornerstone of life in St. Lucy. Its presence is evident everywhere, from the imposing Anglican church that towers above the cane fields near the entrance to the parish to the modest meeting halls wedged between houses in virtually every village. In one form or another people are exposed to religion everyday. During the week gospel music from tapes, compact discs, and daily radio programs spills into the streets. On Sundays and many weeknights the sounds of rhythmic clapping, tambourines, and exclamations of "Hallelujah" and "Praise the Lord" fill the air. Schoolchildren begin each day with prayer and in the course of their studies learn a repertoire of religious songs including "Only Fools Don't Believe in His Power." On Sunday mornings the roads are lined with women walking to church or waiting at the bus stops in brightly colored, satin sheen dresses, hats, and high heels—Bible in hand, well-groomed children in tow. Scattered among them are churchgoing men wearing neatly pressed suits. In this chapter we provide some historical context, but the focus is on contemporary religious practice. What role does the church play in the lives of men and women in St. Lucy? What are some of the tensions surrounding present-day religious life?

Historical Background

British settlers brought the Church of England, or Anglicanism, to Barbados in 1627. Within a decade the island had been divided into six "parishes," which served as ecclesiastical and governmental units, each with its own church.[1] For the next three hundred years Anglicanism dominated the religious life of the white community.[2] Relatively little is known about the religious beliefs and practices of the early black population. The intermingling of people from different cultures meant that a single, intact African religious system never existed in

Pentecostal church in Pie Corner. (Photo by Ellen Frankenstein.)

Barbados, although many beliefs and rituals were retained. In their research on Barbadian slave culture, Jerome Handler and Frederick Lange have noted numerous African religious features including:

> the concept of the great gods, including a creator god; nature deities; the general responsiveness of deities to human actions; propitiation and veneration of ancestors, the ancestral cult and the active role of the dead in the living; oaths and ordeals involving ancestors or other deities; . . . souls (including multiple souls); religious ritual associated with medical practices; the profound belief in witchcraft and sorcery; and the central role and significance of the funeral and rites attending the disposition of the dead.[3]

Mortuary practices displayed particularly strong African influence, including the custom of making food offerings and small animal sacrifices (particularly chickens) at the grave site and "the value attached to locating burial sites close to the houses of the living and interment under the houses."[4]

African-derived beliefs and practices are still found in St. Lucy. Many people, for example, believe in the existence of spirits, or "duppies," that bring bad luck and harm. Villagers once claimed that the "coolie man" (itinerant peddler) would seek revenge on any debtors who failed to repay him by sending duppies to stone their doors. People still report seeing duppies; a few older villagers try to ward them off with strategies such as scattering sand around the house. Folk expressions testify to the prominent place they have held historically in people's imagination: *duppy-agent* for undertaker and *duppy-pinch* for a bruise of unknown cause.[5]

Some people also believe in the existence of "obeah," or witchcraft.[6] In pre-emancipation days the term *obeah* was used to refer to a variety of practices performed by ritual specialists—including drumming, dancing, and trance—to contact the supernatural, and diagnose and treat illness. Such rituals are characteristic of shamanistic performances in many cultures. Over the course of the slave period, obeah had many meanings and "was not necessarily viewed negatively by the slaves themselves."[7] It was, however, viewed negatively by the plantocracy, which passed legislation to ban it.[8] As a result, many practices associated with obeah went underground, especially once

Christianization was fully under way, and it evolved into a form of secret magic. Obeah men and women were consulted by slaves and, later, by free villagers to cure illnesses, interpret omens, and make amulets or potions for a variety of uses, such as keeping an unfaithful husband at home, securing a lover, or exacting revenge. One of the substances they used for the latter purpose was "duppy-dust," powdered bones from the graveyard.

While there are very few obeah specialists in Barbados today, the belief in the presence of obeah and its power lingers. Obeah has become a folk idiom through which many Bajans, not only people in St. Lucy, express their fears and anxieties and explain misfortune, madness, illness, and death.[9] When a young boy in a nearby village died under tragic and seemingly mysterious circumstances during our fieldwork, relatives concluded that he had been the victim of "witchcraft and devil worship." Another villager we know attributed the string of bad luck his family had been having to obeah worked by envious neighbors. A common explanation given for a person's odd or unexpected behavior is to say, "It look as if somebody give he something [magic potion] to eat."[10]

The first direct exposure slaves had to Christian beliefs occurred in the seventeenth century, when Quakers invited those living near them to their meetings. It was not until the late eighteenth century, however, when United Brethren (Moravian) and Wesleyan missionaries arrived in Barbados, that real attempts to convert the black population to Christianity began.[11] Later the Anglican Church also sent missionaries and schoolmasters from England to Barbados—through the Incorporated Society for the Conversion and Religious Instruction and Education of Negro Slaves in the British West India Islands—to open charity schools for slave children. Until that point the native Anglican Church had done little work with slaves. Barbados' Parliament had forbidden their religious instruction on the grounds that it would encourage "notions of equality," and Barbadian-born clergy had been socialized to accept slavery on the island. They also depended upon the goodwill of parish vestries for their support.

Although some Christian baptisms and burials were performed for slaves before active missionization began, only a small number of marriages were sanctified. According to historian Hilary Beckles, the plantocracy apparently regarded marriage as more threatening to "the ideological structure they had imposed" than either baptism or burial.[12] Some Anglican clergy and planters, however, were critical of polygyny and believed the best way to encourage monogamy was to Christianize the slaves and marry them in the church. One such early marriage took place in St. Lucy. After the Reverend W. M. Harte had performed the ceremony, the couple insisted that they now be addressed as "Mr." and "Mrs.," much to the irritation of white parishioners, who objected to their presumption of equality. Parishioners also disliked what they regarded as their rector's ongoing attempts to "alienate their slaves from a sense of their duty."[13]

By the end of slavery white attitudes were changing. In 1824 Parliament decided that religious training should be a part of slaves' preparation for emancipation. With the arrival of Bishop William Hart Coleridge and the passage of the "Sunday and Marriage Act" in 1826, a concerted effort by Anglicans to convert slaves began. Anglicanism soon became the dominant religion of black Barbadians. It was not seriously challenged until the late 1800s, when Protestant fundamentalists from North America began missionary work on the island. The Christian Mission (Pennyites) began proselytizing in 1891, followed by the Church of God, Pilgrim Holiness, Salvation Army Society, and others. By the 1920s revivalist churches of many stripes were capturing the imaginations and souls of rural villagers. Despite the white iconography of these churches, their work has been characterized as an attempt to form a genuine "people's ministry."[14] Today fundamentalist churches are viewed as the "folk," or people's, religion in Barbados. As yet, African-inspired religions with black iconography such as the Jerusalem Apostolic Spiritual Baptist Church and Rastafarians have relatively few adherents, especially in St Lucy.[15]

Religion in Everyday Life

Islandwide, 58 percent of Barbadians attend church regularly; in rural areas like St. Lucy attendance is higher than in urban parishes like St. Michael and Christ Church.[16] Fully three-quarters of St. Lucy's residents claim a religious affiliation. All belong to Christian denominations, with Anglicanism having the greatest number of adherents, followed by various Pentecostal sects, and Seventh Day Adventism (see table 2). Rastafarians constitute a tiny, yet significant, religious minority in the parish.

Women are more involved in organized religion in the parish than

TABLE 2. Religious Affiliation

	Percentage of Adherents[a]	
Religious Denomination	St. Lucy Parish	All Barbados
Anglican	24	33
Pentecostal	14	13
Seventh Day Adventist	11	5
Methodist	4	6
Salvation Army	3	.4
Church of God	2	2
Baptist	1	2
Jehovah Witness	1	2
Roman Catholic	1	4
Brethren	.3	1
Rastafarian	.2	.4
Moravian	.1	1
"Other"	13	8
"None"	24	20

Source: 1990 Census of Barbados, Table 2.06: Population by Parish, Sex and Religion, pp. 148–51.
[a]Percentages do not add up to 100 because of rounding.

are men; 85 percent of women in St. Lucy claim a religious affiliation, compared to 66 percent of men.[17] This gender difference is also apparent in church attendance. At evening prayer meetings, for example, older women predominate; singing, praying, and perspiring in the tropical heat to the accompaniment of tambourines and guitar. Church is many women's primary social outlet—the one place they can meet friends, sing and listen to music, and, for a few hours, escape their everyday responsibilities and routines. Perhaps because village men have more opportunities to gather—at the rum shop and sporting events, for example—they feel less need to attend church. In the parish, church is clearly regarded as women's domain. According to a village friend, "Bajan men think you're soft if you go to church. They feel like more a man if they shy away from religious things." Sociologist Graham Dann found that Barbadian men are less likely than women to believe that religion is the most important thing in life or that the church had helped them achieve their goals.[18]

Anglicanism

Villagers equate Anglicanism with respectability and elite status. Anglicans are "proper" and said to be better off than most members of the community, although many poor villagers also belong to the church. Remnants of Barbados' class system are still evident in services, in which, as one person characterized it, "The lower class sits with the lower class, and the upper class sits with the upper class."[19] The church's historical dominance in Barbados is apparent on holy days like Ash Wednesday, when schoolchildren are bused to Anglican churches for worship regardless of their own religious affiliation.

Anglicanism is "high church." The appearance of its church buildings says as much. Most are impressive structures built of solid coral block with bell towers and stained-glass windows. The church itself is hierarchically organized and its services filled with formal ritual. Services are led by a robed priest assisted by a sexton, altar boys (and, today, girls), and full choir. Centuries-old rituals employing holy water, incense, and bells punctuate the ceremony. One student characterized the setting and service as "majestic," although she also thought the congregation looked "bored" in contrast to those in other churches she had attended: "Other congregations put so much more spirit, rhythm, and joy in their songs." At St. Lucy's Parish Church, however, not every service is staid. Wednesday night meetings and some Sunday services could quite easily be mistaken for Pentecostal with their use of tambourines and exuberant singing.

Generally, however, Anglican services are comparatively subdued. Most consist of hymns accompanied by organ and choir, readings from the Bible and Book of Common Prayer, communion (the symbolic and communal partaking of the Body and Blood of Christ), and a sermon, which typically stresses the importance of leading a righteous life and discusses a current social issue such as decaying moral values and drugs. "I feel the Lord should be worshiped in solitude and seriousness," explained Randolph Broomes, defending the solemnity of Anglican services. "The singing and raving of the others [Pentecostals]—it's like a festival, like Crop Over. Shouldn't there be a distinction between worship and festivity?"

Pentecostalism

After Anglicanism, Pentecostal churches have the greatest number of adherents in the parish. As suggested earlier, their services are lively, intense affairs. The churches are also democratic in style and organization. One village friend, who used to be Anglican but recently joined a fledgling Pentecostal sect, explained her decision: "The [Anglican] priest used to tell us what to do, and I'd just listen. This is the first church where I really feel that I can approach God on my own. That he cares about me." At Pentecostal services all members of the congregation participate. Many begin with an open prayer session, during which congregants call on the Lord and shout his name each in their own fashion. Loud, joyous gospel singing is also a central feature of the service, as people, with arms outstretched, sway, clap, and harmonize to the accompaniment of tambourines, guitar, and drums. A letter to the editor in the daily newspaper, the *Advocate,* bemoaning the corrupting influence of dub music on Barbadian culture, accused some congregations of having gone too far in the direction of entertainment—doing everything from "jump and wave to 'roll yah bam-bam,' 'lift ya leg up,' 'bump,' 'boogie,' and 'jam it'" in their services.[20]

Enthusiastic worship expresses the Pentecostal's commitment to the Lord and gives full reign to the Holy Spirit. One of our students described the effect a Pentecostal service had on her:

> I had to force myself not to cry at one point because I have never had such a gratifying spiritual experience in a church. These people knew where it came from. The words they spoke and sang came from deep down inside their souls and burst out in utter joy. If these people don't truly believe with every ounce of conviction that God is their Lord and Savior, then I don't know where on earth to find people that do. I found myself singing the choruses and clapping along with them, although I tried not to make too much of a spectacle of myself. There were already a lot of people looking at me, including a little girl in the pew in front who stared at me literally for a full hour. She analyzed every move I made, watching my mouth when I sang, my hands tapping on the bench, and even got down on the floor to look at my legs underneath the bench.

A significant doctrinal difference from other Christian churches is the Pentecostals' belief that "holiness," or a sinless state, can be attained by all who exert self-control. Adult baptism and sanctification means that even women with children born outside of marriage are not excluded from full church membership and that their status as unwed mothers does not carry a lasting stigma. Women involved in a current sexual union, whether living with their boyfriend or not, can hope eventually to be sanctified by regularizing the union through marriage.[21]

Pentecostals believe in the power of the Holy Spirit to enter and cleanse them and to help them resist the devil. Spiritual healing is a critical component of worship. During services people with physical ailments are called forward to "let the Lord minister" to them. Amid the congregation's calls of "Oh, God!" and "Oh, dear Jesus help them," each person is "anointed" with the Holy Spirit by an elder or the pastor, who vigorously rubs olive oil on their foreheads, arms, and neck while entreating the devil to leave them. Many of those treated walk away crying, later testifying to feeling much better. God also reveals himself to worshipers through dreams and revelations, and the Holy Spirit sometimes manifests himself at services when congregants experience glossolalia (speaking in tongues).[22] During periods of intense praying, as people begin to chant, raise their arms, and dance, some slip into a trance-like state and speak in tongues. "You have to be inspired," explained one man. "You just feel these words that you can't put into a natural language. . . . It's a direct prayer." If the congregant has received the gift of interpretation, a message from the Holy Spirit may also be imparted to the rest of the congregation.

Pentecostals believe in a literal interpretation of the Bible. Mark 16:17, for example, is the scriptural foundation for glossolalia: "And these signs shall follow them that believe; In my name shall they cast out devils; they shall speak in new tongues." The church stresses the importance of knowing the Scriptures; part of being properly dressed for Sunday service is having your Bible in hand. One congregation begins its morning devotions by "breaking the Bible"—that is, allowing the Bible to fall open and the Lord to inspire the verse selection for the day. Sermons typically consist of reading the Scripture and then elaborating on its meaning. Members are reminded to "study the word of God" so that they will know it by heart and be better able to resist the temptation and sin that surrounds them—movies and parties, drinking and smoking, gambling and cheating, adultery, and even other churches. At one service the pastor cautioned people to be wary of the "enemy," denominations as diverse as Seventh Day Adventists, Jehovah's Witnesses, and the Tie Heads (members of the Jerusalem Apostolic Spiritual Baptist Church). He warned them not to speak to such people: "Just get them out of your house as fast as you can and tell them never to come back!"

In some churches the young are called forward to join hands while the congregation prays for them. Many of those called forward are visibly moved by the experience and join in, crying out, "Touch me Lord!" and "I feel Jesus!" At least once a week all members are invited to give public "testimony" to what God has done for them. At the close of Sunday service, after the offering is taken, new people introduced, community announcements made, and the benediction given, the congregation files out, members greeting one another with further exclamations of "God bless you" and "Praise the Lord." Pentecostal services emphasize emotional release and community.

Seventh Day Adventists

Seventh Day Adventism is also a significant part of St. Lucy's religious community, being the third most popular religion. Adventists observe Saturday Sabbath because this is believed to be the day on which God rested. From sundown on Friday until sundown on Saturday the devout refrain from all work and secular distractions: they do not cook, watch television, or operate electrical appliances. It is a holy day, devoted to the Lord. Adventists believe in denial and moderation. Members are discouraged from eating meat (especially pork) and shun alcohol and caffeine. They are not supposed to smoke, wear jewelry or makeup, or go to movies. Many parents censor television and videos for violence and other bad influences. Some believe that birthdays should not be celebrated with gifts, since they mark a child's entry into a world of sin. Seventh Day Adventists, like other fundamentalists, believe in a literal interpretation of the Bible. They look forward to the Second Coming of Christ and to the Last Judgment, which they believe to be imminent. Salvation is achieved through perfection, and the church stresses the need to forgive the sins of others, for only then can people expect forgiveness for themselves. Once people are able to forgive others and not sin themselves, they will have achieved perfection and will "enter God's kingdom."

Sabbath is devoted to worship. Many Adventists spend most of the day at church. Services are typically more restrained than those of Pentecostals and usually begin with a hymn, followed by Sabbath school, during which the congregation—divided into age groups or classes—studies a weekly lesson (e.g., "What is friendship and evangelism?"). This is followed by the "divine service" for the entire congregation, which consists of hymns, prayers, Scripture reading, and sermon. Some congregations then share a communal lunch, before conducting a second, afternoon service. The youth service is typically more casual and, at one church, consists of hymn singing and religious quiz games, followed by a discussion of a religious topic.

Like Pentecostals, who send "missionaries" out into the community, Adventists emphasize the recruitment of new members. Above the altar in the Adventist church in the village of Grape Hall are the words "Tell the whole world, Jesus and the Family." "Bible workers" regularly go to people's homes to discuss Adventist doctrine and distribute pamphlets such as "The Prophecies of Daniel and the Revelation." At least once a year a major "crusade" is held from a large tent. These open-air services are held for several weeks "to give the people in the area an idea of what we believe in," explained one man. Attracted by the music and activity, local people and passersby, no matter how casually dressed, are invited into the tent, where they are given literature on Adventism and told about the church. At the end of the crusade a graduation ceremony is held, and new members are baptized and their names "read into the church."

Rastafarianism

Although Rastafarianism has a tiny following in the parish, its members are highly visible and the subject of considerable local comment. Rastafarians also represent an attempt to create a black-inspired religion and have been important in heightening black Barbadians' awareness of the African part of their heritage. In comparison to the religions just discussed, Rastafarianism lacks organizational and doctrinal clarity. It was inspired by the teachings of Marcus Garvey, the Jamaican-born founder of the Universal Negro Improvement Association, who in the 1920s and 1930s advocated self-reliance for blacks and a "back to Africa" consciousness. Garvey denounced the colonial mentality that had taught blacks in the Caribbean, United States, and other parts of the world to be contemptuous of their African heritage. Redemption was equated with repatriation to Africa. His prophecy that a black king would be crowned, signaling deliverance, appeared fulfilled in 1930, when Ras Tafari was installed as Emperor Haile Selassie I of Ethiopia. In the following years, as Rastafari beliefs and religious culture developed, the movement was spread by Jamaican activists among the poor of that country and then expanded throughout the Caribbean, into parts of Kenya and Ethiopia and urban areas of the United States, England, Canada, Australia, and New Zealand.[23]

Rastafarianism was introduced to Barbados in the early 1970s. Its popularity is said to have been heightened after a visit to the island by the Jamaican band Third World. In the 1980s a colony of about thirty orthodox male adherents began living in caves south of Cove Bay near two St. Lucy villages. A handful of men remained in the mid-1990s. Other Rastafarians in the parish live with their parents or in their own homes in the villages. Some Rastafarians in other parishes, like the members of the Order of Nyabinghi in St. John, have formed organized congregations, which meet regularly for worship.

To most people in St. Lucy, Rastafarians are an undesirable element. They are accused of stealing clothing from people's lines and of pilfering fruit and vegetables from their gardens. During the 1980s local antipathy in the eastern part of the parish was so strong that one man placed poison in his cucumbers and succeeded, it is claimed, in poisoning two Rastafarians. A few villagers told us they stopped growing kitchen gardens in order to eliminate a food source for the "Rastas." Local experiences have coincided with press reports of crimes committed in other parts of the country by "dreadlocks" (so named for their tresses of uncombed hair), many of whom are criminals who have adopted the appearance but not the religion of Rastafari.

Most villagers actually know very little about Rastafarianism. Those who do, distinguish between "true Rastas" and those people who have merely grown "dreads" and wear "tams" (hats with the Rastafarian colors of green, gold, and red, symbolizing African patriotism). "Rastas are okay people," concluded one woman. "Those other people with the dreadlocks are into drugs and not religion. True Rastas know the Scriptures of the Bible." Rastafarians are also admired for their knowledge of plants and herbs, vegetarianism and healthy lifestyle, and rejection of the materialism and the false values of "Babylon" (outside world). Many Bajans admire the craftsmanship of those who make and sell leather goods and drums in Temple Yard in Bridgetown. Some people are also aware of the achievements of prominent Barbadian Rastafarians as artists, academics, musicians, and sports figures. But for most middle-aged and older villagers, Rastafarians are considered to be little more than lazy dropouts and borderline criminals.

Some younger villagers have difficulty relating to the Rastas' self-denial and rejection of material wealth.

One of our students, Johanna, developed a friendship with a Rasta and learned the hard way about the attitudes of villagers toward Rastafarianism.[24] She met Joseph, a twenty-four-year-old Rasta, on the street outside the primary school in her village. They began talking while watching the children play. At the end of the conversation they arranged to meet the following week in front of the village store. When Johanna's seven-year-old host sister returned from school later that day, however, she told Johanna that the children at school had been upset: "Oh no, that man is going to take Johanna into the mountains and kill her!" they had said. Her teacher also told her to warn Johanna not to talk to Rastas. Even though Joseph had grown up in the parish and was known to some villagers, he was considered undesirable.

Despite the warnings, Johanna met Joseph the following week, and they left the village together to visit "Creation"—the secluded caves where he and four other orthodox Rastas lived. Johanna learned that Joseph had first become interested in Rastafarianism while smoking ganja (marijuana) and listening to Bob Marley's "Redemption Song." He visited the Rasta colony and talked to the brethren, who explained their religion to him. He learned much about plants and herbal medicines from the founding member of the colony, who is a knowledgeable "bush doctor," with both Rasta and non-Rasta clients. Once he decided to join, he gave away all his belongings, left his parents' home, and moved to Creation, where he lives in a simple cave and collects and grows most of his food and cooks in calabash pots, like most of St. Lucy's families once did. While in Creation, Joseph and the other orthodox Rastas do not wear clothes. They do not drink alcohol or smoke, except for sacramental ganja.

Johanna visited Joseph a number of times and was accepted by the Rastas as a "daughter" and "woman of consciousness." But, as the days went by, she noticed that people in her village were becoming less friendly. "What was once a hearty greeting from across the road has become a malicious stare," she recorded in her journal. A group of young village men who had verbally harassed her at the beginning of her stay, but who stopped once they had gotten to know her, had begun to treat her as a sexual object again. One day, as she passed the local rum shop, a loud voice called her "the devil's child." On another day an elderly woman mocked her as she walked by, asking, "You goin' to the cave to have a time [sex]?"

When Johanna's host mother learned of her visits, she called her into her room and shut the door. "Have you been up with the Rastas?" she asked. "The way she reacted, frightened me . . . looking so desperate and disappointed," Johanna reported. "I don't think I ever realized the stigma attached to Rastas until this moment." Her host mother then told her that people in the village were talking, saying she was smoking marijuana and bathing naked. "I don't want my house and my children connected with these things," she informed her. "I know you only have a little time left in Barbados, but I have to live here for the rest of my life." As Johanna wrote in her journal:

> The gravity of what I was doing was suddenly apparent to me. She was kind enough to have me stay in her house, and now I was jeopardizing her reputation and the reputations of her children. We talked about it. How the fact that I was a woman alone made it ten times more despicable than if I were a male or with a group of people. "See those people sittin' around the shops?" she said. "They'll all be sayin', 'That Johanna is a drug addict.'" Indeed, they did.

Rastafarianism's African iconography and emphasis on the righteousness of black people is interpreted from numerous biblical references, especially in the books of Isaiah, Romans, Corinthians, and Numbers. Its teachings appeal primarily to men; it is the only religion in Barbados to have a higher male than female membership.[25] Women clearly occupy a subordinate role in the religion. They can only be called to Rastafari through a male and must seek men's guidance in spiritual matters. Orthodox female Rastafarians must also observe numerous behavioral restrictions. When menstruating, for example, they cannot prepare meals for men, nor can they approach a male ritual gathering. They must also keep their heads covered at all times in contrast to men's flowing dreadlocks. Rastafari's central symbol—the majestic, powerful lion—is clearly linked to men and not to women.

Secularization

Despite the ubiquity of religious activity in St. Lucy, older villagers claim that religion is losing ground. In their day every child went to

Sunday school. "You wake up on Sunday mornings, and you know you had to go to Sunday school," remembers Marcus O'Neale. "You wasn't asked if you wanted to go. You got up and get ready!" Sunday school teachers sometimes came to the homes of families whose parents were not practicing Christians in order to bathe their children and bring them to church. They even provided clothing if parents could not afford something suitable. Today villagers say that fewer children are being socialized into a faith. Fewer go to Sunday school or accompany their parents to worship services. Most people think this reflects a general breakdown in parental discipline. Now that parents no longer routinely "lash" their children, say elders, children no longer fear their authority and are no longer as obedient. Threats of other-worldly punishment no longer work either. "Years ago if a child didn't go to Sunday school," explains Marcus O'Neale, "you'd tell it, 'You going to hell. The devil will burn you in the fire. The fire going to burn you up.' Things like that. Children don't believe that nowaday."

Many middle-aged and younger adults are also disillusioned with religion. Villagers usually attribute this to a failure in church leadership. Whether true or not, many claim that clergy no longer set as good an example for their congregations as they once did. "They are backing away from the truth, the actual Christianity of the church," claimed Theo Thornhill, who went on to explain:

Church is actually something like a business today, like a supermarket. I'm building a supermarket so I can stuff it with food, so people will all come in and shop and make it great. With a church, I'm building a church so everybody going to come in and listen to a few words of the Bible and bring some envelopes with money. Some pastors are visiting more than one church. They can make a hundred dollars just to make a guest appearance. It's a business. It's not like years ago where you find church as an encouragement to push you on further in life, to give you something to hold onto, to relax your mind when you got a problem.

Years ago you find religious people getting groups [of people together] sitting down together on the lawn or under the streetlight preaching religion, preaching it. But nowadays every pastor want to build a church to teach religion. And every pastor that has a church have an office in it, and the office has a secretary, and a treasurer controls the money. . . . Twenty-five years ago if you see a pastor on the road walking, you would stop and say, "You know something, Pastor? I really got to talk to you." And he'd say, "Okay, I listen now." Today you say, "Pastor, I got a problem. I got to talk to you." He'll say, "Okay, call my secretary, and she'll make an appointment for you to see me. Right now, I'm in a hurry."

This perception may be true of some clergy, but it is also contradicted by the behavior of others who devote hours each week and sacrifice much of their personal lives to counseling their parishioners. One Pentecostal pastor we know, for example, spends many hours on the telephone each day and regularly receives early-morning and late-night visits from members of his congregation who come to seek his advice, all in addition to his preaching duties and full-time job.

Villagers accuse some clergy of wrongdoing, notably "committing fornication"—that is, being more interested in sex and the young women in their congregations than in religion. Still other people are disillusioned with sermons in which pastors' accuse members of the congregation of misbehavior and use their pulpit as a platform to air personal grievances and to pursue private agendas rather than to teach the Word of God.

The perception among St. Lucy residents that there is a declining interest in organized religion is borne out by national census data. In 1970, over 99 percent of the population gave a religious affiliation. In 1990, 77 percent did. The largest decline has occurred among Anglicans, though Moravians and Methodists also lost membership. The Pentecostals, however, doubled their adherents islandwide—from 6 percent to 13 percent. Seventh Day Adventists, Jehovah's Witnesses, and Baptists also gained followers.

The changes are linked to modernization. Religion is no longer the sole solace or source of information that people turn to for guidance. Many older villagers still read the Psalms to find spiritual comfort and advise one another to "Trust in the Lord," but today people work outside the village and often seek advice and suggestions from colleagues and friends. Barbadians are also better educated and more widely read; most now graduate from secondary school. And everyone is exposed to television, film, and radio. Consequently, people are better informed about social issues. One study found that, when Barbadians were asked who they turned to for advice on a variety of issues—including concerns such as death, the future, and marriage, which normally fall into the religious domain—only 10 percent mentioned their minister; another 15 percent reported praying. Friends were much more likely to be consulted.[26]

The mass media, new forms of recreation, and better transportation also make the local church a less vital social institution. "Back in the fifties," recalls eighty-two-year-old Pastor Emerson Yearwood with sadness, "you would meet people flocking to Sunday schools learning the Scriptures. . . . [It was] a subject like math or English. You would never see a cricket team on the field or a football team on the field on a Sunday. People used to like going to the churches." In the past even nonmembers often walked to church on Sundays to listen outside. "Used to be everybody strewn around the churches to see what was going on," remembers Marcus O'Neale, "even if you wasn't a member of that church. They [sermons] carried more meaning. It [religion] was more sacred than today." Such observations are supported by research, which indicates that it is young, single, and better-educated Barbadians, as well as those with higher incomes, who are the least interested in organized religion.[27] Despite the decline in the number of people who claim a religious affiliation, however, a large majority (86 percent) of Bajans believe that they possess "spiritual well-being." Apparently, a growing number of people perceive spiritual well-being as something that can exist independently of organized religion.

Chapter 8

The Global Village: Television, Tourism, and Travel

Most people in St. Lucy are aware that Barbados is continually changed by its contact with the outside world. They know that events and political decisions made thousands of miles away in North America and Europe can have a profound effect on the island's economy—setting the price of sugar, determining the demand for hotel rooms, and, more recently, dictating structural readjustments that resulted in major civil service layoffs. In addition to the nearly half-million foreign tourists who stay on the island each year, many Bajans leave the country to work or study abroad or to visit relatives in North America and Europe. Both population movements introduce new ideas. On a daily basis television brings world news and North American popular culture directly into people's homes. "We're no longer an island," opined journalist Charmaine Gill. "Through telecommunications we belong to the world. We're part of the global village."

Philosopher Marshall McLuhan coined the term *global village* in the 1950s to refer to the single homogeneous world culture he believed the electronic media was creating. In many respects his prophecy seems to have come true, although it is due to more than just the spread of electronic media. Multinational corporations place legal and operational demands on small nations that they have little power to resist. At the local level, however, when people talk about the outside influences that most affect their lives, they identify three: television, tourism, and travel. In this chapter we examine the impact of these forces on people's lives. How much exposure do people in rural St. Lucy have to these phenomena? What changes do they think have taken place as a result? Although it is nearly impossible to separate the role played by television from that of tourism or foreign travel, there can be no doubt that, collectively, they have a profound impact on both the island and parish.

Television

Television arrived in Barbados in the 1960s; most people in St. Lucy acquired it a decade later. Today virtually every parish household has TV, and many people also own VCRs. Foreign lifestyles that were once the subject of speculation based on information gleaned from emigrants' letters home and returnees' tales are now displayed through talk shows, sitcoms, and films. World news is a part of everyday life. People in St. Lucy watched Nelson Mandela become president of South Africa and O. J. Simpson on trial. All homes receive the Caribbean Broadcasting Corporation (CBC) channel, which carries both North American and local programming. Since the late 1980s a subscription television service (STV) has been available, making U.S. networks such as the Cable News Network (CNN), the Entertainment and Sports Programming Network (ESPN), and Turner Network Television (TNT) available for a fee. At least 75 percent of Bajan households subscribe, although far fewer in St. Lucy than elsewhere in the island.[1] In 1996 a new digital satellite system was being introduced, promising its subscribers hundreds of additional channels.[2]

Most villagers are avid television and video watchers. In many homes the television set is constantly on, the sound seldom turned down. And, while it is still common to see neighbors talking together outside in the early evening, many more people are inside watching TV. Many families eat while watching TV. During our fieldwork so many people watched the nightly broadcast of "Days" ("Days of Our Lives"), an American soap opera, that telephoning someone between 6 and 7 P.M. was virtually taboo. An elderly woman we know was so absorbed in the drama that she yelled at the program's villains, fretted about the safety of her favorite character—"She just got to be careful 'cause I don't trust he. I don't trust he at'all, at'all, at'all"—and commiserated with a friend over the telephone immediately following each episode. Once darkness falls many villages seem eerily deserted; disembodied dialogue drifts through open windows into the street, and houses radiate a flickering blue glow.

North American shows dominate the television programming that Bajans watch and prefer. All of the channels available through subscription television originate in North America, as does most of the programming on Barbados' CBC.[3] The most frequently watched and popular television programs are American soap operas, action series, and situation comedies, many of the latter with African-American stars.[4] Many Barbadians worry about North American cultural penetration. "Man, we're the fifty-first state!" exclaimed one return migrant from the States.

> I came back home because I wanted my children to grow up in an unspoiled environment, but now Barbados is the same as the States. My kids want to wear American clothes, eat American food, do American things, play American games. They're even watching American football and baseball on TV.

In the opinion of Sandra May Shorey of the Barbados National Trust, television programming should be controlled:

> Television should be tempered with more Barbadian and Caribbean-influenced programs. It's obviously easier to get "Days of Our Lives" and "Dallas" than something from Trinidad or Jamaica. Those countries produce very little, and what they have produced might not yet be of a standard high enough for the tastes of Barbadian viewers. But we don't really make an effort to get anything else. . . . We've never made an effort to develop programs, to explore our culture, because there's this ready-made culture, and we can just buy it.[5]

Because commercial sponsors buy advertising time on programs they know are popular, the money to develop local programming remains limited. Nor can the government afford to support expensive program development. "We haven't got the money to do good programming—the gloss and the glitter. The government can't afford it," explained one man. "So how can we retain our culture? How can we compete with the rest of the world?"

Despite the enjoyment that television brings, villagers blame it for a variety of social ills. Communities and families, they say, are no longer as close. "People don't visit one another place like before—that gone," said an elderly neighbor of ours. "They visit more before TV." Television has made even children less sociable and less active. Instead of playing outside with their friends, many stay indoors to watch television alone or with their siblings. Research done by Monica Payne found that secondary school students watch an average of nineteen hours of television and videos each week. With time spent in school and travelling back and forth, there is little time left for socializing with friends. Villagers also hold television partially responsible for the growing alienation between the generations because children now spend less time talking to their parents and grandparents. The stories they once enjoyed are now considered "boring" in contrast to TV.

Bajans sometimes describe themselves as "quick to want and to acquire." Television fosters materialism and status striving. "It's impossible to see the equivalent of 'Dynasty' and 'Knots Landing' every night of the week, month after month, without assuming that you, the viewer, are also entitled to this standard of life," explained columnist and author John Wickham. Anxious to "improve" their lives, many people feel it is important to keep current with what is shown on TV. Some women watch television in order to track the latest North American fashions as well as to follow their favorite programs. Many young women in the parish flatly refuse to leave their homes to attend a party or concert unless they can dress in the latest style. Men are not immune. In the mid-1990s teenagers and young adults walked around the villages wearing Nike sweatbands and sport shoes, baggy name-brand jeans, and T-shirts emblazoned with American sports team logos. The son of a maid and a security guard we know begged his parents to buy him an expensive pair of Nike pump shoes—the equivalent of a week's combined wages—so he would feel comfortable at school. They gave in, reasoning that their modest income should not prevent him from being "happy." Advertising, of course, is based on creating dissatisfaction in viewers and linking happiness to a product.

Many villagers, like many Americans, believe that television and films contribute to violence and crime. The film *Colors,* which graphically portrayed the activities of a Los Angeles gang, is singled out as having spawned a number of mimic gangs in Barbados in the late 1980s. The parish's first reported gang made its appearance in 1989. Calling itself the "CBC gang," the youths reportedly broke bottles in the streets, stole coconuts, made noise, and hassled passers-by. Expressing the shock of other residents, a resident of Broomefield said: "Well, we know that they have drugs all over Barbados. . . . But I never thought we would have lawless young people in St. Lucy walking about making other people miserable. You only hear about that kind of thing in Bridgetown."[6] Gang names suggest media influence. In Bridgetown and neighboring areas the major gangs in the early 1990s were CNN, Vietnam, Beirut, and Q-8 (after Kuwait); in St. Lucy, CBC. Two are names of television networks, while three are countries or cities in which televised wars and violence had recently taken place.

Although the research findings are mixed, psychologists believe that television promotes aggression and violence in a number of ways. When violence is rewarded on TV, there is a greater tendency for children and adolescents to imitate it. The sheer frequency of violent acts and images on television normalizes violence and desensitizes children to real people's suffering. Both violent and high-action programs arouse their viewers, which can contribute to violent behavior in aggression-prone individuals. In a U.S. study, which followed children over a twenty-two-year period, from third grade through adulthood, Leonard Eron and Rowell Huesmann found that heavy television viewing was more predictive of later aggression than any other factor, including poverty, grades, single-parent homes, or exposure to real violence. When Barbadian police are interviewed about crime and youth gang activity, however, they emphasize the more direct influences of unemployment and drugs.[7] Indeed, most crime and gang activity in Barbados is found not in rural St. Lucy but in Bridgetown and the more urban parishes of St. Michael, Christ Church, and St. James, where drugs and opportunities for crime are greatest, due to the large number of tourists.

Some people in the parish worry about the moral tone of much television programming and its long-term effect on the country. Many shows glorify material wealth, greed, corruption, casual sex, and power striving at any cost. "Adult programming," or pornography, available on satellite TV, is a particular concern to some. Although the number of parish households with satellite TV is currently small, those that have it receive fifteen adult channels from Canada. "It sickens me," said one father. "You wouldn't believe what you can see—I was talking to my friends about it this morning—it's gone past pornography. And who's to stop the children from seeing it? We're creating a sick society."[8]

Television has a good side, of course, and this is the side that most villagers see. It provides inexpensive entertainment and can also play a positive educational role. Locally produced public service announcements, aired throughout the day, provide lessons on a variety of topics such as proper parenting, environmental awareness, and good citizenship. Documentaries and international news brought via CNN increase

Bajans' awareness of social issues outside the country, although with an obvious American bias. "Before Anita Hill," claims one professional woman, "there was no concept of sexual harassment in Barbados. There was no name for it. I know I got no sympathy when I complained [five years earlier], so I dropped it." Bajans' current interest in diet and fitness is also attributed to the influence of North American TV. Barbadians speak highly of once-popular programs like "The Fresh Prince of Bel Air" and "The Cosby Show" and of the positive images of family life they portrayed. Some people wish, however, that their positive social messages were emulated. "You see on "The Cosby Show" a lot of familial communication and families sitting down to eat [together], but this isn't adopted here," said one woman, "only the clothes."

Tourism

Tourism also ties Barbados to the outside world, bringing large numbers of foreigners to the island. In the early years tourists came to Barbados to recover their health in the island's warm air and salubrious sea breezes. Most stayed in small guest houses or in private homes. In 1751, for example, George Washington brought his older brother Lawrence, who was suffering from tuberculosis. They stayed for nearly seven weeks in country lodgings about a mile outside Bridgetown. Almost two centuries later tourist guidebooks still extolled the island's virtues as a "health resort," referring to Barbados as "the sanitorium of the West Indies."[9]

By the early 1900s tourism had become a "notable feature" of Barbados' economy. No fewer than eleven steamships made regular calls.[10] These early visitors tended to be wealthy, since transportation costs were high and the trip was long. They also stayed for substantial periods of time, weeks or even months. Although some large hotels had been built, most visitors stayed in guest houses or at small, exclusive "colony" or "club" resorts made up of individual bungalows, which fostered an intimate friendliness between visitors and local staff.

All this changed in the late 1950s and 1960s as the era of mass tourism got under way.[11] With the jetliner travel was made faster and easier. Postwar affluence and the adoption of guaranteed holidays with pay for most North American and European workers gave people time off and money to travel. Sophisticated travel agencies and tour opera-

Cruise ships moored in the deepwater harbor near Bridgetown. (Courtesy of the Barbados Tourism Board.)

tors sprang up to package and promote Caribbean vacations. They popularized the idea of winter vacations in "exotic" tropical places and helped bring Caribbean holidays within the price range of many middle-income North Americans. Today nearly 400,000 tourists arrive in Barbados each year; an even greater number visit briefly aboard cruise ships.[12]

Tourism now touches nearly everyone on the island. Many people in St. Lucy are employed in the industry as maids and security guards, waitresses and barmen, receptionists and gardeners. Others are self-employed food vendors, beach vendors, jet ski operators, and "beach boys." Still other people sell locally-grown produce to hotels and restaurants that cater primarily to the tourist market. The rest of the population experiences the indirect effects of tourism on Barbados' infrastructure, environment, and social climate.

Some of these effects are positive. By creating consumers for art and entertainment, tourism has encouraged the development of local music, dance, performance, visual arts, and crafts. The quantity and quality of live entertainment on Barbados is said to be high considering the island's small population.[13] At the parish level this benefits primarily those young who can afford to visit hotels and nightclubs. Despite the availability of good local entertainment, however, many hotels and nightclubs persist in staging manufactured tourist shows such as limbo dancers and in playing North American Top 40 music rather than that of local artists. Tourism is responsible for the creation of a major cultural event that has been embraced by Bajans. "Crop Over" was originally a celebration held among plantation workers at the end of the sugarcane harvest. This "tradition" was introduced as a national celebration in 1974 to promote tourism during the slack summer season. Held at first in hotels with dancers dressed in colorful Trinidad-style carnival costumes, the new holiday was later reoriented to the local market and further developed by the National Cultural Foundation. It is now a popular national holiday that entices even Barbadians living abroad back home.

One negative consequence of tourism is its effect on the environment. Much of the south and west coasts of the island are covered with hotels and condominiums and tourist-oriented businesses such as restaurants, boutiques, and gift shops. While these provide local people with employment opportunities and offer some new services, they have created visual pollution. Along some stretches of coastline it is difficult for local people to catch a glimpse of the sea; most coastal property has been priced out of their reach. Only the steep cliffs, scarcity of beaches, heavy surf, and strong undertow along St. Lucy's coastline have saved it from similar development. Water pollution from hotel sewage and detergents are killing the reefs and eroding the beaches.[14] Tourism also produces an enormous amount of garbage, which has overburdened the island's landfill, just as increased traffic overburdens the roads.[15]

From the visitor's point of view, however, tourism is benign. It is simply a temporary trip away from home, for the purpose of rest or recreation, that brings money and employment to the island. Barbados promotes itself as a tropical paradise with a friendly population, the perfect place to get away from it all. The country's beauty lies "not only in its special location but in the relaxed hospitality of the Bajans—an intelligent, proud, and free people who cheerfully share their home with visitors from all over the world."[16] In large measure Barbadians live up to their tourism industry image. Behind their rather reserved exteriors most people are friendly and surprisingly tolerant, often excusing tourist misbehavior with an indulgent "They're just here to have fun."

Yet tourism does place a social burden on the host population. While escaping their own obligations and commitments, tourists demand that local people fulfill theirs—serving food, cleaning rooms, entertaining, transporting, and providing a stress-free environment for sometimes boorish "guests." Tourists expect to be treated well no matter how they act, and they expect local people to be cheerful and courteous no matter how they feel. "I was startled to be spoken to in a gruff manner by a man behind the counter," groused a surprised Canadian tourist in a letter of complaint to a local newspaper, "telling me that I had no business coming in there [his shop] without a shirt."

The fact that most tourists are white and most Barbadians are black influences many tourist-local interactions.[17] Racism—or expectations of it based on the country's colonial history and many Bajans' personal experiences as emigrants living in England, the United States, and Canada—can complicate interactions between tourists and locals. Some hotel employees, for example, render service to tourists indifferently. As one manager explained, "Too many of my people . . . equate service with servitude." A focus of training within the tourism industry has been teaching employees to be friendly and courteous. As

Richard Haynes, then leader of the opposition, warned, "I urge . . . [Barbadians] to reflect on the damage which even a ten to fifteen percent decline in tourism expenditure will do to the Barbados economy and to further reflect on . . . the impact of such [racial] confrontation on tourism activity elsewhere in the Caribbean. . . . National pride, yes. Racism no."[18]

The tourism industry in Barbados, however, has its own record of racism. "Until the 1960s," according to E. D. Archer, "black Barbadians were routinely refused service (or given the slowest service) in tourist hotels and restaurants."[19] Hotel management still remains disproportionately white. Such discrimination made tourism a prime target of the short-lived student Black Power movement of the late 1960s. Many resorts continue to discourage locals from using their facilities. The nearest resort to St. Lucy, for example, recently adopted an all-inclusive plan in which tourists arrive having prepaid for everything, including food, drinks, and entertainment. Nonguests are no longer allowed onto the hotel's premises to eat in its restaurants, drink at its bars, or dance in its nightclubs, effectively banning all locals. The new plan also harms local businesses, since fewer tourists venture off hotel grounds. The presence of hotel security guards on the beaches discourages locals from using the public beach along the hotel's waterfront.

Race is sometimes overtly manipulated by both Bajans and tourists. Beach vendors occasionally use it as a sales strategy. A male vender of shell necklaces, for example, challenges tourists with the accusation, "You don't want to buy from me because I'm black." "Beach boys" (gigolos) who prey on female tourists similarly say: "Hi, I called to you earlier, but, when you didn't answer, I thought maybe it was because you don't like us black boys."[20] Tourists, too, may introduce race into their interactions with local people. Some make overtly racist remarks to hotel staff. Martin Boyce, a former hotel entertainment director from St. Lucy, recalls the English tourist who criticized his speech: "I'm sure he was racist. . . . He wanted me to speak the way he was speaking. He wanted me to pronounce words the way he did. Like, I'm speaking bad. So I said, 'That's your English; this is my English. It's all English. I can understand you. If you can't understand me, I'm sorry!" Other tourists simply make statements or ask questions that reveal how salient race is to them. One of us listened in surprise, for example, as an American tourist walked directly up to two hotel

The scene most tourists come to Barbados to experience. (Courtesy of Barbados Tourism Board.)

barmen and asked: "How do you guys feel about waiting on white people? Does it bother you?"

"Treat them well and they'll come back," advise public service announcements on television.[21] The Caribbean Tourism Research Center (CTRC) holds workshops for teachers so that they can introduce tourism into Barbados' school curriculum. Heading the CTRC's list of recommendations is to teach students to be aware of their demeanor and of the need to change their deportment in order to match the expectations of visitors.[22] The fact that people have to be told how to act indicates something of the unnatural strain tourism places on the local population. When tourists display their ignorance of Barbados, residents are annoyed and offended. Chupsing and raising his eyebrows, a hotel worker from St. Lucy said: "Tourists often tell me, 'I never heard of Barbados before I came here.' They don't have the slightest idea what Barbados is. They ask me about the size, what type of people live on the island, our language. Man, why they come?" According to a beach vender we know: "They think it [Barbados] somethin' like de wilderness of Africa. They expect to see de people runnin' round with a cloth about de waist." "People are surprised when I speak," the owner of a small restaurant reported. "They say, 'My, but you speak well.'" "Their ignorance was sometimes profound," remembers a former hotel manager:

> They'd come and ask where they can get stamps. I'd tell them, "There's a little shop around the corner that sells stamps." They'd come back, "Well, they don't sell American stamps. We want to post a letter to the States." I'm telling you, it's absolutely amazing. Any five-year-old in the Caribbean would know that, and they don't because to them the U.S.A. is the whole world. . . . Some of these people have saved up a long time to come to the Caribbean, and, when they get here, they figure everybody here has to be more ignorant than they are. They're just the tops, and aren't we glad they came!

Bajans who have prolonged contact with tourists sometimes benefit financially. Hotel workers and vendors who get to know a tourist well over a period of days or weeks may be given a substantial tip or gift at the end. In rare instances relationships between tourists and residents develop into friendships that are maintained over the years through letters and return visits, with the tourist sometimes helping finance a home improvement or business venture. One St. Lucy man we know was able to set himself up in the water ski business because of the financial help from a woman friend. Occasionally, Bajans travel with a tourist back to their home country to work or visit. A young St. Lucy woman who had looked after an American couple's children during their two-week vacation returned with them to the States to work as a live-in babysitter. Beach boys have traveled to Canada, the United States, and Europe to move in with their lovers. In *Colonial Madness* Lawrence Fisher discusses the role that relationships with tourists can play in creating jealousy and envy among villagers. He quotes a hotel maid:

> People come to visit me from the hotel at my house. They come to see me, or maybe they would bring me up [home] if the rain fall. If they have a party, they would come for me, an' I would work for them. . . . [my neighbor] say "De white people think you are somebody, but they wouldn't know you aren't nobody."[23]

The most intimate and visible tourist-local relationships are those between female tourists and "beach bums," or beach boys. These relationships are so well-known that many Bajans believe that any foreign woman who arrives on the island without a male companion has come with more than tourism's "three Ss"—sun, sand, and sea—in mind. While some women undoubtedly do have sex in mind, other women fall into romantic relationships with local men, which they believe are genuine and unique.[24] "Romance tourism," as anthropologists Deborah Pruitt and Suzanne LaFont note in a study of beach boys in Jamaica, is not just a gender inversion of the "sex tourism" found in underdeveloped countries like Thailand or the Philippines, in which male tourists travel explicitly to avail themselves of the paid services of local prostitutes, most of whom have been forced into prostitution by poverty.[25] Relationships between beach boys and female tourists, in contrast, even if paid, are voluntary and "constructed through a discourse of romance and long-term relationship."[26] Unlike the local Filipina or Thai woman, the Barbadian beach boy in many respects has the upper hand. As sociologists Cecilia Karch and Graham Dann point out, he is the person who is on familiar ground, while the tourist is in a foreign land.[27] He is knowledgeable about such relationships, while she may be unfamiliar with them. (Indeed, all she may know about local men is that the travel literature describes Bajans as "friendly.") Ironically, the beach boy may even act as a male protector, since foreign women often feel threatened by the hissing and explicit sexual comments many Bajan men direct at them. It is the female tourist who ultimately has control of the relationship, however, since she pays the bills, can break it off, and will leave the island to return home. She may be emotionally vulnerable, but it is the local beach boy who is financially dependent and who must show deference and appreciation in order to maintain the relationship.

Fantasy notions of "the Other" play a part in beach boy–tourist interactions.[28] For the white tourist there is the idea of romance with a black man who she is likely to regard as "exotic," "natural," and more sexually endowed than a white man (according to the familiar saying "once you go Black, you never go back"). Most local beach boys are young and muscular and prowl the beaches in revealing swimsuits. Some wear dreadlocks, enhancing their exotic and natural appeal. Female tourists who at home might be considered plain, overweight, or too old for such a young man may be especially vulnerable to the beach boy's "sweet talk." "You married? You have a special friend?" he asks. "A beautiful girl like you should have a boyfriend," he responds, no matter how she has replied. "You need a Bajan boyfriend," he insists. "How you goin' to experience Barbados if you never sleep with a Bajan man?" Many beach boys now directly address the fear of AIDS, reassuring potential partners, "Don't worry, I practice safe sex." One jet ski operator and beach boy's motto is, "No accidents during the day, no AIDS at night!"[29] For some women the offer presents an opportunity to experiment with their sensual sides while risking relatively little. Being a tourist is a liminal experience during which a person's behavior does not really count; she need never return to Barbados, and no one at home need ever know what she has done.

For the local beach boy, some of whom live in St. Lucy, relationships with tourists provide money, sex, intimacy with a foreigner, short-term comforts (e.g., dinner, drinks, a nice room), and enhanced status among their peers—as self-styled nicknames like "Dr. Love" suggest. Bajan masculinity is defined largely by sexual prowess, which includes the ability to satisfy women; what better evidence than the highly visible ability to attract foreign women. For many men such relationships mean money and even help with emigration. Most local people, however, regard beach boys as disreputables who are too lazy to find honest work. Yet they have a pragmatic attitude toward this special tourist-local relationship. "The people that are being approached are not innocent," claimed one villager. "They're both getting what they want [sex]. It's like trying a different type of food." According to a young woman we know: "The guys get a good time out of it. It's good for them. The only time it's a problem is when they [female tourists] mess with my guy." Being a beach boy is a young man's occupation, and most men move on to more respectable work by their thirties.

Other kinds of tourist-local encounters are undoubtedly more in keeping with the Tourism Board's assertion that "social interaction between people of diverse origins and cultural backgrounds" brings "positive benefits."[30] We have both overheard many conversations in which tourists and local people shared information about their personal lives and their countries' customs, economy, and politics. A young hotel worker from St. Lucy, for example, struck up a conversation one afternoon with a Venezuelan couple who were swimming in a hotel pool. As they clung to the side, he practiced his Spanish with them, and they asked him to explain Bajan dialect. Together they talked about the need for people to learn other languages so they can better understand one another's cultures. The Mighty Gabby, Barbados' famous calypsonian, frequently talked to tourists during his early career as a singer on tour boats: "They'd talk about things I had no experience of—fascinating things, like countries, the size of them, the fastness of them, the kind of things that you could do there. . . . I was a young man having all this information fed to me. . . . I was fascinated, and I wanted to go see for myself."[31]

What degree of contact do St. Lucy's residents have with tourists? Those who work in the industry, of course, have daily contact with tourists. But most people's exposure is limited to brief encounters and observations they make on the streets or in the stores of Bridgetown and Speightstown. One tourist behavior of which Bajans disapprove is their practice of wearing beach clothing in public. Locals interpret this as disrespect. "They walk around in these skimpy bathing suits. . . . Even in supermarkets you see men walking around without shirts and the ladies in only their swimwear," commented a woman with distaste.

"A Bajan would be arrested if they were caught walking around with the lack of clothing that tourists walk around in." Local people are far from prudish; they just think that businesses and the streets of town are not the proper place. Some store owners have put up signs informing tourists: "No bare backs" and "No scantily dressed persons allowed in the store."

Few tourists stay in St. Lucy. To begin with there are no hotels. In the 1960s a large resort with an Olympic-size swimming pool was built at North Point, but management problems and its isolation from the centers of tourist activity led to its closing. Exposed to salt spray and strong winds for many years, it is now in bad condition. Tourists do visit the parish to enjoy its natural beauty. Most people go to the Animal Flower Cave, a wave-eroded underground cavern that opens beneath the cliffs onto the sea.[32] Others come to see scenic Cove Bay with its view of Pico Teneriffe, a craggy rock spire just south of the bay.[33]

Tourists who visit St. Lucy as part of an island-wide bus tour have minimal contact with villagers, speeding by on their way to the Animal Flower Cave or Cove Bay. They only leave the bus to see the sights and take pictures and are soon back on board. Those who travel in a hired taxi may see more and linger longer, but they too generally have limited contact with local people. Only tourists who rent "mokes" (open cars) and spend time exploring the island actually talk to villagers, typically while buying a cold drink at a rum shop or stopping to admire the view. It is not uncommon, however, to see even these more adventuresome tourists parked on the roadside bent over a map while glancing nervously in the direction of local people who could easily aid them. Some communities in the parish are never visited by even the most intrepid traveler, and thus the impact of tourism on many villagers remains indirect.

Tourism, like television, nevertheless transfers outside values and patterns of behavior to Barbadians through its "demonstration effects." Tourists become a reference group for the host society; they are living manifestations of the wealth St. Lucy's residents and other Barbadians so frequently see in film and on TV. Tourism thus contributes to a sense of relative deprivation. Even people who do not work in tourism have heard stories about how much hotel rooms cost. "Do you know at Sandy Lane that some people pay as much as two thousand dollars U.S. a day!" a member of Barbados' police force exclaimed during an interview about tourism and crime.[34] Hotel workers watch as tourists purchase drinks and food at inflated prices, wasting much of it. Going to a restaurant for most villagers is an extravagance, done only to celebrate major family events such as a child's passing the Common Entrance Examination, graduating from college, or getting married. Tourists staying at the best hotels wear expensive clothing and jewelry. Others seem to flash their cameras, sports equipment, and money around. Many locals envy not only the tourists' ability to travel but also their possessions and apparent wealth. "The locals see what the tourists have and how they're living, and they want it," explained one hotel worker. "They don't see the fifty weeks of work behind it. They think it's easy."

One consequence of tourism that many people worry about is its effect on the work ethic of Bajan youth. Tourism is believed to raise expectations and the desire for material goods, at the same time giving some youths an opportunity to make "easy" money quick. The beach boy phenomenon is one example. Another is through drugs and crime, especially burglary and theft. According to one St. Lucy resident, the attitude of a growing number of youths is, "Why should I work all week when I can make the same money in one drug deal or hustling the tourists?" "There's a feeling out there among the younger guys," elaborated a professor at the University of the West Indies,

> that there's a lot of money to be had and that "We want part of it, and we want it now." Serious steady work is not fast enough for them and doesn't pay well enough. So there's a tendency to hustle and perhaps cut corners for it [money]. There's a thin line between hustling and cutting corners and doing illegal things. . . . I think [tourism] has had that kind of impact, although it's hard to separate this from the impact of television, which has changed expectations—expectations that are unrealistic given the resource base of this country.[35]

Because tourists have money and come to Barbados to have a good time, villagers reason, they provide a ready market for drugs. Selling to them has become a quick way for unemployed youths to make money. Indeed, the first four drug arrests in Barbados (for marijuana) occurred in 1971 just as mass tourism was getting under way; three of the four individuals arrested were tourists.[36] By the 1980s cocaine and "rock" (crack) had also arrived on the island. Most drug dealing and crime occurs in areas with heavy concentrations of tourists, in the parishes of St. Michael, Christ Church, St. James, and, secondarily, in St. Joseph around the community of Bathseba. But St. Lucy is also affected. Barbados is one of many drug transshipment sites in the Caribbean, although a minor one compared to the Grenadines and Antigua, with couriers taking premium marijuana and crack to North America via airlines, yachts, and cruise and container ships. Drugs are often landed on isolated beaches—Maycock's, Duppies, Stroud Bay—along St. Lucy's coast.

Travel and Emigration

Foreign travel is also a major link to the outside world and a significant source of change at both the national and parish level. Emigration, prompted by poverty at home and opportunities abroad, has a long history on the island and was one of the earliest outside influences to affect the average Bajan. Today many people still travel abroad to work or study. Others go as tourists or to visit relatives overseas. Indeed, many people are members of "transnational families"—a term used by Rosina Wiltshire to describe Caribbean families who are spread across national boundaries, with relatives living on both sides of the Atlantic forming a network of linkages through which the normal family functions of economic support, decision making, and nurturing are shared.[37] Approximately a quarter of St. Lucy's households currently have children living abroad. Most people regularly receive mail, telephone calls, and visits from family members living overseas. Many people visit relatives living in the United States, especially in Brooklyn, each year. Aileen Allman, introduced in chapter 4, travels to England and Tortola every year to visit her far-flung family.

Most early emigration from Barbados was to other islands in the Caribbean and to South America. From the mid-1800s to early 1900s an estimated fifty thousand people left Barbados to work as seasonal agricultural laborers in British Guiana (Guyana) and Trinidad.[38] Others emigrated to Suriname, St. Croix, and Cuba. During the construction of the Panama Canal an estimated forty-five thousand to sixty thousand people, including many from St. Lucy, left to work as "pick and shovel men" for ten cents an hour.[39] Other Bajans emigrated to England, Canada, and the United States. They were fleeing the kind of poverty the Reverend F. Godson described in the parish in 1916:

In Crab Hill and neighboring villages I came in contact with the worst poverty and destitution I ever saw up to then—except perhaps in one village in St. Kitts. It was a specially dry year, even for that area; there was little work on the plantations around and very little money; the people's own gardens were bare; and the price of imported foodstuffs, together with sugar, were soaring. So I met with hunger, rapes, dilapidated shacks, idling, and praedial larceny on an exceptional scale.[40]

Emigration tides have waxed and waned over the years in response to conditions at home and the needs and policies of other nations. In 1924, for example, emigration to the United States virtually stopped as a result of legislation that placed national quotas on the number of immigrants allowed in. The entire British West Indies was limited to two hundred people; only five from Barbados.[41] By the 1930s most emigration outlets in the Caribbean had also closed. One villager remembers those years: "There was nothing coming in terms of food. We ate sweet potatoes morning, noon, and night. It was a very hard time." Opportunities for emigration did not open up again until World War II, when Britain, Canada, and the United States needed workers to help in war industries and alleviate manpower shortages in agriculture. Some Barbadians also went to Britain as volunteers in the armed forces.

After the war large-scale emigration began once more. Many people, like Siebert Allman, went to Britain on the Sponsored Workers Scheme. British companies and government agencies including the London Transport Executive and the British Hotel and Restaurant Association sent recruiters to Barbados, and people from all over the island, including St. Lucy, traveled to Bridgetown to be interviewed. If they measured up, as most did, they were assigned a job, trained, and transported to England. Many women went to Britain to become nurses or work in light industry in cities like Manchester, Liverpool, and Birmingham. The Barbados government provided some people with travel loans. Between 1955 and 1961 nineteen thousand Barbadians left for Britain, nearly forty-five hundred as "assisted migrants."[42]

In the 1960s the emigration tide shifted to Canada and the United States, which had eased their immigration restrictions, at the same time that Britain, through the Commonwealth Immigration Act (1962), was closing its doors to immigration.[43] Although U.S. and Canadian poli-

This young woman was one of 700 West Indians to disembark on 9 June 1956 at the port of Southampton on the south coast of England. (Courtesy of BBC Hulton Picture Library.)

cies favored skilled workers and professionals, some unskilled workers managed to obtain "labor certification" to become domestic workers and seasonal agricultural laborers. One of our neighbors in Josey Hill went to the United States six times during the 1960s to pick fruit in the Northeast. Another villager cut sugarcane in Florida for five years. Emigration continues today. Student household surveys in five St. Lucy villages in 1994 and 1996 found that nearly one-fifth of household heads had lived abroad and that a quarter of the households currently had one or more children living abroad.[44] According to both our own and our students' interviews with teachers and students over the years, the majority of St. Lucy secondary students would like to emigrate to the United States after graduation to find work or further their education.

The influence of emigration is felt as soon as people leave. Families at home must readjust; young children often move in with a granny or aunt. Emigrants soon begin sending home "remittances" as well as goods and news from North America, England, and elsewhere. Roosevelt Griffith, profiled in chapter 4, managed to save a large part of his income and return home to build a wall house. In 1991 remittances to Barbados amounted to $11,716,000 BDS.[45] Men living on their own sometimes send back as much as half their pay to their mothers or wives. Many people in St. Lucy still receive cartons of clothes and other goods at Christmas each year. An older villager remembers that, even if the carton contained only hand-me-downs or clothes bought secondhand, "no matter how old, from America, it look new." Barbadians abroad also help family members when they emigrate or visit. When villagers we know visit their relatives abroad, the cost of their plane ticket is often reimbursed on arrival. With the foreign currency villagers buy clothing and household goods to bring home.

Most people who emigrate intend to stay only a few years and then return. "On the way over to England," remembers Roy Campbell, who grew up in the village of Rockfield, "my thinking was that I'd be away no more than five years. I had a goal of saving a certain amount of money and then coming back to Barbados and getting a little house." A good indication of most Bajans' strong attachment to home and of their intention to return is the fact that they have one of the lowest naturalization rates of any foreign-born immigrant group in the United States.[46]

When Bajans return home they become agents of change. Their

Large wall house being built in Josey Hill by a villager living in England. (Photo by George Gmelch.)

influence starts when they send back money to their relatives to hire a contractor to build a house. Most return with substantial capital from their savings and the sale of overseas assets, sometimes a house and car, which they invest in housing at home. In St. Lucy the most substantial wall houses have been built by returnees, the earliest with "Panama money." Today returnee housing is almost invariably large and of high quality, setting a standard to which others in the parish aspire. Early returnees also introduced material innovations. Those who came back from Panama, for example, are credited with introducing better household sanitation and window screens.[47] North American returnees have brought back wall-to-wall carpeting. Today, however, because of the pervasive influence of television and film, there is little new in the way of material objects that returnees can introduce that villagers are not already familiar with.

Returnees do, nevertheless, continue to be an important source of information. In the words of Valenza Griffith, who lived in England:

When I was a child the people that came back from overseas were accepted back into the community [Coles Cave, St. Lucy]. We were eager to learn things from them—what the houses were like, what the education was like, do they write like us. . . . Today people know a lot more about America and England than they did in my time. But some people still asked me some weird questions [when I returned in 1973], like if you get false teeth for free in England or if they really bury three and four people in the same grave or if people's toes drop off in England from the cold.[48]

In an earlier survey of Barbadian returnees, one of us found that nearly half of those who took jobs at home believed that they had been able to introduce changes at their workplace based on knowledge they had acquired abroad. An American-trained certified public accountant, for example, introduced the electronic processing of financial accounts to a Bridgetown firm. A nurse trained in England introduced new techniques for monitoring babies before birth. A former rector of the St. Lucy Parish Church instituted policies he learned in England that expanded his parishioners' participation in church services. In some fields major innovations can be attributed to the influence of return migrants. A movement to deinstitutionalize childcare in Barbados came from returnees working in the Ministry of Social Services who had become familiar with new approaches while working in Canada. While most of these changes have taken place outside the parish, they still have an indirect affect on many villagers' lives.

Some returnees, of course, have a direct impact on the parish. Siebert and Aileen Allman opened a small general store in the village of Sutherland. Another St. Lucy couple shipped three buses home from England and set up a mini-bus service. Although such enterprises typically do not employ many people, they do provide needed services and contribute to the smooth running of the parish economy and the convenience of its residents.

Villagers who have lived abroad return with acquired values: an appreciation for promptness and efficiency, familiarity with a faster pace, and more materialistic goals. They are also considered more "worldly" than those who have never gone away. Some evidence suggests that returnees heighten other villagers' political awareness and racial consciousness. Returnees tell family and friends about the racial remarks and incidents they experienced while living abroad. Not only did Siebert Allman experience racism while working on the buses in England; he and Aileen were turned away from an apartment in Canada even though the landlord had told them over the telephone that it was available. Writer George Lamming, in *The Castle of My Skin,* contrasts the protagonist's own naive lack of awareness with the racial consciousness acquired by his friend Trumper while in the United States: "If there was one thing I thank America for, she teach me who my race wus. . . . None o' you here on this islan' know what it mean to fin' race."[49] Anthropologists Constance Sutton and Susan Makiesky believe that return migrants in the village they studied had greater influence on people's racial and political consciousness than either middle-class Barbadians or student radicals.[50] The emigration experience, for many people, also strengthens a regional identification with other West Indians whom they have lived with in London and New York.

The influence that returnees have at the local level, however, is much less than it could be. Many returnees encounter jealousy and resistance to their new ideas. Some of Valenza Griffith's ideas were rejected by her fellow nurses:

The standard of nursing in England is completely different. . . .
Up there you are exposed to more equipment and teaching than

here, and you have more different kinds of cases there. But you can't apply what you learned up there without being criticized. They'd [fellow nurses] soon tell you, "You should've stayed up there."[51]

A civil servant who had worked in England believes his colleagues ignored his ideas "because . . . they feel threatened. They don't want to admit that maybe you have the answer, especially when you've only been on the job half as long." A teacher recalls the way her colleagues would "push up their faces" (skeptically grimace) at her suggestions. Another frustrated returnee explains: "We [returnees] have the same ideas as North Americans who live here. The difference is that people will listen to what the foreigner has to say but not to their own kind. They'll say, 'Who the hell is he to tell us what to do? He's only Barbadian like us.' "

One difficulty in assessing the influence returnees have, either at the national or local level, is trying to disentangle their role as agents of change from the many other external influences, such as television and tourism, that bombard people each day. In the aggregate we believe that emigration introduces many new ideas and has been a significant force for change. Certainly, migrants who return to Barbados come back as changed individuals. If nothing else, those villagers who interact with them are bound to observe and perhaps to absorb, even if reluctantly, some of their new attitudes and ways.

Today many Bajans travel abroad themselves for pleasure and to visit family and friends. In 1993, for example, U.S. Emigration issued nonimmigrant visas to twenty-five thousand Barbadians, or nearly 10 percent of the population, so they could visit the United States.[52] Other popular destinations include Canada and England and, to a lesser extent, South America and other Caribbean islands. Barbadians also take advantage of airline promotions and inexpensive package trips to go to Puerto Rico, Miami, St. Martin, and Margarita Island, off the coast of Venezuela, on short shopping trips.[53] Most take long shopping lists from family and friends along and return with bags packed with clothing, fabric, linens, and small appliances purchased at a fraction of what they cost at home. Street vendors who sell on Swan Street in Bridgetown may travel as often as six times a year to purchase popular clothing items such as designer jeans. School groups from St. Lucy visit Puerto Rico, Venezuela, and Disney World. Although fund-raisers help

Robert Quintyne, who earned his degree in leisure and tourism management in London, now runs an adventure tourism company. (Photo by Emily Sparks.)

defray the costs, many parish children cannot afford to go. Despite all this travel, some people seldom leave the parish—one elderly man we know claims never to have been to Bridgetown—and most have never left the island. This difference captures a very real feature of the parish, which is the growing gap in experience among people. It was not so long ago that most people worked on the same plantations, lived in the same modest houses, and shared the same experiences. Today this is no longer true.

Wind-powered mill for grinding sugarcane (ca. 1930). (Photo by E. Fitzpatrick, courtesy of The Barbados National Trust.)

Final Thoughts

The modern phenomena of globalism is actually a continuation of a much older reality. Barbados and other Caribbean societies have a long history of involvement in the world system, as anthropologist Sidney Mintz and other social scientists have pointed out.[1] Their cultures emerged out of a colonial encounter with the West that involved the exploitation of the region for staples such as sugar, the decimation of aboriginal populations, and the introduction of new ones from Africa, Europe, and Asia. After emancipation, globalism was further fostered by the widespread emigration of Caribbean people to Europe and North America. Today telecommunications play a key role.

Despite Barbados's long-term involvement in the outside world, the focal point of most people's daily lives until comparatively recently was the village. People were connected to their village and to one another by kinship, friendship, economic cooperation, and the homogeneity of their experiences and beliefs. Today many of these ties remain, but it is also true that "community" is becoming increasingly detached from place; the village is no longer the focal point of life for most people. More than ever before, people belong to "relational communities" that are geographically dispersed and include people living outside the village and parish, in other parts of the island and in other countries in the Caribbean, North America, and Europe. In the new jargon families are becoming "transnational" and Barbadian culture increasingly "deterritorialized."[2]

The Caribbean today is less a part of the Third World than "the First World's first annexe."[3] According to the United Nations Development Program's human development index, living standards in Barbados rank twentieth in the world, ahead of several European nations, including Spain, Greece, Ireland, and Italy. With this increasing affluence—despite periodic setbacks such as those caused by economic restructuring in the early 1990s—more villagers are directly participating in the world economy, buying imported consumer goods, watching foreign television, and traveling off the island for pleasure. Barbados' beautiful environment and comfortable standard of living attract hundreds of thousands of foreign tourists each year who create job opportunities and desires, as well as new problems. Similarly, the island's political stability, legal system based on English common law, disciplined work force, high literary rate, and telecommunications links lure international business.

Does this growing international orientation on the part of Bajans and U.S. cultural penetration threaten Barbadian culture? When villagers are asked to describe Bajan "culture," most people are hard put to think of anything to say. There is little they regard as uniquely Bajan except foods—flying fish and coucou—and folk traditions such as Land Ship and Crop Over.[4] It is fairly common to hear Barbadians claim that "Barbados has no culture." The suspicion that Bajans may be "mimic men," versions of someone else rather than truly themselves, is a recurring theme in the former colonies of the Caribbean.[5] It is an unfair, although understandable, characterization given the island's heritage of colonization, forced labor, and the destruction and transformation of traditional African lifeways. Despite the devastation brought by slavery, however, Barbadians, like other Caribbean peoples, created their own creole culture out of a mix of European colonial culture and their African past.[6] Black Barbadians became "Barbadians"; they did not remain Africans, nor were they ever imitation Britons, despite the country's past appellations as "Little England" and "Bimshire."

The issue of cultural identity in Barbados took on special meaning in the late 1960s with the island's independence and the end of its economic and emotional dependency on Great Britain—"the mother country." These events coincided with a shift in emigration to North America, the development of mass tourism, which brought many more North Americans to the island, and the introduction of television, which remains dominated by North American programming. Today, as we have seen throughout this book, the signs of U.S. cultural penetration are everywhere. American popular music competes with dub, dancehall, ragga soca, reggae, calypso, and other Caribbean sounds. Basketball beamed into Bajan homes over STV rivals cricket and soccer for interest among the young. The cultural hegemony of North America came at a bad time—so close on the heels of independence. Just when Barbadians were free to examine the roles their African and British heritages had played in creating their creole culture and identity and to forge stronger regional ties, they were overwhelmed by North America.

Caribbean countries were colonized by diverse European powers, yet their shared historical experience unifies the region.[7] They share broad social frameworks resulting from the plantation system, coerced labor, and the process of creolization. Today a common curriculum emphasizing Caribbean history, geography, and literature prepares students for higher education, replacing the old European-based curricula. It has introduced new, unifying concepts—oppression, colonization, colonialism, slave mentality—and a more critical analysis of the past. Regional church, tourism, university, sports, and development organizations and associations are also beginning to unite neighboring islands.[8] Carifesta, a regional creative arts festival organized every four years and hosted by different Caribbean countries, celebrates the creativity and popular traditions of the region through art displays, drama, dance, and music. Held in Barbados in 1981, it is credited by many people with strengthening Bajans' awareness of their shared heritage with other Caribbean nations.

Coinciding with this growing regional identification has been an interest, especially among Bajan intellectuals, in exploring Barbados' African heritage. For several years during the 1970s, for example, a private group called Yoruba House worked to educate the public about Africa, providing a venue and forum for artists and writers. Today Africa House, the cultural arm of the Sons of God Apostolic Spiritual Baptist Church, fulfills a similar mission by organizing speakers and events for Black Civilization Day. Its executive director, Archbishop Granville Williams, has exhorted Afro-Barbadians to recognize Africa as their "ancestral home" and to realize the extent to which their future is shaped by an awareness of their past.[9] The Africa wing of the Barbados Museum, created in the 1980s to help balance the strongly European focus of its collection, now educates schoolchildren about this part of their heritage.[10] Other African influences that have increased awareness and interest among black Barbadians include Rastafarianism; world political events such as the successful struggle of black South Africans; and the revitalization of interest in Africa among African Americans. The annual festival Crop Over, similar in many respects to Carnival in Trinidad and other islands, has grown in popularity, serving as a symbolic affirmation of the island's "Afro-Caribbean" identity.

On a daily basis in the villages and in many urban neighborhoods, of course, African influences are expressed through the use of Bajan dialect, African-derived proverbs and folk beliefs, traditional foods, and herbal remedies.[11] It is still rare, however, for people in St. Lucy to connect such everyday practices to Africa. Indeed, many villagers harbor negative stereotypes about the continent; it is more likely to bring to mind images of poverty, famine, and war than cultural pride. As yet, few people in the parish other than Rastafarians strongly identify with the African part of their creole heritage. None of the adults from our neighborhood, for example, joined the many people who gathered at nearby Farley Hill park to celebrate Nelson Mandela's release from prison. The African-inspired art, clothing, hairstyles, and names that are found in certain urban circles are still unusual in the parish. Most villagers, indeed most Bajans, are primarily oriented to North America; young people especially are attracted by American sports and popular culture.

This attachment to North America will remain strong, given the economic dominance of the United States, the pervasiveness of its media, and the many personal contacts Bajans have with North America through emigration, tourism, and travel. While Barbadians are not passive recipients of this transsocietal flow of goods, images, information, and people, the relationship that a nation such as Barbados has with the outside world is clearly asymmetrical, given its small size and modest political clout. The future is likely to see a Barbados that is increasingly Americanized. "Come back in twenty years and you will see that we have become the latest outpost of American civilization," said a local teacher with resignation. "The St. Lucy that I grew up in is finished." Clearly, the St. Lucy of his youth is gone. Whether this also means that black Barbadians will lose all sense of their own Afro-Caribbean culture and identity, however, remains to be seen.

Appendix

Students and Barbadians:
Lessons from the Field

In this book we have occasionally referred to the experiences of our students who lived and did their own research in Barbadian villages to support points we were making about village life. Here we look at the students' experiences in terms of what they learned about culture, particularly their own, by living in a Barbadian household and village for ten weeks.[1] Their observations also illuminate some of the differences between middle-class, white American culture and that of rural Barbadians.

Our students arrive in Barbados expecting to learn about how people in another culture live and think. What they do not foresee is that they will also learn a great deal about themselves and about their own society. Nor do they imagine that they will discover attitudes and perspectives that they will take home and incorporate into their own lives.

Rural Life

Over 80 percent of our students come from suburbs or cities and have never lived in the countryside before. For them a significant part of their experience in Barbados is living closer to nature and among people who are close to the land. Students often share their bedrooms with a green lizard or two and sometimes mice, cockroaches, and frogs. They are struck by the darkness of the sky and the brightness of the stars with no city lights to diminish their intensity. A student from Long Island described it as "like living in a planetarium." They become aware of how different are the sounds of the countryside. Each morning, before dawn, they are awakened by the sounds of animals in the yard. Their host families, like most villagers, grow crops and raise animals. The students quickly begin to learn about the behavior of chickens, pigs, sheep, and cows. They witness animals giving birth and being slaughtered. They see the satisfaction families get from consuming food they have produced themselves. One student described her initial surprise at an everyday occurrence:

> I was in Mrs S.'s kitchen and she was making sugar cakes. The recipe calls for a lime, and, when she didn't have any in the kitchen, she just walked into the yard and pulled a few off the nearest tree. It was nothing to her, but I was amazed, and I thought how in that situation I would have had to drive to the supermarket.

The social world of the village is also unlike anything most students know. In doing a household survey, for example, they discover that not only does everybody seem to know everybody else and that most families are related to others in the village, but that they know one another in more than one context; people are tied to one another in multiple ways. Relationships are not single stranded, as they often are in the urban America the students come from.

Students have never known a place of such intimacy, in which relationships are so embedded with different meanings and a shared history. Some students reflect upon and compare the warmth, friendliness, and frequent sharing of food and other resources with the impersonality, individualism, and detachment of urban life at home. But they also learn the drawbacks to living in small communities: there is no anonymity. People are nosy—unduly interested in the affairs of their neighbors. As the students become integrated into the community, they soon discover that they too may be the object of local gossip. One year several female students learned from village friends that there were stories afoot that they were either mistresses to their host fathers or sleeping with their host brothers. The gossip hurt, for the students had worked hard to gain acceptance, greatly valued the friendships they had made, and naturally were concerned about the damage such rumors might do to their reputations (even though the students spend only ten weeks in their villages and many will never return, they still care greatly about what villagers think of them).

One of the biggest adjustments students must make to village life is to its slow pace; the diversions and entertainment that they are accustomed to at home are absent, and early in their stay there seems to be little to do apart from their research. In the first weeks there are times when they are desperate to escape the village, but they are not allowed to leave except on designated days. The outcome of their forced isolation from other students is that they must satisfy their needs for companionship and recreation within their communities. They must learn to be resourceful in finding ways to entertain themselves. They spend a good deal of time just "liming" (hanging out), socializing with people in the village, a practice that strengthens friendships and results in a good deal of informal education about culture. By midway through the term most students have adapted so well to village life that they no longer report being bored or feel a strong need to get away. Many no longer leave the village on their day off.

Materialism

Many students arrive at a new awareness of wealth and materialism. One of the strongest initial impressions the students have of their villages is that people are poor—that most of their houses are tiny, that their diets are restricted, and that they have few of the amenities and conveniences the students are accustomed to. Even little things may remind students of the difference in wealth, as Betsy, an anthropology major, recounted after her first week in the field:

> At home [Vermont] when I go into a convenience store and buy a soda, I don't think twice about handing the clerk a twenty dollar bill. But here when you hand a man in the rum shop a twenty dollar bill [equal to ten U.S. dollars] he often asks if you have something smaller. It makes me self conscious of how wealthy I appear, and of how little money the rum shop man makes in a day.

The initial response of the students to such incidents and to the lower standard of living they see around them is to feel embarrassed and even guilty that they, like many Americans, have so much in comparison. Such feelings are short-lived, however, for, as the students get to know the families and their communities better, they no longer see poverty; even the houses no longer seem so small. They discover that most people not only manage quite well on what they have but are reasonably content as well. In fact, most students eventually come to believe that the villagers are, on the whole, actually more satisfied with their lives than are most Americans. Whether or not this is true, it's an important perception for students whose ideas about happiness have been shaped by an ethos that measures success and satisfaction by material gain. About his host family Dan said:

> I ate off the same plate and drank from the same cup every night. We only had an old fridge, an old stove, and an old TV, and a few dishes and pots and pans. But that was plenty. Mrs. T. never felt like she needed any more. And after awhile I never felt like I needed any more either.

Many students say that after Barbados they became less materialistic. Many said that when they returned home they were surprised at how many possessions they owned and that when they returned to campus they didn't bring nearly as many things with them as they had before. A few went through their drawers and closets at home and had given the Goodwill and Salvation Army the things they didn't really need. Most also said they would no longer take for granted the luxuries, such as hot showers, that they are accustomed to on campus and at home. Amy said:

> When I came back I saw how out of control the students here are. It's just crazy. They want so much; they talk about how much money they need to make, as if these things are necessities and you'll never be happy without them. Maybe I was like that too, but now I know I don't need those things. Sure I'd like a great car, but I don't need it.

When alumni of the program were asked in a survey—conducted years after their return from Barbados—how their attitudes had been changed by their experience in a Bajan village, most said they were less materialistic today than their friends who have not had a similar experience. Some compared their attitudes with those of acquaintances who had served in the Peace Corps.

Gender

Female students quickly learn that gender relations are quite different in Barbados. Indeed, the most difficult adjustment for many female students is learning how to deal with the frequent and aggressive advances of Bajan men. At the end of her first week in the field Jenny described a common plight of female students:

> When I walk through the village, the guys who hang out at the rum shop yell comments. I have never heard men say some of the things they tell me here. My friend Andrew tells me that most of the comments are actually compliments. Yet I still feel weird. . . . I am merely an object that they would like to conquer. I hate that feeling, so I am trying to get to know these guys. I figure that if they know me as a person and a friend, they will stop with the demeaning comments. Maybe its a cultural thing they do to all women.

Many Barbadian men feel it is their right as males to accost women in public places with hissing, appreciative remarks, and offers of sexual services. This sexual bantering is tolerated by Barbadian women, who generally ignore the men's comments. Most women consider it harmless, if annoying; some women may enjoy it. Students like Jenny, however, are not sure what to make of it. They do not know whether it is being directed at them because local men think white girls are "loose" or whether Barbadian men behave in this fashion toward all women. Anxious to be accepted and not wanting to be rude or culturally insensitive, most female students tolerate the remarks the best they can while searching for a strategy to politely discourage them. Most find that, as people get to know them by name, the verbal harassment subsides. But they still must get accustomed to other sexual behavior. For example, when invited to their first neighborhood parties most are shocked at the sexually explicit dancing, in which movements imitate intercourse. One female student wrote, after having been to several such fêtes:

> I was watching everyone dance when I realized that even the way we dance says a lot about culture. We are so conservative at home. Inhibited. In the U.S. one's body is a personal, private thing, and when it is invaded we get angry. We might give a boyfriend some degree of control over our bodies, but no one else. Bajans aren't nearly as possessive about their bodies. Men and women can freely move from one dance partner to the next without asking and then grind the other person.

Students discover that, to an even greater degree than in the United States, women are regarded by most men as both subordinates and sexual objects. Masculinity is based in large part on men's sexual conquest of women and also on their ability to give them pleasure. Being sexually active, a good sex partner, and becoming a father all enhance young men's status among male peers. As time passes, the students discover male dominance in other areas of Barbadian life as well—that women typically earn less than men, that they have higher unemployment rates at all ages, and that far fewer seek or attain political office. Generally, they conclude that, while the United States is clearly sexist, there are other societies that are far more so.

Race

In Barbados our students become members of a racial minority for the first time in their lives. Virtually everyone in the villages in which they live is black, while nearly all of our students so far have been white. Before going to Barbados, many of the students have had little contact with African-Americans, and as a result they feel awkward. The students have never experienced racial prejudice themselves. During their first few weeks in the field, however, they become acutely aware of their own "race," of being white while everyone around them is dark. Students are often called "white boy" and "white girl" by people in the village until they get to know the students personally. Village children ask if they can touch the students skin or hair. They marvel at the blue veins that show through the students' white skin and sometimes ask those with freckles if they have a skin disease. One student's homestay mother asked her how she managed to drink from a glass with such a "big nose." During the second week one student wrote, characteristically:

> I have never been in a situation before where I was a minority purely due to the color of my skin and treated differently because of it. When I approach people I am very conscious of having white skin. Before I never thought of myself as having color.

A few students become hypersensitive to race during the early weeks of their stay. When they leave their villages, they must travel by bus which are often crowded. The student is usually the only white

Student Peter DiCerbo with his host parents, Calvert and Esther Blankett, and their children. (Photo by George Gmelch.)

person on board. Often he or she is stared at (sometimes because as the buses head into the countryside of St. Lucy, the passengers worry that the student has taken the wrong bus). The students notice that, as the bus fills up, the seats next to them are often the last to be taken, and some react with feelings of shame or guilt. Here is the extreme reaction of one female student who, during her first week in Barbados, had gone by bus to a remote area, where she had an encounter with a local woman that disturbed her:

> The woman glared at me as if she was seeing the evil white woman who has been responsible for the oppression of her people. I felt like I had chained, maimed, and enslaved every black person who had ever lived. The feelings were so strange . . . somehow I felt responsible for the entire history of the relationship between blacks and whites. I carried this woman's face with me for the rest of the day. When I got on the bus to go back to my village I felt very alone and very unwanted, like the mere presence of my color was making a lot of people very uneasy.

But concerns about race, even the awareness of race, diminishes rapidly as the students make friends and become integrated into their villages. In fact, by the end of the term most said they were "rarely" aware of being white. Several students described incidents in which they had become so unaware of skin color that they were shocked when someone made a remark or did something to remind them of their being different. Sara was startled when, after shaking the hand of someone in her village, the woman remarked that she had never touched the hand of a white person before. Several students reported being surprised when they walked by a mirror and got a glimpse of their white skin. One student wrote that, although she knew she wasn't black, she no longer felt white.

What is the outcome of all this? Do students now have more of an understanding of what it means to be a minority, and does this translate into their having more empathy at home? We think so. A majority of the students from the previous Barbados programs whom we questioned about the impact of their experiences mentioned a heightened empathy for blacks and, for some, other minorities as well. Several said that when they first returned home they wanted to go up to many of the African-Americans they saw and have a conversation. "But I kept having to remind myself," said one student, "that most blacks in America are not West Indians, and they wouldn't understand where I am coming from." Another admitted that her first naive, reaction upon coming home and seeing black people was to want "to hug every one of them."

Social Class

American students, particularly compared to their European counterparts, have little understanding of social class. Even after several weeks in Barbados most students are fairly oblivious to class and status distinctions in their villages. The American suburbs in which our students grew up are fairly homogeneous in social composition and housing; most homes fall in the same general price range. In contrast, Barbadian villages today exhibit a spectrum of housing, from the large two-story masonry homes of return migrants to the tiny board houses of small farmers who eke out a living from a small plot of sugarcane and a kitchen garden.

It is largely from comments that their host families make about other people, that students become aware of village status distinctions. Equally, however, they learn about class and status by making mistakes, from violating norms concerning relationships between different categories of people. Kristen learned that there are different standards of behavior for the more affluent families after she walked home through the village carrying a bundle on her head: "Mrs. C. told me never to do that again, that only poor people carry things on their heads, and that my doing it reflected badly on her family."

As in most field situations, the first villagers to offer the student friendship are sometimes marginal members of the community, and this can create special problems when a student is a guest in the home of a "respectable" or high-status village family. The host parents become upset when they discover their student has been seeing a disreputable man or woman (e.g., beach bum, drug user, or sexually permissive woman). In the early years of the field program, some female students dated lower-class local men. The women entered into these relationships oblivious to what the local reaction might be and equally oblivious to how little privacy there is in a village in which everyone knows everyone else's business. One student said she wrongly assumed that people would look favorably upon her going out with a local man because it would show she wasn't prejudiced and that she found blacks just as desirable as whites. Earlier (chap. 7) we discussed the female student who befriended some orthodox Rastas and the negative reaction of her host family and some other residents of her village. About this experience she wrote, "I have discovered the power of a societal norm: nice girls don't talk to Rastas. When girls who were formerly nice talk to Rastas, they cease to be known as nice. Exceptions, none."

New Perspectives on North America

In learning about Barbadian society, students inevitably make comparisons with American culture. Especially in the early stages of fieldwork students think about Barbadian customs in terms of how similar or different they are from those at home. The students are often assisted in such comparisons by villagers who, as we have seen, know a lot about the United States from television, tourism, travel, and, for some, emigration. Students quickly discover, however, that the villagers' perceptions about the United States are often at odds with their own. Based on a steady diet of American soap operas, many villagers, for example, believe that all the students are wealthy, own late-model cars, vacation in exotic places, and so on. Early in the term they find themselves defending the United States from criticism. For example, one student described getting very annoyed when a guest at his host family's dinner table criticized the United States and talked about the chemical adulteration of American chicken. He knew this to be true, but later he said: "I couldn't take it anymore and fought back. I felt like an idiot afterward, defending American chicken."

Over time the students become less eager to defend their own society. Indeed, many become quite critical of the United States, or at least aspects of it. Why? What makes them question their own society after a few months in Barbados? Part of the answer is found in their growing appreciation for Barbadian life and their identification with local people. They come to see many things from the perspective of their village friends. Another factor is the students' exposure to North American tourists. When they go to the beach or town on their free day, they encounter tourists and are sometimes disappointed or embarrassed by what they see and hear—tourists entering shops and walking the street wearing revealing beach attire or their loud and intrusive voices. From a variety of sources students learn about the negative social impacts of tourism—drug trafficking, materialism, crime, environmental damage, and U.S. cultural penetration (as discussed in chap. 8). Viewing tourism as part of a broader "Americanization" of the region, many students become critical not only of tourists but of the United States' presence abroad generally.

Fieldwork and Education

Students learned about more than just cultural differences from their experience of living and doing anthropology in a Caribbean village. Most returned from Barbados with a more positive attitude toward education. This appears to stem both from their own experiences in doing research and from seeing the high value that villagers place on formal education, which is the chief means of upward mobility in Barbados. They see that they are accorded respect and adult status largely because they are working toward a university degree. Also, as the weeks pass, most students become deeply involved in their own research. They are surprised at how much satisfaction they get from doing something that they previously regarded as "work." A number of the students from past terms have said that they didn't see education as an end in itself, something to be enjoyed, until doing fieldwork in Barbados. One student wrote about her attitude after returning from the field:

> I feel isolated from many of my old friends on campus, and I no longer feel guilty missing social events. . . . I appreciate my education more and I do much more work for my own understanding and enjoyment rather than just for the exam or grades. I find myself on a daily basis growing agitated with those who don't appreciate what is being offered to them here. Several of my classmates blow off class and use other peoples' notes. A lot of what I feel is from seeing how important education was to my Bajan friends, compared to the lax attitude of my friends here.

Students spend much of their time in the field talking to people. A good part of each day is spent in conversations which they must direct toward the topics that they are investigating. To succeed at their studies they must learn to be inquisitive, to probe sensitively and dig deep into another person's knowledge or memory of particular events or aspects of culture, and to concentrate, to listen to what they are being told, and later to be able to recall it so that they can record it in field notes. The students become proficient at maintaining lengthy conversations with adults and at asking pertinent questions. These are interpersonal skills they bring back with them and make use of in many aspects of their own lives.

While the students spend a semester discovering and making sense of the differences between their own culture and that of the Barbadians around them, most end up concluding that, beneath differences in race and culture, Barbadians and Americans are basically alike, that beneath the veneer of custom there is a shared "human nature." In the words of one student, who is now an anthropologist:

> If I had to sum up my whole trip in one experience it would be this. It was late at night, a full moon, and I sat in a pasture with a local Rastafarian. After hours of talking, about everything from love to politics, the two of us came to an interesting conclusion. Although we lived a thousand miles away from each other, and that our skin color, hair style, and many personal practices were quite different, at heart we were the same people.

While this may seem like common sense, it is, surprisingly, not a notion that many college students who have not lived abroad share today. Our students are like the proverbial fish that does not know what water is until it is taken out of it. For them getting to know another culture is to look in a mirror and catch a glimpse of themselves as cultural beings, of who they are as Americans and human beings.

Notes

Chapter 1

1. Moxly, *Account of a West Indian Sanitorium and a Guide to Barbados*, 25.

2. St. Lucy has a population density of 256 per square kilometer, the second lowest density of the eleven parishes on the island.

3. The eleventh parish is Christ Church.

4. Fraser et al., *A–Z of Barbadian Heritage*, 129; Editorial, "Parish Boundaries," 131.

5. *West India Royal Commission Report*, 393.

6. The island was then divided into three areas governed by councils: Bridgetown, the Southern District, and the Northern District, which incorporated St. Lucy. These were abolished in 1967.

7. An exception are the residents of the capital and larger towns like Oistins and Speightstown who often give the name of their town rather than the parish.

8. A few motorists, however, register their plates in parishes other than the ones in which they live.

9. See, for example, *Barbados Insight Guide*, 207.

10. Recently, it has been established that plant species with small, easily airborne seeds can be carried by trade winds all the way from Africa, about three thousand miles away. Hurricanes, which, unlike trade winds, blow from different directions, may have also brought plants from lands lying to the west, such as Central America. The shores of Barbados are also washed by a major ocean current coming from Africa, which is capable of carrying seeds and fruits over great distances. Despite the various routes by which plants may have arrived in Barbados, the island only has seven hundred native species, which is low for a tropical region. Gooding, *Plant Communities of Barbados*, 13.

11. There are an estimated 300 miles of gully on the island.

12. There are an estimated five thousand to eight thousand monkeys on the island, according to the Barbados Wildlife Reserve.

13. In 1680, for example, St. Lucy had 430 property holders, the largest number on the island; however, nearly half of these (205) were freeholders or persons owning just 10 acres of land (Campbell, "Barbados Vestries, 1627–1700," 177).

14. While the plant was under construction in 1985, one of our anthropol-

ogy students, Ellen Lawton, examined its impact on the nearby community of Checker Hall. Many homes had to be moved, and people lived with dust and air pollution for many months. But most villagers tolerated the degrading of their environment without much complaint, since government and plant officials promised jobs and much needed foreign exchange for Barbados' Treasury. Their projections, however, were overly optimistic; the two hundred million–dollar plant was overbuilt and is capable of producing far more cement than the eastern Caribbean requires. It employs far fewer local people than promised. In 1995 the government sold the plant to a Trinidadian corporation to cut its losses.

15. See Beckles, *History of Barbados*, 110–12. Some tenants were able to rent a house spot from churches that had land holdings and from small land owners; others braved the uncertainties of immigration. Over time some tenants were able to buy the land on which their houses sat from humanitarian owners and plantations in need of cash. But it was not until the Tenants Act of 1980 that all residents of the tenantries were given the opportunity to buy their land at affordable prices.

16. In addition to these ethnic groups, sixty people were unclassified.

17. All but one of the students in our anthropology program in Barbados have been white.

18. Some of the landowners were absentee, residing primarily in England. Ten percent of the owners in the 1689 census were women, with the largest of them, Elizabeth Pickerin, owning 220 acres, with five white servants and ninety-five black slaves.

19. The census of 1712 reported 1,208 whites and 2,742 blacks. Most of the poor whites live in the eastern part of the parish, in the Pie Corner area (P. Jackman, "St. Lucy under the Lens: A Socio-economic View from 1680–1900" [MS, University of the West Indies, Caribbean Studies Collection]).

20. See Beckles, *History of Barbados*, 21; and K. Watson, *Civilized Island, Barbados*.

21. The number of whites declined sharply in the decades following the end of slavery. During slavery plantations were required to employ whites, who could serve in the militia when there was a need. The government stipulated that there should be one white for every thirty acres of plantation land, so a planter with one hundred acres had to employ about three whites. After emancipation the militia was disbanded, and many of the white tenants were cast off. Those living outside the plantations became a marginal class of peasant agriculturists, fishers, and underemployed laborers. With emancipation it was difficult for them to compete with the large number of blacks now on the labor market. Some moved out of St. Lucy to other parishes and to Bridgetown; others migrated to the neighboring islands of St. Vincent, Bequia, and Grenada; and a few went to more distant locations. The Barbados government resettled four hundred poor whites in Dorsetshire Hill, St. Vincent. Another settlement of poor whites from Barbados had established itself at Mount Pleasant in Bequia by 1870, although it is possible that they originated from the St. Vincent settlement (Price, *Behind the Planter's Back*, 36). By 1891 there were only 509 whites left in the parish. Over the next century the number dwindled further.

22. *Village* is the term Barbadians use when referring to rural communities. For North Americans the term often has the connotation of a preindustrial, pastoral community with a certain timelessness, which, as will be evident in later chapters, is not entirely accurate for Barbados.

23. This was the pattern stamped on the native population by Franciscan and Dominican missionaries from Spain, who wanted every Indian in the New World to live within the sound of churchbells. The centralized village laid out at right angles to the church also represented their idea of what a utopian community should look like.

24. H. Fraser and R. Hughes, *Historic Houses of Barbados*, 70.

25. Ibid.

26. Purple heart and green heart are hard woods that are resistant to termites. They also weather better than pine. But pine is the most common wood used because it is less expensive and easier to saw and nail. The imported timber—pine from the United States and Canada and green heart and purple heart from Guyana and Belize—is shipped in standard lengths ranging from twelve to twenty feet.

27. Recently, area rugs have become more common, and some return migrants from the United States have installed wall-to-wall carpeting. An American medical anthropologist looking for the cause of the sharp increase in the number of Barbadians with allergies found a link to the growing popularity of carpeting, which harbors mites.

28. The average rent per house plot in 1992 was about fifteen dollars (BDS) per week. The rent for land that produces crops is much higher. Owners who wish to remove their tenants to reclaim their land usually do so by raising the rent. Most villagers own no more than their house plots, which are typically less than a half-acre in size. Others own up to about three acres. Whatever the amount of land, it has only been in recent time that most villagers have become landowners. The 1980 Tenants Act greatly increased land ownership. Under this act landlords who wish to sell their land must offer it first to their tenants. And under no circumstances can they evict a tenant from rented property in order to sell the land to someone else. Hence, landowners wishing to sell their land to other family members or neighbors are often unable to do so. Many owners now hesitate renting land to anyone but a family member, in case they later need it to help support a returning relative or a newlywed child. New couples looking for a house plot of their own must now think in terms of buying land rather than renting.

29. In contrast, those who wish to grow crops on someone else's land usually pay rent because most crops remove nutrients from the soil.

Chapter 2

1. This chapter is based primarily on the following works: Beckles, *History of Barbados* and *Afro-Caribbean Women and Resistence to Slavery in Barbados;* Handler and Lange, *Plantation Slavery in Barbados;* Knight, *Caribbean;* Ligon, *True and Exact History of the Island of Barbados;* Dickson, *Letters on Slavery;* and K.

Watson, *Civilized Island, Barbados*. We have ignored the poor white community of Barbados during the period of slavery because of limited space and because none of their descendants remain in the parish of St. Lucy. For similar reasons we give little attention to the small population of "free coloureds." See Handler, *Unappropriated People*, for an excellent treatment of them.

2. The date of the first European landing on Barbados is uncertain. Barbados appears on a Spanish chart in 1542. But there is an earlier written reference to Barbados when, in 1518, Charles V of Spain sent Rodrigo de Figueroa to Espanola "to ameliorate the condition of indians sent there as slaves" (Drewett, *Prehistoric Barbados*, 1). In this document Barbados is referred to as the "Isla de Barbudos."

3. Henry Powell, an English ship captain, who sailed to Guyana just weeks after he had delivered the first group of English settlers to Barbados, is said to have taken thirty Amerindians on board and brought them back to Barbados. They arrived as freemen but were later enslaved. There are also early accounts of Amerindians from St. Vincent, ninety-two miles away, sailing to Barbados on their own in long, dug-out canoes. Richard Ligon (1657), who lived in Barbados from 1647 to 1650 and provided the most thorough descriptions of Barbadian life in his period, notes that the Indians constituted only a "slight fraction" of the total Barbadian population.

4. Handler, "Amerindians and Their Contributions to Barbadian Life in the Seventeenth Century," 195–97.

5. Ibid., 204.

6. Wolf, *Europe and the People without History*, 202.

7. Beckles, *History of Barbados*, 13.

8. Ibid, 13.

9. Ibid, 14.

10. Ibid.

11. Dutchman Pieter Blower, who had learned to grow and process sugarcane in Brazil, was the first to introduce sugarcane to Barbados, around 1637 (Beckles, *History of Barbados*, 20).

12. Ibid., 21.

13. Quoted in Knight, *Caribbean*, 115.

14. Handler and Lange, *Plantation Slavery in Barbados*, 16.

15. Coming from tropical Africa, the new arrivals, it was also said, were more resistant to diseases such as malaria.

16. Quoted in Beckles, *History of Barbados*, 28.

17. By 1670 the bulk of white servants coming to the West Indies chose to go to Jamaica and the Leeward Islands instead, where opportunities to own land someday were greater (ibid., 31).

18. Wolf, *Europe and the People without History*, 195–202; Parry et al., *Short History of the West Indies*, 67.

19. Not all blacks were slaves, as Handler notes in *Unappropriated People*, 73. He refers to a decree issued in 1636 by the governor of the colony and his council that stated that "Negroes and Indians, that came here to be sold, should serve for life, unless a contract was before made to the contrary." This suggests

that a few Africans may have had the same legal status as white indentured servants.

20. Quoted in Mintz, *Sweetness and Power*, 42.

21. Beckles, *History of Barbados*, 43.

22. Handler and Lange, *Plantation Slavery in Barbados*, 27. The Caribbean received nearly one-half of all Africans brought to the Americas in the 350-year span of the organized transatlantic slave trade (Knight, *Caribbean*, 111).

23. As Thorton notes in *Africa and Africans*: "The institution of slavery was widespread in Africa and accepted in the all the exporting regions. And the capture, purchase, transport, and sale of slaves was a regular feature of African society. This preexisting social arrangement was as much responsible as any external force for the development of the Atlantic slave trade" (97).

24. Quoted in Beckles, *Afro-Caribbean Women and Resistance to Slavery*, 35.

25. Parry et al., *Short History of the West Indies*, 89.

26. Beckles, *Afro-Caribbean Women and Resistance to Slavery*, 35.

27. Ibid, 36.

28. *Traders, Planters and Slaves*, 39.

29. Edwards, *Equiano's Travels*, 32.

30. Quoted in Beckles, *Afro-Caribbean Women and Resistance to Slavery*, 19.

31. Karl Watson notes, in *The Civilized Island, Barbados*, that, while the demographics of Barbados have yet to be carefully worked out, it is clear that the pattern is quite different from that of the other islands. By 1700, for example, Barbados had a balanced sex ratio and a high percentage of Creoles.

In support of the notion that Barbados had eliminated its need for imported slaves by 1780, Watson notes that by the end of the eighteenth century only about 5 percent of the black population of Barbados was African born, compared to approximately 55 percent in Trinidad. Moroever, the Barbados Assembly had supported passage of a bill in the English Parliament to abolish the slave trade. Barbados was the only colony to do so, and in correspondence some Barbadian planters openly expressed the wish that it had been abolished years earlier (personal communication).

32. During most of the period of plantation slavery in Barbados (1650s to 1834) there were about four hundred medium to large plantations that had holdings between 60 and 300 acres in size, and another six hundred or so smaller plantations or farms, depending upon the time period (Handler and Lange, *Plantation Slavery in Barbados*, 38–46).

33. Later in the slave period many plantations also had a small infirmary, or "sick house," descriptions of which range from a "horrible unhealthy hole" to one planter's exaggerated claim in 1823 that "there is a good hospital on almost every estate." See Handler and Lange, *Plantation Slavery in Barbados*, 98.

34. Handler and Lange, *Plantation Slavery in Barbados*, 77.

35. Ibid.

36. *Mitigation of Slavery*, 85.

37. In 1789, notes Karl Watson, a Barbadian male or female field slave cost between eighty and one hundred dollars, whereas an imported slave was valued at fifty pounds (Watson, *Civilized Island, Barbados*).

38. This was due to lower mortality rates among slaves as well as planters, recognizing the advantages of producing their own workers, having adopted policies (such as material incentives and sometimes neonatal care) that encouraged women to have more children. On the Newton Plantation, the most thoroughly studied estate in Barbados, birthplace data show that, of the 255 slaves who lived there in 1796, 98 percent were born at Newton, 1 percent were born elsewhere in Barbados, and 1 percent (all over the age of fifty) had been born in Africa. Handler and Lange, *Plantation Slavery in Barbados*, 68.

39. The sex ratio on the eighty-nine Barbadian plantations that Jerome Handler and Frederick Lange analyzed stood at forty-eight males for every fifty-two females (ibid.).

40. Beckles, *Afro-Caribbean Women and Resistance to Slavery*, 15; Watson, *Resistance*, 17–18.

41. Quoted in Beckles, *Afro-Caribbean Women and Resistance to Slavery*, 15.

42. Beckles, *History of Barbados*, 61, 17.

43. Quoted in Watson, *Civilized Island, Barbados*, 91.

44. Ibid.

45. Rawlin 1699; quoted in Handler, *Unappropriated People*, 91.

46. Watson, *Civilized Island, Barbados*, 73.

47. Beckles, *History of Barbados*, 35.

48. Quoted in Watson, *Resistance*, 33.

49. Ibid.

50. Quoted in Beckles, *Afro-Caribbean Women and Resistance to Slavery*, 64.

51. Ibid.

52. Handler, *Unappropriated People*, 16.

53. In 1731 an act was passed that penalized anyone assisting runaways in their flight. The penalty for first-time offenders who "wilfully entertain, harbour or conceal any runaway slave" was "twenty lashes on their bare backs, " for a second offence "thirty and nine lashes," and for a third offence "thirty and nine lashes" and a branding on the right cheek.

54. Some slaves also served in the militias, as Jerome Handler describes in "Freedmen and Slaves in the Barbados Militia."

55. Watson, *Resistance*, 28–29.

56. Beckles, *History of Barbados*, 56.

57. Quoted in Watson, *Civilized Island*, 84.

58. Handler and Lange, *Plantation Slavery in Barbados*, 214.

59. Ibid., 33, 214.

60. Some months later another account of the insurrection, by an anonymous author, figured that "a little short of 1,000 slaves were killed in batttle and executed by law" (Beckles, *History of Barbados*, 80).

Chapter 3

1. Sugarcane may originally have been cultivated as a garden plant for chewing. Hagelberg, "Sugar in the Caribbean," 88.

2. Until the 1600s sugar was such a scarce commodity in Europe that it was considered a luxury import. The development of the vast sugar plantations in the West Indies, however, made sugar an affordable everyday item, and its use spread to all social classes and outward to other regions of the world.

3. Hagelberg, "Sugar in the Caribbean," 87.

4. Sugarcane is grown from "cuttings" called ratoons. Shoots, snipped off the tops of mature plants, are planted in November or December and are ready to be harvested thirteen months later. Like other grass species, sugarcane will grow back several times after it is cut. In Barbados up to five crops are normally produced, one each year, before the fields must be reconditioned and replanted.

5. When the market is glutted with a particular crop, prices are depressed, and it can be difficult to find a buyer at all.

6. But before the crop begins the Barbados Workers Union must agree to a new contract with the sugar producers. Negotiations take place every other year.

7. There are two types of harvesting machines. The "Carib Cutter" cuts and knocks the cane down; workers follow behind, pick up the canes, and lop off the leafy tops. The "Toft Cutter" chops the cane into eight-inch lengths called billets and shoots them into a trailer towed behind the harvester. The Toft Cutter also separates out the trash, shreds it, and spits it back onto the ground.

8. They cut off a section, peel back the hard husk, and bite or cut off a piece of the cream-colored, sucrose-saturated fibers. Chewing the cane releases the juices. When the liquid has been extracted, the fibers are spit out. Beyond the fields, in the villages all across the island, children and adults chew cane during crop time.

9. Handler, "Small Scale Sugar Cane Farming in Barbados."

10. In the past, when peasants didn't have machines that could drive into the fields and load the canes directly onto trucks, women were used as "headers"; that is, they carried bundles of cane on their heads to the nearest road. Headers, notes Jerome Handler, in "Some Aspects of Work Organization on Sugar Plantations in Barbados," were an important part of the work force because the planter had to get his canes out of the fields and to the factories expeditiously; sitting in the fields in the hot sun the canes would dry out and lose weight and value.

11. An average worker can cut 3 to 3½ tons of cane per day, which is more than half a truckload. (On average an acre of ratoon sugarcane yields from 23 to 25 tons, although the figure may vary considerably depending upon rainfall.) In 1996 cane cutters earned from about $300 BDS per week, with a high of $500 to $600.

12. The cane first passes through a shredder to be crushed. The wet brown mass then passes through a series of grooved rollers, which squeeze out the sucrose liquid. This raw sugar juice is then heated to evaporate the water, leaving molasses containing sugar crystals. The molasses solution then goes through several different centrifuges, where the sugar crystals are spun out

(Hagelberg, "Sugar in the Caribbean, 88–90; Mintz, *"Sweetness and Power,* 19–74).

13. One ton of wet bagasse is roughly equivalent to one barrel of oil. New sugar factories produce enough energy to meet all their own needs as well as to put some electricity into the national grid.

14. Handler, "Small Scale Sugar Farming in Barbados," 264.

15. Ibid.

16. The number of arable acres under active management declined from 66,000 acres in the late 1960s to less than 40,000 acres in 1990. Since some of the land in a given year is out of production, this figure differs from the acreage that is reaped.

17. Increasing mechanization of the cane harvest is likely soon to eliminate future need for foreign workers.

18. Colin Hudson, personal communication.

19. Yields in the years following burning are lower. Instead of five or more crops from a planting, a planter may get only three before the canes become spindly and must be replaced. Also, burned cane loses its sugar content more rapidly than green cane and must be processed within twenty-four hours. When cane fires get out of control, far more acreage of cane is burned than can be reaped and transported to the factory before the canes spoil. While most fires are set by vandals, some are started by workers wishing to make their task easier, as the fire burns off the "trash" and destroys the prickers and cow itch, which irritate the skin. The practice of burning canes is said to have been introduced by migrant cutters from the neighboring islands of St. Lucia and St. Vincent, who first learned it while working in Florida's cane fields. But, again, most fires today are the work of malicious youths and hooligans.

20. Rising labor costs and very heavy rains, which resulted in some crops not being harvested, demoralized some planters (Colin Hudson, personal communication).

21. Notably, the European Union, with its very favorable prices.

22. For the moment, however, Barbados is somewhat insulated from fluctuations in world prices for sugar because of guaranteed markets, such as in Europe. In fact, Barbados does not produce enough sugar to meet the quotas with its established markets.

23. The allocation was raised to almost 17,000 tons in 1990 (*Nation,* 23 February 1990).

24. During the seventeenth and eighteenth centuries little attention was paid to education for the masses. Most of the white planter families sent their children to England for schooling; what few schools existed in Barbados were religious institutions under the control of the clergy. Slaves received no education, other than the few who were taught a skill on their plantations. After the 1870s, however, following recommendations of a government-appointed commission, some improvements were made. Although these primarily benefited the middle and upper classes, government spending on schools for the poor was also greatly increased. The government now proclaimed education as

desirable for all, but school fees effectively made anything beyond a few years of primary school out of reach of most families. All that changed in the 1960s and 1970s.

25. Dann, *Quality of Life in Barbados,* 90.

26. To cite just one recent example, a well-known agro-industrialist, writing in the *Nation,* called for educational reform to "remove, once and for all, the stigma that agriculture is a slave oriented vocation. . . . Right now, no primary school student wants to work in agriculture. Little is taught in secondary school on the subject, and even less in our university" (reference lost).

27. Handler, *Unappropriated People,* 117.

28. The exact numbers for 1995 were 422,102 "long-stay" arrivals (over twenty-four hours) and 484,620 cruise ship arrivals (Barbados Tourism Authority).

29. Doxey, "Tourist Industry in Barbados," 120.

30. Holder, *Caribbean Tourism,* 210.

31. Occupational data were obtained from household censuses, randomly administered in four St. Lucy villages by ourselves and students in our field program. The sample consisted of 212 households.

32. Freeman, "Designing Women: Corporate Discipline and Barbados's Off-Shore Pink-Collar Sector," 184.

33. "It is a condition," Comitas wrote, "wherein the model adult is systematically engaged in a number of gainful activities which form for him an integrated economic complex" (qtd. in Rubenstein, *Coping with Poverty,* 132).

34. For example, Wilson, *Crab Antics* and Horowitz, *Morne Paysan.*

35. Stewart, *American Cultural Patterns,* 38.

36. The data were gathered by us and our students as part of a household census. The households were selected randomly. In each household the interviewer listed all occupations of every adult living in the household who was no longer in school. We did a similar occupational survey in Josey Hill in 1992, and the percentages of different occupations produced in that survey are in line with those gathered by the students, suggesting a degree of reliability.

37. The Barbados Statistical Service divides occupations into twenty-six different categories. For clarity we have collapsed these into the six broad categories shown in table 1, after discussions with Eric Strong, director of the service.

38. Eric Strong, personal communication. Clustering may also arise when a particular type of work is in close proximity to the community; the village of Josey Hill, for example, has an unusually large number of cotton pickers due to the presence of plantation cotton fields on two sides of the village.

39. Islandwide 5.1 percent of Barbadians in the fourth quarter of 1993 gave their primary occupation as working in agriculture and sugar. This figure comes from the quarterly occupational survey done by the Barbados Statistical Service. Although based on a household census, the data are not very comparable because the Statistical Service only records the primary occupation stated by the respondent; in our survey we tried to elicit all types of work engaged in by each respondent.

40. The most common crops are cucumbers, beets, lettuce, cabbage, and beans. Less common are peas, potatoes, yams, squash, carrots, sweet peppers, "ground nuts" (peanuts), cassava, okra, *eddoes,* and a variety of herbs.

41. Breadfruit was introduced to the West Indies from the Pacific to provide a staple diet for slaves (Fraser et al., *A–Z of Barbadian Heritage,* 25).

42. In 1994 the prices obtained for livestock were approximately $1,000 to $1,500 for cows, $500 for pigs, $100 to $150 for sheep, and $75 for goats (BDS).

43. In the third quarter of 1993 10 percent of working adults were employed in the tourism sector of the economy, according to the Barbados Statistical Service's household survey.

44. Massiah, "Women Who Head Households," 63.

45. French, "Colonial Policy towards Women after the 1938 Uprising: The Case of Jamaica", 44–45.

46. National unemployment figures are calculated from a quarterly household survey of 2 percent of the island's households conducted by the Barbados Statistical Service and are regarded as reliable, although the political party in opposition is prone to saying that such "government figures" are understated, and, conversely, the party in power is prone to claiming that the "actual employment picture" is rosier or that employment has risen in recent months but has not yet shown up in the Statistical Service's official figures. The unemployment rates for 1993, 1994, and 1995 were 24.3 percent, 21.9 percent, and 19.7 percent, respectively.

Chapter 4

1. Barbados Statistical Service, 1990 Census.

2. The company representative that I interviewed about Barbara's work, however, claimed that the only eyestrain employees suffer is due to their failure to get or wear prescription glasses.

3. Barbados Statistical Service, 1990 Census.

Chapter 5

1. This discussion deals only with heterosexual relationships. Little is said openly about homosexuality in Barbados, and in the villages most homosexuals remain closeted. Many people regard homosexuality as an abomination in the sight of God. Even popular culture is homophobic. Recent dub lyrics by Buju Banton in "Boom Bye Bye," for example, promote eliminating homosexuals because, as the song goes, they are responsible for AIDS.

2. These are characterized, although in exaggerated form, by the same directness that is true of other village speech. Our students are always taken aback, for example, when they are first ordered to "Come" (come here or come in), told abruptly to "turn off de light," or matter-of-factly informed by a village friend that they are "fat" or that another student is "prettier." Even Bajan

newspaper descriptions can seem blunt to an outsider: "Police are seeking the public's assistance in locating a missing girl. She . . . is five feet four inches tall, stockily built, full-breasted, knock-kneed, has short black hair and pierced ears."

3. Sutton and Makiesky-Barrow, "Social Inequality and Sexual Status in Barbados," 492.

4. Bajan proverbs reflect men's utilitarian attitude toward women: "Dirty water does cool hot iron," meaning "Once a man is aroused, any woman, good or bad, can satisfy his desire"; and "De new broom sweep cleaner, but de ole broom know de corners," meaning both new women and familiar women have their advantages (Hoefer and Wilder, *Barbados*, 256–57).

5. Errol Barrow, a native of St. Lucy, became Barbados' prime minister in 1961 and led the country to independence in 1966. He served until 1976 and then spent ten years as leader of the opposition. In 1986 he was reelected but died suddenly a little more than a year later. His birthday, 21 January, was declared a national holiday in 1989.

6. Pudding and souse is a popular Barbadian dish. A blood sausage made of pig's intestine stuffed with sweet potato and seasonings is eaten with pickled breadfruit and pigs' feet.

7. Dann, *Barbadian Male*, 43–44.

8. As of 1994, there were 865 known cases of AIDS in Barbados; 323 people had died. This gave Barbados the highest per capita death rate (77 percent) from AIDS in the West Indies and the world; the worldwide death rate at the time was 60 percent (Henrick Ellis, public lecture, 1994).

9. In sociologist Graham Dann's study of male attitudes toward sex and related issues (which was conducted in 1985 and based on in-depth interviews with a random sample of 185 men between the ages of eighteen and forty), 49 percent of men who had never been involved with a woman who had had an abortion considered it "totally wrong," while only 32 percent of those who had been intimate with such a women did. A national poll based on 950 male and female respondents found that 48 percent of the population opposed abortion.

10. Senior, *Working Miracles:Women's Lives in the English-Speaking Caribbean*, 189.

11. The child of an unwed mother typically takes the mother's surname. Christian names reflect the parents' interests and identification: Wesley for a famous cricketer, Kareem for a basketball player, Latoya for an entertainer, Esther for a biblical figure, Maggie after a soap opera character, Kashida for those with an African identification, or a combination of the parents' own first names, such as Dennika, from Dennis and Monika, and Sater from Sarah and Peter.

12. Barrow, "Male Images of Women," 58.

13. For the Caribbean as a whole the figure is 40 percent (Stuart, "Whither the Family," 3). The term *matrifocality* has been the subject of considerable debate since it was coined by R.T. Smith in 1956 to describe the female-headed households he observed among lower-class Guyanese. Smith focused on two

characteristics: women's dominant domestic role as mothers and household decision-makers and their male partners' marginality to the household and family. Later authors cautioned that, by stressing women's domestic role, their work outside the home can be mistakenly minimized. There is also a risk of underestimating the role that other men—such as uncles and brothers—play in the household.

14. Powell, "Caribbean Women and Their Response to Familial Experiences."

15. Dann, *Barbadian Male*, 150.

16. At age eleven all children take the Common Entrance Examination. Their score determines which secondary schools they will be allowed to enter. Girls, who are believed to mature earlier and therefore have an academic advantage over boys, must score ten points higher on the exams. Older schools like Harrisons, Queens, Combermere, and Lodge are recognized as being superior to schools like St. Lucy Secondary and are usually selected by parents as their child's top choices. This system separates the academically talented and privileged children—those raised in middle-class and more affluent homes—and reproduces inequality, since some schools end up with student bodies made up entirely of children with top test scores, while others primarily have children scoring at the bottom. (The prestige of the secondary school a child attends also carries great weight later in life.) Many village friends now become separated, since they travel to different parts of the island to attend secondary school—the school they attend (and its prestige) clearly evident from their uniforms. In 1996 a "zoning" system was being discussed, but it will not radically alter the current system.

17. Queen's College is the only secondary school, at the time of writing, to have banned corporal punishment.

18. Children once made all their own toys: kites from sugarcane stalks, newspaper, and string; scooters and toy trucks from wood and tin cans; cricket bats from pieces of wood; balloons from a pig's bladder; "rollers" from a bike rim rolled along the street with a stick; and rag dolls. Homemade toys are still played with today, but most children also have manufactured toys—handheld video games are popular—which they tend to keep safely indoors. Make-believe games like "father and mother" are common. Group games like hide-and-go-seek, "sticky" (freeze tag), "camp fight" (capture the flag), marbles, "pick-ups" (jacks), hopscotch, blind man's bluff, "frog in the sea can't catch me" (keep away), Simon says, and skipping rope are still played, but television has also taken hold, cutting into the time children spend together outdoors.

19. Sea eggs are the edible sex organs of the white sea urchin (*Tripneustes ventricosus*). It was a popular food until the sea urchin population declined in the 1970s. Folklore maintains that sea eggs enhance virility and fertility.

20. Chiggers (*Tunga penetrans*) are a skin-burrowing flea, once common in Barbados. After mating, the female burrows into a person's skin, usually between the toes, and remains there while her eggs developed. The pressure created by the swelling flea and developing eggs eventually breaks through the skin, leaving a sore that can become gangrenous (Fraser et al., *A–Z of Barbadian Heritage*).

Chapter 6

1. Most corn mills were privately owned. Villagers typically ground 5 to 8 gallons of corn at a time, repaying the owner for use of the mill with a pint or two of flour. The owner also got what flour remained in the mill at the end of the day, which was unusually fine.

2. Some villagers cooked in clay or cast iron "coal pots" (Dutch ovens) fueled by coal.

3. Many springs and ponds have dried up, although there are still over 270 natural ponds on the island.

4. Information from Vestry Minutes, 3 September 1885; cited in P. Jackman, *St. Lucy under the Lens: A Socio-economic and Political View from 1680–1900*, 27.

5. Information from the 1990 Census, "Table 9.09: Occupied Dwelling Unites by Parish, Type of Water Supply and Type of Toilet Facilities", 320. Nationally, 94 percent of Barbadian homes have piped water.

6. Cassava was shredded and juice wrung from the shavings. The starch was allowed to sink to the bottom. It was later mixed with water and spread on the clothes, which were then rinsed and laid out to dry.

7. *Warri* is an African pit and pebble game still played by some villagers, using a board with two rows of six cuplike depressions and forty-eight horse-nicker seeds or pebbles for counters. After World War II Barbadians returning from the United States popularized dominoes, which replaced *warri* as the game of choice.

8. Quoted in Jackman, "Barbadian Games of Yesterday," 44–45; from an interview conducted in 1978.

9. 1990 Census, "Table 9.11: Occupied Dwelling Units by Parish, Materials of Outer Walls and Type of Lighting", 326.

10. Parish households had access to Rediffusion, a wired radio service, as early as 1935. Radio greatly facilitated communications. "After radio," according to one villager, "we no longer needed to send someone to walk all over the island to tell everyone about a funeral." Radio also informed villagers of national news—cricket scores, election results, and more. Many people learned of the imminent arrival of Hurricane Janet in 1955 from the radio.

11. A random household survey conducted in five St. Lucy villages by our students in 1996 asked how many households in the village the interviewee's household was related to; results ranged from zero to twenty households, with an average of five. One-quarter of those interviewed, however, reported not being related to any other household in the village.

12. Similar rotating credit associations are found in Africa, Asia, and among immigrant populations in the United States and Britain as well as in other parts of the Caribbean. In Trinidad and St. Lucia, for example, they are known by the Yoruba name "su-su." In Jamaica they are known as "partners" and in Guyana and Antigua as "box-hands."

13. A source of external credit that still plays an important role in the economic strategies of some poor households is the traveling Indian salesman,

long referred to as the "coolie man." Once or twice a week these salesmen—who are based in Bridgetown but originally emigrated to Barbados from Trinidad, Guyana, India, and Bangladesh—drive into St. Lucy's villages to sell clothing, fabric, and kitchen supplies. They also take special requests for large items such as mattresses and televisions. Despite the existence of public transportation and delivery services, which makes the stores of Speightstown and Bridgetown accessible, poorer villagers continue to buy from these salesmen. They offer convenience and easy credit. Most allow their customers to pay for goods in small weekly installments, usually ten dollars but sometimes as little as two. Despite the pejorative-sounding label, most villagers speak positively of the coolie man. Currently, at least three itinerant salesmen visit St. Lucy's villages.

14. See Stoute and Ifill, "Rural Rumshop: A Comparative Case Study."

15. Ibid., 162.

16. Men living in villages without sufficient flat land for a decent playing field, like Josey Hill, play for nearby communities such as Rock Hall or Pie Corner.

17. The Barbados Cricket League organizes village cricket throughout the island, grouping village "clubs" into divisions, which in turn are grouped into zones and a "Super League." Teams representing companies and government agencies can also participate.

18. Corbin, "Picnics in Barbados."

Chapter 7

1. Church wardens and a parish-based vestry system of local government administered parish affairs and maintained order. By 1653 all eleven of today's parishes were in place.

2. Jews and Quakers constituted important minorities within the propertied class during the seventeenth and early eighteenth centuries. Many early white indentured servants were Roman Catholics, but it was only after a military garrison asked for a Catholic chaplain in 1839 that a Catholic mission was established in Barbados. Until disestablishment in 1969—one hundred years later than in the rest of the British West Indies—the Anglican bishop and clergy were paid by the state out of general taxation.

3. Handler and Lange, *Plantation Slavery in Barbados*, 214.

4. Ibid., 210.

5. Frank Collymore, *Barbadian Dialect*, 35.

6. For discussions of obeah in Barbados, see Handler, "Slave Medicine and Obeah in Barbados"; and Fisher, *Colonial Madness*. Constance Sutton's dissertation, "Scene of the Action," provides examples of obeah beliefs in the village of Endeavor.

7. Handler and Jacoby, "Slave Medicine and Plant Use in Barbados," 76.

8. Acts prohibiting obeah were enacted from the seventeenth century to the nineteenth centuries. In 1806 "an Act for the punishment of such slaves as

shall be found practicing obeah" was passed, replaced in 1818 by "an Act for the better prevention of the practice of obeah" (Watson, *Civilized Island, Barbados*, 88, 97).

9. Fisher, *Colonial Madness*, 105.

10. Watson, *Civilized Island, Barbados*, 88.

11. The Moravians arrived in 1765, establishing their first mission in the parish of St. Thomas in 1799. Wesleyan missionaries arrived in 1789.

12. Beckles, *Natural Rebels*, 130.

13. Schomburgk, *History of Barbados*, 122.

14. Austin-Broos, "Pentecostals and Rastafarians."

15. The former is also referred to as the Sons of God Apostolic Spiritual Baptist Church. Its members are commonly known as Spiritual Baptists, or "Tie-heads," for the cloth head wraps they wear. This is Barbados' only indigenous religion. It was founded in 1957 by Granville Williams. During a sixteen-year stay in Trinidad, he was exposed to the Spiritual Baptists, a revitalization movement with African roots. After experiencing his own revelation, he returned to Barbados to preach. The church now has an estimated seven thousand members, including a small number of St. Lucy residents.

16. Dann, *Quality of Life in Barbados*, 177.

17. 1990 Census of Barbados, "Table 2.06: Population by Parish, Sex and Religion," 148–51.

18. Ibid., 180–84.

19. Before disestablishment, in 1969, a system of pew rents maintained class-, if not race-, segregated seating.

20. *Advocate*, 7 February 1996.

21. See Austin-Broos, "Pentecostals and Rastafarians," for a good discussion of such gender issues in religion in Jamaica.

22. *Glossolalia* refers to the patterned vocalizations church members make when they slip into a trancelike state. These vocalizations are very similar cross-culturally due to the regular, rhythmical tightening and relaxation of the muscles of the vocal apparatus that occurs while in trance. They also share a characteristic intonation pattern.

23. See Lewis, *Soul Rebels*.

24. Johanna Campbell has granted permission to quote from her journal and fieldnotes and to describe this incident (see also Gmelch, "Nice Girls Don't Talk to Rastas").

25. According to the 1990 census, 79 percent of Rastafarians are male.

26. Dann, *Quality of Life in Barbados*, 180.

27. Ibid., 176, 182.

Chapter 8

1. In 1993 there were over eleven thousand subscribers on the island ("85 percent STV Subs by Year End," *Nation*, 15 February 1993, 13).

2. Satellite television became available in Barbados in the 1980s, although

its high cost meant that only a few people in St. Lucy acquired it. The first system operated on an analog signal that required the purchase of a large satellite dish and receiver (minimum 10 feet diameter), which had to be turned to pick up the signal from one of eighteen satellites. Some people built their own receivers, but even then the cost was considerable. The new digital system, called Direct TV, uses a less expensive 18-inch dish and permits immediate access to all satellites. In 1996, 60 channels were being introduced from North America and Latin America, with the promise of 250 soon after and the possibility of hundreds more in the future.

3. Direct TV, a digital satellite system introduced in 1996, will bring in some Latin American programming. A licensing arrangement being negotiated the same year between the South African Broadcasting Corporation (SCBC) and DIMPEX, a black-owned U.S. company, may also bring in programming from South Africa ("TV Shows to Emanate from South Africa," *Barbados Advocate*, 8 February 1996, 6).

4. In 1994 "Days of Our Lives" and "The Bold and the Beautiful" dominated in the first category; "Kung-Fu: The Legend Continues" and "MacGyver" in the second; and "Cheers," "Roc," "The Fresh Prince of Bel Air," and "Family Matters" in the last. Other popular programs were "Beverly Hills 90210," "Living Single," "Hanging with Mr. Cooper," and "Oprah Winfrey."

5. Personal interview, 1994.

6. Boyce, "'Gang' Trouble Reported in St. Lucy," *Daily Nation*, 10 October 1989.

7. In 1996 the unofficial unemployment rate was 30 percent.

8. Even though households receiving satellite television can block certain channels, most adolescents can find a way around it. As the owner of a satellite television business explained by analogy: "Do you know how to program your VCR? No. But your kids do."

9. Barbados Improvement Association, *Tourist Guide to Barbados*, 11.

10. Cave, Shepherd, and Co. *Barbados (Illustrated)*, 17.

11. In 1956 Barbados had passed the Hotel Aids Act, which permitted the importation of duty-free construction materials and gave tax relief to the new tourism industry.

12. Exact numbers for 1993 were 395,979 "long-stay" arrivals (over twenty-four hours) and 428,611 cruise ship arrivals (Barbados Tourism Authority).

13. Cynthia Poon, personal interview, 1990.

14. Although treated waste water is not a public health risk, the large amount of phosphates and nitrates remaining in treated water stresses living corals. The particulate matter in sewage also retards their growth by blocking sunlight. (The run-off from fertilizers and pesticides used in modern agriculture also harms them.) Over time the corals die, and the reef begins to break down. With no reef barrier to absorb wave energy, there is nothing to prevent beach erosion. And without healthy, growing corals there is nothing from which new beaches can be generated.

Hotel developers have unwittingly hastened the demise of their beaches by building too close to the shoreline. At high tide the waves strike hotel seawalls instead of the beach, preventing the sand particles that would normally drop out of the water as the waves run up the beach from doing so. The government has established set-back requirements for coastal construction, but these are often ignored.

Scuba divers damage the reefs every time a dive boat drags its anchor and breaks off the fragile coral heads. Not only is an important underwater tourist attraction diminished in this way, but, because corals are nurseries for many fisheries, their deterioration threatens another resource, namely, reef fish (Wayne Hunte, personal interview, 1992).

15. Hotels and restaurants bring in large quantities of heavily packaged imported food in order to feed tourists in the manner to which they are accustomed. Many tourists, however, are aware of the consequences of pollution. Through conversations with local people and frequent letters to the editor, they remind Bajans of the beauty of their island and the costs of degrading it, even while they contribute to its pollution.

16. Barbados Board of Tourism, "Barbados: The Warmest Welcome in the Caribbean."

17. Not all tourists are white. Some African Americans and blacks from other countries visit Barbados, but their numbers are small. Likewise, not all Barbadians are black; 5 percent are white. To differentiate themselves from tourists, some white Bajans and white expatriates for a time wore T-shirts announcing, "I'm not a tourist, I live here."

18. In his speech to Barbados' hoteliers in 1989 Richard Haynes also stated, "Our people are sensible enough to distinguish between service and servitude and to recognize the key role which professionally trained workers play in the industry."

19. Archer, *Effects of the Tourist Industry in Barbados, West Indies*, 83.

20. Karch and Dann, "Close Encounters of the Third World," 250.

21. Other recent slogans have included "Make a friend for Barbados today" and "Tourism is our business, let's play our part."

22. CTRC, "Report: Tourism Education Workshop for Teachers."

23. Fisher, *Colonial Madness*, 116–17. Fisher reports that anthropologist Clayton Press Jr. also found that tourism and the wealth it brings to certain villagers created jealousy. He provided the example of a maid who was given a house and enough money to put in piped water and electricity by a female tourist and, as a result, lost her local friends; she was said to have earned the "envy hatred" of people in her village.

24. Some beach boys are homosexuals or bisexuals who cater to gay tourists, but the dominant beach boy–tourist relationship is a heterosexual one.

25. Pruitt and LaFont, "For Love and Money: Romance Tourism in Jamaica."

26. Ibid., 432.

27. Karch and Dann, "Close Encounters with the Third World."

28. Ibid.

29. AIDs is also blamed on tourism. At a public awareness meeting sponsored by the Barbados Family Planning Association a member of the audience rose to declare angrily that tourists were responsible for bringing it to the

island. No one dissented. "Disease has a lot to do with international travel," one of the panelists explained calmly, "and sex is part of what happens with tourism."

30. Richard C. Haynes, speech to Barbadian hoteliers, 1989.

31. Quoted in Gmelch, *Double Passage*, 184.

32. Its name came from the small sea anemones that once grew profusely in its rocky pools. Trampled and poked at by visitors, few remain.

33. On the earliest maps of Barbados it was named Mt. Pisga (Pisgah), the biblical mount from which Moses saw the Promised Land. No one is certain why the name was changed to Pico Teneriffe. There is no known connection between Barbados and the Canary Islands, nor does Teneriffe have such a peak (Colin Hudson, personal communication).

34. Room rates at the time of the interview ranged from $700 to $2,000 (U.S.) a night.

35. Wayne Hunte, personal interview, 1990.

36. Superintendent John Sealy, personal interview, 1994.

37. Wiltshire, *The Caribbean Transnational Family*.

38. Marshall, "History of Caribbean Migrations," 6–7.

39. Richardson (*Panama Money in Barbados, 1900–1920*) reports that sixty thousand Barbadians emigrated to Panama between 1904 and 1914. D. Lowenthal places the figure at forty-five thousand between 1880 and 1914 (*West Indian Societies*, 216). The Royal West India Commission reported that the total population of Barbados had declined by twenty thousand between 1896 and 1921 (*Royal West Indian Commission Report*, 243).

40. *Royal West Indian Commission Report*, 11.

41. The U.S. Immigration Act of 1917 imposed a literacy test and a gradation system, which placed West Indians at the bottom of the list of those allowed in.

42. Chamberlain places the emigration figure at twenty-seven thousand for the period 1955–66 ("Family and Identity: Barbadian Migrants to Britain," 1). Although Barbadians represented a minority of the overall number of migrants, they had a large impact on British society, since so many were employed in public transport and the hotel industry where they came into frequent contact with the British public.

43. The act came in response to a widely publicized campaign by right-wing groups, which claimed that Britain's "New Commonwealth" immigrants were taking away British jobs and creating a "race problem" in the country. Ironically, its impending passage created a short-term surge in immigration; from 1960 through the first half of 1962 West Indians emigrated to Britain in large numbers to get in before the act went into effect. Many Bajans living in Britain who had been considering returning home decided to stay for fear they might never be allowed back.

44. In 1993, 3,774 residents of the eastern Caribbean emigrated to the United States; an estimated 65 percent, or approximately 2,400, were from Barbados (U.S. Emigration, personal communication, 1994).

45. Given in Barbados dollars; one Barbados dollar equaled $1.98 U.S. (Bar-

bados Statistics Department, "Finance—Table 35: Selected Remittances from Abroad," 42).

46. In 1977, 2,756 Barbadians were admitted into the United States, but by 1989 only 805, or 29 percent, had become naturalized U.S. citizens (Best, "Proud to Be a Barbadian," *Nation*, 11 September 1992).

47. Richardson, *Panama Money in Barbados, 1900–1920*.

48. Quoted in Gmelch, *Double Passage*, 125.

49. Lamming, *In the Castle of My Skin*, 295.

50. Sutton and Makiesky, "Migration and West Indian Racial and Political Consciousness."

51. Quoted in Gmelch, *Double Passage*, 122.

52. The total figure of nonimmigrant visas issued in 1993 for the eastern Caribbean was 46,514, of which an estimated 50 percent were Barbadians (U.S. Emigration, personal communication, 1994).

53. In 1994 a round-trip ticket to San Juan cost only $320 BDS; to Miami, approximately $630 BDS; and to Margarita Island, off the coast of Venezuela, $250 BDS.

Final Thoughts

1. See Mintz, "So-called World System: Local Initiative and Local Response"; and Mintz and Price, *Caribbean Contours*.

2. See Olwig, *Global Culture, Island Identity*.

3. Besson, "RAI News (Summary of Sidney Mintz's 1994 Huxley Memorial Lecture)," 27.

4. Coucou, served with flying fish, is considered Barbados' national dish. It is an African-derived dish made of corn flour paste and okra. Landship societies have waxed and waned in popularity for more than a hundred years. They are "friendly societies" in which members contribute annual fees in return for sickness and death benfits. Landship members wear naval regalia, parade, and dance, their movements imitating a ship and its crew at sea. Their dances also show African influence (see Fraser et al. *A–Z of Barbadian Heritage*).

5. The term *mimic men* comes from V. S. Naipaul's novel about Trinidad, *Mimic Men*. See D. Miller's discussion of modernity and identity in *Trinidad in Modernity: An Ethnographic Approach*.

6. Barbadians have a self-satisfied, smug reputation within the Caribbean (see Wickham, "The Thing about Barbados"; and Hearne, "What the Barbadian Means to Me"). For a discussion of the development of Bajan creole culture, see Welch, "In Search of a Barbadian Identity."

7. See Mintz, *Sweetness and Power;* and Mintz and Price, *Caribbean Contours*.

8. Barbados has become more involved in the regional economy and polity, developing ties with its neighbors in the Leeward and Windward Islands. In 1973 it joined with several other Caribbean countries to found the Caribbean Community (CARICOM). Today CARICOM is composed of fourteen English-speaking countries and Surinam. Barbados is also a member of the newly

formed Association of Caribbean States (ACS), a group of twenty-four nations in the Caribbean Basin, whose goal is to form a trade bloc.

9. See, for example, "Granville: Be Fully Aware of Our Past," *Advocate,* 31 January 1996, 15.

10. It was initiated by an American Peace Corps volunteer who was a graduate student in anthropology.

11. See Collymore, *Barbadian Dialect;* Fraser et al., *A–Z of Barbadian Heritage;* and Handler and Jacoby, "Slave Medicine and Plant Use in Barbados."

Appendix

1. One of us studied the experiences of our students in Barbados during the 1990 field term. Using a variety of techniques, including questionnaires, tape-recorded interviews, and analysis of their daily field notes and journals, he examined their adjustment to the new culture and to being student anthropologists as well as what they learned about their own culture while living in Barbados. See G. Gmelch, "Learning Culture," 245–52.

Bibliography

Allen, S. 1971. *New Minorities and Old Conflicts.* New York: Random House.

Alleyne, W., and Fraser H. 1988. *The Barbados-Carolina Connection.* Basingstoke: Macmillan Caribbean.

Archer, E. D. 1980. Effects of the Tourist Industry in Barbados, West Indies. Ph.D. diss., University of Texas, Austin.

Austin, D. 1983. Culture and Ideology in the English-Speaking Caribbean: A View from Jamaica. *American Ethnologist* 19(2):223–40.

Austin-Broos, D. J. 1987. Pentecostals and Rastafarians: Cultural, Political and Gender Relations of Two Religious Movements. *Social and Economic Studies* 36(4):1–19.

Barbados Improvement Association. 1913. *The Tourist Guide to Barbados.* Bridgetown: Barbados Improvement Association.

Barrow, C. 1976. Reputation and Ranking in a Barbadian Locality. *Social and Economic Studies* 25(2):106–29.

———. 1977. Migration from a Barbados Village: Effects on Family Life. *New Community* 5(4):381–91.

———. 1983. Ownership and Control of Resources in Barbados: 1834 to the Present. *Social and Economic Studies* 32(3):83–120.

———. 1986a. Finding the Support: A Study of Strategies for Survival. *Social and Economic Studies* 35(2):131–76.

———. 1986b. Male Images of Women in Barbados. *Social and Economic Studies* 35(3):51–64.

———. 1988. Anthropology, the Family and Women in the Caribbean. In *Gender in Caribbean Development,* ed. P. Mohammed and C. Shepherd, 156–69. Mona: University of the West Indies.

Basch, L. 1987. The Politics of Caribbeanization: Vincentians and Grenadians in New York. In *Caribbean Life in New York City,* ed. C. Sutton and E. Chaney, 160–81. New York: Center for Migration Studies.

Basch, L., N. G. Schiller, and C. Szanton Blanc, eds. 1994. *Nations Unbound: Transnational Projects, Global Predicaments, and Deterritorialized Nation-States.* New York: Gordon and Breach.

Beckles, H. 1989a. *Afro-Caribbean Women and Resistence to Slavery in Barbados.* London: Karnak House.

———. 1989b. *Natural Rebels: A Social History of Enslaved Black Women in Barbados.* New Brunswick, N.J.: Rutgers University Press.

———. 1989c. *White Servitude and Black Slavery in Barbados, 1627–1715.* Knoxville: University of Tennessee Press.

———. 1990. *The History of Barbados.* Cambridge: Cambridge University Press.

Beckles, H., and V. Shepherd. 1991. *Caribbean Slave Society and Economy.* New York: New Press.

Besson, J. 1995. Rai News (Summary of Sidney Mintz's 1994 Huxley Memorial Lecture). *Anthropology Today* 2(2):27.

Besson, J., and J. Momsen, eds. 1987. *Land and Development in the Caribbean.* London: Berlin.

Bolles, A. L. 1981. "Goin' Abroad": Working Class Jamaican Women and Migration. In *Female Immigrants to the United States: Caribbean, Latin American and African Experiences,* ed. D. Mortimer and R. Bryce-Laporte, 56–85. Occasional Papers no. 2. Washington, D.C.: Smithsonian Institution, RIIES.

Brooks, D. 1975. *Race and Labour in London Transport.* London: Oxford University Press.

Brown, A., and R. Sanatan. 1987. *Talking with Whom? A Report on the State of the Media in the Caribbean.* Seminar report. University of the West Indies, Cave Hill.

Bryce-Laporte, R. S. 1979. New York City and the New Caribbean Immigration: A Contextual Statement. *International Migration Review* 13(2):214–34.

Bryce-Laporte, R. S., and D. Mortimer, eds. 1976. *Caribbean Immigration to the United States.* Occasional Papers no. 1. Washington, D.C.: Smithsonian Institution, RIIES.

Bullen, R. P. 1966. Barbados and the Archaeology of the Caribbean. *Journal of the Barbados Museum and Historical Society* 32:16–19.

Bush, B. 1990. *Slave Women in Caribbean Society: 1650–1838.* Bloomington: Indiana University Press.

Campbell, P. F. 1984. Barbados Vestries, 1627–1700, pt. 2. *Journal of the Barbados Museum and Historical Society* 37(2):174.

Carnegie, C. V. 1982. Strategic Flexibility in the West Indies: A Social Psychology of Caribbean Migration. *Caribbean Review* 2(1):10–13, 54.

Cave, Shepherd, and Company. 1911. *Barbados (Illustrated): Historical, Descriptive and Commercial.* Bridgetown: Cave, Shepherd and Company.

Chamberlain, M. 1994. Family and Identity: Barbadian Migrants to Britain. In *Migration and Identity,* ed. R. Benmayer and A. Skotnes, 119–36. London: Oxford University Press.

Chandler, A. A. 1946. The Expansion of Barbados. *Journal of the Barbados Museum and Historical Society* 13:106–16.

Chaney, E. 1987. The Context of Caribbean Migration. In *Caribbean Life in New York City,* ed. C. Sutton and E. Chaney, 3–14. New York: Center for Migration Studies.

Clarke, A. 1980. *Growing Up Stupid under the Union Jack.* Toronto: McClelland and Stewart.

Clarke, E. T. 1981. Mental Illness among Barbadians in Barbados and England. Ph.D. diss., University of Surrey.

Coleridge, H. N. [1836] 1970. *Six Months in the West Indies.* New York: Negro Universities Press.

Collymore, F. 1955. *Barbadian Dialect.* Bridgetown: Barbados National Trust.

Corbin, B. 1979. Picnics in Barbados. In *Everyday Life in Barbados: A Sociological Perspective,* ed. G. Dann, 103–23. Leiden: Royal Institute of Linguistics and Anthropology.

Cross, M. 1979. *Urbanization and Urban Growth in the Caribbean.* Cambridge: Cambridge University Press.

Cumper, G. E. 1957. Working Class Emigration from Barbados to the U.K. *Social and Economic Studies* 6(1):76–83.

Cutsinger, L. 1990. Informal Marketing in Barbados, West Indies. Ph.D. diss., Department of Anthropology, Washington State University.

Dann, G. 1979. *Everyday Life in Barbados: A Sociological Perspective.* Leiden: Royal Institute of Linguistics and Anthropology.

———. 1984. *The Quality of Life in Barbados.* London: Macmillan.

———. 1987. *The Barbadian Male.* London: Macmillan.

Davison, R. B. 1962. *West Indian Migrants: Social and Economic Effects of Migration from the West Indies.* London: Oxford University Press.

———. 1966. *Black British: Immigrants to England.* London: Oxford University Press.

Deere, C. D., et al. 1990. *In the Shadows of the Sun: Caribbean Development Alternatives and U.S. Policy.* Boulder: Westview Press.

Dickson, W. 1789. *Letters on Slavery.* London: J. Phillips.

———. [1814] 1970. *Mitigation of Slavery.* London. Westport: Negro Universities Press.

Dominquez, V. 1975. *From Neighbor to Stranger: The Dilemma of Caribbean Peoples in the United States.* New Haven: Yale University Press.

Drewett, P. L. 1987. Archaeological Survey of Barbados. First Interim Report. *Journal Barbados Museum Historical Society* 38(1):44–80.

———. 1988. Archaeological Survey of Barbados. Second Interim Report. *Journal Barbados Museum Historical Society* 38(2):196–204.

———. 1989. Archaeological Survey of Barbados. Third Interim Report. *Journal Barbados Museum Historical Society* 38(3):338–52.

———. 1991. *Prehistoric Barbados.* London: Institute of Archaeology, University College London and Barbados Museum and Historical Society.

Dunn, R. 1972. *Sugar and Slaves: The Rise of the Planter Class in the English West Indies, 1624–1713.* Chapel Hill: University of North Carolina Press.

Ebanks, G. E., P. M. George, and C. Nobbe. 1974a. Fertility and Number of Partnerships in Barbados. *Population Studies* 28(3):449–61.

———. 1974b. Patterns of Sex-Union Formation in Barbados. *Canadian Review of Sociology and Anthropology* 11(3):230–46.

Editorial. 1988. Parish Boundaries. *Journal of the Barbados Museum and Historical Society* 38(2):131–36.

Ellis, P., ed. 1986. *Women in the Caribbean.* Kingston: Kingston Publishers.

Equiano, O. 1967. *Equiano's Travels: His Autobiography: The Interesting Narrative of the Life of Olaudah Equiano or Gustavus Vassa, the African.* London: Heinemann.

Eriksen, T. H. 1990. Liming in Trinidad: The Art of Doing Nothing. *Folk* 32:23–43.

Family Welfare Association. 1960. *The West Indian Comes to England.* London: Routledge and Kegan Paul.

Fisher, L. E. 1989. *Colonial Madness: Mental Health in the Barbadian Social Order.* New Brunswick, N.J.: Rutgers University Press.

Foner, N. 1978. *Jamaica Farewell: Jamaican Migrants in London.* Berkeley: University of California Press.

———. 1979. West Indians in New York City and London: A Comparative Analysis. *International Migration Review* 13(2):284–97.

Forde, G. A. 1988. *Folk Beliefs of Barbados.* Barbados: National Cultural Foundation.

Franck, H. A. 1920. *Roaming through the West Indies.* New York: Century.

Fraser, H., et al. 1990. *A–Z of Barbadian Heritage.* Kingston: Heinemann Publishers (Caribbean).

Fraser, H. and R. Hughes. 1982. *Historic Houses of Barbados.* Bridgetown: Barbados National Trust.

Freeman, C. 1993. Designing Women: Corporate Discipline and Barbados's Off-Shore Pink-Collar Sector. *Cultural Anthropology* 8(2):169–86.

French, J. 1986. Colonial Policy towards Women after the 1938 Uprising: The Case of Jamaica. *Caribbean Quarterly* 34(3–4):38–76.

Galenson, D. 1986. *Traders, Planters, and Slaves.* Cambridge: Cambridge University Press.

Gmelch, G. 1980. Return Migration. *Annual Review of Anthropology* 9:135–59.

———. 1985. Barbados Odyssey: Some Migrants Fulfill Their Dreams by Returning Home. *Natural History* 94(10):34–38.

———. 1987. Work, Innovation, and Investment: The Impact of Return Migrants in Barbados. *Human Organization* 46(2):131–40.

———. 1992. *Double Passage: The Lives of Caribbean Migrants Abroad and Back Home.* Ann Arbor: University of Michigan Press.

———. 1992. Learning Culture: The Education of American Students in Caribbean Villages. *Human Organization* 51(3):245–52.

Gmelch, G., and S. B. Gmelch. 1995. Gender and Migration: The Readjustment of Women Migrants in Barbados, Ireland and Newfoundland. *Human Organization* 54(4):470–73.

———. 1996. Barbados's Amerindian Past. *Anthropology Today* 12(1):11–15.

Gonzalez, N. S. 1961. Family Organization in Five Types of Migratory Wage Labor. *American Anthropologist* 63(6):1264–80.

Goodall, E. A. 1977. *Sketches of Amerindian Tribes, 1841–1843.* London: British Museum Publications.

Gooding, E. 1974. *The Plant Communities of Barbados.* Barbados: Ministry of Education.

Graburn, N. 1978. Tourism: The Sacred Journey. In *Hosts and Guests: The Anthropology of Tourism,* ed. V. Smith, 17–31. Oxford: Blackwell.

Great Britain. 1945. *West India Royal Commission Report.* Command Paper, 6607. London: His Majesty's Stationary Office.

Greenfield, S. 1966. *English Rustics in Black Skin.* New Haven: Yale University Press.

Greenwood R., and S. Hamber. 1979. *Arawaks to Africans.* London: Macmillan.

Griffith, D. C. 1985. Women, Remittances, and Reproduction. *American Ethnologist* 12(4):676–90.

Griffith, W. 1990. CARICOM Countries and the Caribbean Basin Initiative. *Latin American Perspectives* 17 (1:63):33–54.

Griswold, W. 1994. *Cultures and Societies in a Changing World.* Thousand Oaks, Calif.: Pine Forge Press.

Hackenberger, S. 1988. An Abstract of Archaeological Investigations by the Barbados Museum, 1986. *Journal of Barbados Museum Historical Society* 38(2):155–62.

———. 1987. *Archaeological Investigations, Barbados, West Indies.* MS, Barbados Museum.

Hagelberg, G. B. 1985. Sugar in the Caribbean. In *Caribbean Contours*, ed. S. Mintz and S. Price, 85–126. Baltimore: Johns Hopkins University Press.

Handler, J. S. 1966. Small Scale Sugar Cane Farming in Barbados. *Ethnology* 5(3):264–83.

———. 1969. The Amerindian Slave Population of Barbados in the Seventeenth and Early Eighteenth Century. *Caribbean Studies* 8(4):38–64.

———. 1970. Aspects of Amerindian Ethnography in Seventeenth Century Barbados. *Caribbean Studies* 9(4):50–72.

———. 1972. An Archaeological Investigation of the Domestic Life of Plantation Slaves in Barbados. *Journal of the Barbados Museum and Historical Society* 34(2):64–72.

———. 1974. *The Unappropriated People: Freedmen in the Slave Society of Barbados.* Baltimore: Johns Hopkins University Press.

———. 1977. Amerindians and their Contributions to Barbadian Life. *Journal of the Barbados Museum and Historical Society* 35:189–210.

———. 1982. Slave Revolts and Conspiracies in Seventeenth-Century Barbados. *New West Indian Guide* 56(1–2):5–42.

———. 1984. Freedmen and Slaves in the Barbados Militia. *Journal of Caribbean History.* 19(1):1–25.

———. 1994. Slave Medicine and Obeah in Barbados. In *The Lesser Antilles in the Age of European Expansion*, ed. R. Paquette and S. Engerman. Gainesville: University of Florida Press.

Handler, J. S., and J. A. Jacoby. 1993. Slave Medicine and Plant Use in Barbados. *Journal of the Barbados Museum and Historical Society* 41:74–98.

Handler, J. S., and F. Lange. 1978. *Plantation Slavery in Barbados: An Archaeological and Historical Investigation.* Cambridge: Harvard University Press.

Harlow, V. T. 1926. *A History of Barbados, 1625–1685.* Oxford: Clarendon Press.

Harper, R. 1965. *Colour in Britain.* London: British Broadcasting Corporation.

Harrison, D., ed. 1992. *Tourism and the Less Developed Countries.* London: Belhaven Press.

Hatch. A. 1978. The Salvation Army and the Red Light District. *Bajan* (July): 31–32.

Hearne, J. 1973. What the Barbadian Means to Me. In *Caribbean Essays: An Anthology*, ed. A. Salkey. London: Evans Brothers Ltd.

Hernandez-Alverez, J. 1968. *Return Migration to Puerto Rico.* Berkeley: California Institute of International Studies.

Heuman, G. 1986. *Out of the House of Bondage: Runaways, Resistance, and Ma-roonage in Africa and the New World.* London: Frank Cass.

Higman, B. W. 1976. *Slave Population and Economy in Jamaica, 1807–1834.* Cambridge: Cambridge University Press.

———. 1984 *Slave Populations of the Brititsh Caribbean, 1807–1834.* Baltimore: Johns Hopkins University Press.

Hill, D. R. 1977. The Impact of Migration on the Metropolitan and Folk Society of Carriacou, Grenada. *Anthropological Papers of the American Museum of Natural History* 54(2).

Hoefer, H., and R. Wilder, eds. 1986. *Barbados.* Singapore: APA Productions.

Holder, J. F., ed. 1979. *Caribbean Tourism: Policies and Impacts: Selected Speeches and Papers.* Barbados: Caribbean Tourism Research and Development Centre.

Holder, J. F., and C. Wilson, eds. 1976. *Caribbean Tourism: Profits and Performance through 1980.* Port of Spain: Key Caribbean Publications.

Holmes, C. 1988. *John Bull's Island: Immigration and British Society, 1871–1971.* London: Macmillan.

Hope, R. K. 1982. *Economic Development in the Caribbean.* New York: Praeger.

Hoyos, F. A. 1978. *Barbados: A History from Amerindians to Independence.* London: Macmillan.

Hughes, G. [1750] 1972. *The Natural History of Barbados.* New York: Arno Press.

Hutt, M. B. 1981. *Exploring Historic Barbados.* Nova Scotia: Layne.

Jackman, I. 1979. Barbadian Games of Yesterday. In *Everyday Life in Barbados: A Sociological Perspective,* ed. G. Dann. Leiden: Royal Institute of Linguistics and Anthropology.

Jackman, P. 1993. *St. Lucy under the Lens: A Socio-economic and Political View from 1680–1900.* Caribbean Studies bachelor's thesis, University of the West Indies, Cave Hill.

Karch, C. 1979. *The Transformation and Consolidation of the Corporate Plantation Economy in Barbados, 1860–1877.* Ph.D. diss., Rutgers University.

Karch, C., and G. Dann. 1981. Close Encounters of the Third Kind. *Human Relations* 34:249–69.

Klein, H. S. 1967. *Slavery in the Americas: A Comparative Study of Virginia and Cuba.* Chicago: University of Chicago Press.

Knight, F. 1990. *The Caribbean: The Genesis of a Fragmented Nationalism.* 2d ed. New York: Oxford University Press.

Lamming, G. [1953] 1991. *In the Castle of My Skin.* Ann Arbor: University of Michigan Press.

Lazarus-Black, M. 1991. Why Women Take Men to Magistrate's Court: Caribbean Kinship Ideology and Law. *Ethnology* 30(2):119–33.

Lea, J. 1988. *Tourism and Development in the Third World.* New York: Routledge.

Lent, J. 1990. *Mass Communications in the Caribbean.* Ames: Iowa State University Press.

Levy, C. 1980, *Emancipation, Sugar, and Federalism: Barbados and the West Indies, 1833–1876.* Gainsville: University Presses of Florida.

Lewis, W. 1993. *Soul Rebels: The Rastafari.* Prospect Heights, Ill.: Waveland Press.

Ligon, R. A. [1657] 1970. *A True and Exact History of the Island of Barbados.* London: Frank Cass and Company.

Lowenthal, D. 1972. *West Indian Societies*. New York: Oxford University Press.

Lowenthal, D., and L. Comitas. 1973. *Consequences of Class and Color*. New York: Doubleday.

Lynch, L. 1972. *The Barbados Book*. London: Andre Deutsch.

MacCannell, D. 1976. *The Tourist: A New Theory of the Leisure Class*. New York: Schocken Books.

Makiesky-Barrow, S. 1976. *Class, Culture and Politics in a Barbadian Community*. Ph.D. diss., Brandeis University.

Mandle, J., and J. Mandle. 1994. *Caribbean Hoops*. New York: Gordon and Breach.

Marshall, D. 1982. The History of Caribbean Migrations: The Case of the West Indies. *Caribbean Review* 11(1):6–9, 52.

———. 1982. Migration as an Agent of Change in Caribbean Island Ecosystems. *International Social Science Journal* 34(3):451–67.

Marshall, P. 1959. *Brown Girl, Brownstones*. New York: Random House.

———. 1987. Black Immigrant Women in *Brown Girl, Brownstones*. In *Caribbean Life in New York City*, ed. C. Sutton and E. Chaney, 87–91. New York: Center for Migration Research.

Marshall, T. 1986. Post-emancipation Adjustments in Barbados, 1838–1876. In *Emancipation I*, ed. A. Thompson, 8–108. Barbados: National Cultural Foundation.

Marshall, W. 1971. The Termination of Apprenticeship in Barbados and the Windward Islands: An Essay in Colonial Administration and Politics. *Journal of Caribbean History* 2:1–45.

———. 1987. *Emancipation II: Aspects of the Post-Slavery Experience in Barbados*. Barbados: National Cultural Foundation.

Massiah, J. 1982. *Women and the Family*. Cave Hill: Institute of Social and Economic Research, University of the West Indies.

———. 1983. *Women as Heads of Households in the Caribbean: Family Structure and Feminine Status*. Colchester: UNESCO.

McCullough, D. 1977. *The Path between the Seas*. New York: Simon and Schuster.

Midgett, D. K. 1977. West Indian Migration and Adaptation in St. Lucia and London. Ph.D. diss., Department of Anthropology, University of Illinois at Urbana-Champaign.

———. 1980. West Indian Ethnicity in Great Britain. In *Migration and Development*, ed. H. I. Safa and B. DuToit, 57–81. The Hague: Mouton.

Miller, D. 1994. *Modernity, An Ethnographic Approach: Dualism and Mass Consumption in Trinidad*. Oxford: Berg.

Mintz, S. 1974. *Caribbean Transformations*. Chicago: Aldine Publishing Co.

———. 1977. The So-called World System: Local Initiative and Local Response. *Dialectical Anthropology* 2(4):253–70.

———. 1985. *Sweetness and Power: The Place of Sugar in Modern History*. New York: Penguin Books.

Mintz, S., and S. Price. 1985. *Caribbean Contours*. Baltimore: Johns Hopkins University Press.

Moxly, Rev. J. H. Sutton. 1886. *An Account of a West Indian Sanatorium and a Guide to Barbados*. London: Low, Marston, Searle, and Rivington.

Musgrove, P. 1987. The Economic Crisis and Its Impact on Health and Health Care in Latin America and the Caribbean. *International Journal of Health Services* 17(3):411–41.

Naipaul, V. S. 1967. *Mimic Men.* New York: Macmillan.

Nurse, L. 1983. *Residential Subdivision of Barbados: 1965–1977.* Cave Hill: Institute of Social and Economic Research, University of the West Indies.

Olwig, K. F. 1993. *Global Culture, Island Identity: Continuity and Change in the Afro-Caribbean Community of Nevis.* New York: Harwood Academic Publishers.

Parry, J., P. Sherlock, and A. Maingot. [1956] 1987. *A Short History of the West Indies.* 4th ed. New York: St. Martin's Press.

Pastor, R. 1985. *Migration and Development in the Caribbean.* Boulder: Westview Press.

Patterson, O. 1968. West-Indian Immigrants Returning Home. *Race* 10(1):69–77.

Patterson, S. 1965. *Dark Strangers: A Study of West Indians in London.* Harmondsworth: Penguin.

————. 1969. *Immigration and Race Relations in Britain, 1960–1967.* London: Oxford University Press.

Peach, C. 1968. *West Indian Migration to Britain: A Social Geography.* London: Oxford University Press.

Philpott, S. B. 1973. *West Indian Migration: The Montserrat Case.* New York: Humanities Press.

Portes, A., and R. Rumbaut. 1990. *Immigrant America: A Portrait.* Berkeley: University of California Press.

Powell, D. 1986. Caribbean Women and Their Response to Familial Experiences. *Social and Economic Studies* 35(2):83–130.

Price, N. 1988. *Behind the Planter's Back: Lower Class Responses to Marginality in Bequia Island, St. Vincent.* London: Macmillan Caribbean.

Prior, M. 1993. Matrifocality, Power, and Gender Relations in Jamaica. In *Gender in Cross-Cultural Perspective,* ed. C. Brettell and C. Sargent, 310–17. Englewood Cliffs: Prentice-Hall.

Pruitt, D., and S. La Font. 1995. For Love and Money: Romance and Tourism in Jamaica. *Annals of Tourism Research* 22(2):422–40.

Richardson, B. C. 1983. *Caribbean Migrants: Environment and Human Survival in St. Kitts and Nevis.* Knoxville: University of Tennessee Press.

————. 1985. *Panama Money in Barbados, 1900–1920.* Knoxville: University of Tennessee Press.

Rubenstein, H. 1983. Remittances and Rural Underdevelopment in the English-Speaking Caribbean. *Human Organization* 42(4):295–306.

————. 1986. *Coping with Poverty: Adaptive Strategies in a Caribbean Village.* Boulder: Westview.

Schomburgk, R. H. [1848] 1971. *The History of Barbados.* London: Frank Cass and Company Ltd.

Senior, O. 1991. *Working Miracles: Women's Lives in the English-Speaking Caribbean.* Bloomington: Indiana University Press.

Shepherd, V., B. Brereton, and B. Bailey. 1995. *Engendering History: Caribbean Women in Historical Perspective.* New York: St. Martin's Press.

Sheppard, J. 1977. *The Redlegs of Barbados.* New York: KTO Press.

Smith, M. G. 1965. *The Plural Society in the British West Indies.* Berkeley: University of California Press.

Smith, R. T. 1988. *Kinship and Class in the West Indies.* Cambridge: Cambridge University Press.

Stewart, E. C. 1972. *American Cultural Patterns: A Cross-Cultural Perspective.* Chicago: Intercultural Press.

Stoute, J., and K. Ifill. 1979. The Rural Rumshop: A Comparative Case Study. In *Everyday Life in Barbados: A Sociological Perspective,* ed. G. Dann, 145–67. Leiden: Royal Institute of Linguistics and Anthropology.

Sutton, C. 1969. *The Scene of the Action: A Wildcat Strike in Barbados.* Ph.D. diss., Columbia University.

———. 1992. Transnational Identities and Cultures: Caribbean Immigrants in the United States. In *Immigration and Ethnicity: American Society—"Melting Pot" or "Salad Bowl,"* ed. M. D'Innocenzo and J. P. Sirefman, 231–41. Westport: Greenwood Press.

Sutton, C., and S. Makiesky-Barrow. 1975. Migration and West Indian Racial and Political Consciousness. In *Migration and Development:Implications for Ethnic Identity and Political Conflict,* ed. H. I. Safa and B. DuToit, 113–44. The Hague: Mouton.

———. 1981. Social Inequality and Sexual Status in Barbados. In *The Black Woman Cross-Culturally,* ed. F. Steady. Cambridge: Schenkman.

Thomas-Hope, E., ed. 1984. *Perspectives on Caribbean Regional Identity.* Monograph Series no. 11. Liverpool: Centre for Latin American Studies.

———. 1985. Return Migration and Implications for Caribbean Development. In *Migration and Development in the Caribbean,* ed. R. A. Pastor, 157–73. Boulder: Westview Press.

———. 1988. Caribbean Skilled International Migration and the Transnational Household. *Geoforum* 19(4):423–32.

Thornton J. 1993. *Africa and Africans: In the Making of the Atlantic World. 1400–1680.* New York: Cambridge University Press.

Trouillot, M.-R. 1987. *Women and Children in Barbados: A Situational Analysis.* Bridgetown: UNICEF Caribbean Area Office.

———. 1992. The Caribbean Region: An Open Frontier in Anthropological Theory. *Annual Review of Anthropology* 21:19–42.

UNESCO. 1977. The Effects of Tourism on Socio-Cultural Values. *Annual of Tourism Research* 4:74–105.

Watson, H. 1990. Recent Attempts at Industrial Restructuring in Barbados. *Latin American Perspectives* 17 (1:64):10–32.

Watson, J. L. 1977. *Between Two Cultures.* Oxford: Basil Blackwell.

Watson, K. 1979. *The Civilized Island, Barbados.* Bridgetown: Caribbean Graphics.

Welch, P. L. V. 1992. In Search of a Barbadian Identity: Historical Factors in the Evolution of a Barbadian Literary Tradition. *Journal of the Barbados Museum and Historical Society* 40:37–46.

Western, J. 1992. *A Passage to England: Barbadian Londoners Speak of Home*. Minneapolis: University of Minnesota Press.

Wickham, J. 1975. The Thing about Barbados. *Journal of the Barbados Museum and Historical Society* 35:223–30.

Wilson, P. 1969. Reputation and Respectability: A Suggestion for Caribbean Ethnology. *Man* 4:70–84.

———. 1973. *Crab Antics: The Social Anthropology of English Speaking Negro Societies of the Caribbean*. New Haven: Yale University Press.

Williams, E. 1966. *Capitalism and Slavery*. New York: Putnam.

Wiltshire, R. 1975. *The Status of Jamaican Women in Politics*. Kingston: Three Leaves.

———. 1986. *The Caribbean Transnational Family*. Cave Hill: Institute of Social and Economic Research.

———. 1992. Implications of Transnational Migration for Nationalism: The Caribbean Example. In *Towards a Transnational Perspective on Migration*, ed. N. G. Schiller, L. Basch, and C. Blanc-Szanton, 175–87. Vol. 654. New York: Annals of the New York Academy of Sciences.

Withey, S., and R. Abeles. 1980. *Television and Social Behavior: Beyond Violence and Children*. Hillside: Lawrence Erlbaum Associates.

Wolf, E. R. 1983. *Europe and the People without History*. Berkeley: University of California Press.

Wood, C. H., and T. McCoy. 1987. Migration, Remittances, and Development: A Study of Caribbean Cane Cutters in Florida. *International Migration Review* 19(2):251–77.

Worrell, D., ed. 1982. *The Economy of Barbados, 1946–1980*. Bridgetown: Central Bank of Barbados.

———. 1987. *Small Island Economies*. New York: Praeger.

Index

GEORGE GMELCH studied anthropology at Stanford as an undergraduate and at the University of California, Santa Barbara as a graduate student. He has done extensive research in Ireland, England, Alaska, and the Caribbean, and brief studies in Japan and Austria. He is currently studying the culture of professional baseball in the United States. The author of eight books and sixty articles, he is a professor of anthropology at Union College in upstate New York.

SHARON BOHN GMELCH obtained her Ph.D. in anthropology from the University of California, Santa Barbara. She is the author of five books. Her first, *Tinkers and Travellers*, won Ireland's Book of the Year award, and another, *Nan: The Life of an Irish Travelling Woman*, was a finalist for the Margaret Mead Award. She co-produced an ethnographic film on cultural revitalization among the Tlingit Indians of Southeast Alaska and is currently exploring the early use and impact of photography on the Tlingit. She is a professor of anthropology at Union College.